BREAKUP BOOTCAMP

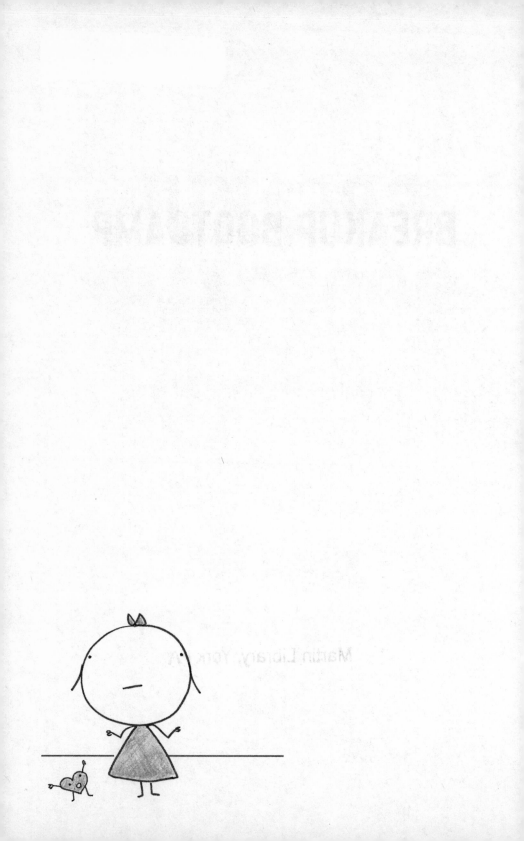

BREAKUP BOOTCAMP

The Science of Rewiring Your Heart

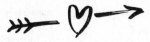

Amy Chan

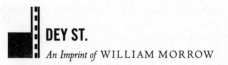

DEY ST.
An Imprint of WILLIAM MORROW

DEY ST.

I have changed the names and identifying characteristics of some individuals discussed in this book, including all Renew participants, to protect their privacy. Some of the individuals I discuss are composites of multiple Renew participants.

While I have thoroughly researched the information contained in this book, the material in this book is for general educational purposes only and should not be considered a substitute for medical treatment, psychotherapy, or advice from a mental health professional. If you are experiencing depression, abuse, addiction, or any other severe emotional illness, please seek professional help immediately.

HarperCollins books may be purchased for educational, business, or sales promotional use. For information, please email the Special Markets Department at SPsales@harpercollins.com.

FIRST EDITION

Designed by Michelle Crowe

Library of Congress Cataloging-in-Publication Data has been applied for.

ISBN 978-0-06-291474-3

20 21 22 23 24 LSC 10 9 8 7 6 5 4 3 2 1

To my family:

Mee Ping, Kay Mau, Alice, Anita, and Paul

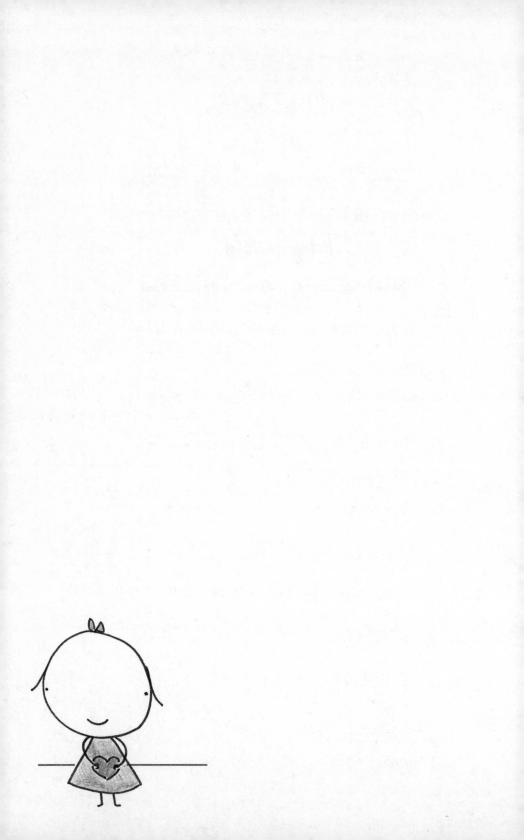

CONTENTS

INTRODUCTION

Just when the caterpillar thought the world was over, it
became a butterfly.

Proverb

After nine months of dating, Adam told me he loved me for the first
time.

After eighteen months of dating, Adam and I agreed that I would
move into his apartment after I suddenly lost my job.

After twenty-four months of dating, Adam cheated on me.

We had just returned from a romantic holiday in Europe, and he
was going to dinner with the boys. But when midnight rolled around
with no sign of Adam, I started to get worried. I texted and called,
with no answer. My angst intensified with each hour that passed, and
when he finally came home at four A.M., I was livid. Crying hysteri-
cally, I interrogated Adam about his whereabouts.

"You're acting crazy," he scolded. He explained that he was with
friends and potential investors, having drinks and talking business.

I didn't want to be *that* crazy girl, so in a puddle of tears, I went to
bed. But the next day, I couldn't help but ask for more clarity on the
previous evening's events.

"Can we just go over what happened, so I can truly put it past me
and not feel the need to bring it up again in the future?" I asked.

But as Adam recounted the events this time, I noticed that some of the details had changed. The story didn't match up with the one from the night before. As I started to push, he got defensive. He stormed into our bedroom and went back to sleep. I knew something was off. And so, for the first time ever, I did what "crazy girls" do. I checked his phone.

It didn't take much scrolling to realize that he hadn't been out with investors until four A.M.

He'd been with another woman.

I fell to the ground, curled into a fetal position, and wept. I was unable to move for hours. I felt dead inside.

One stream of questions looped endlessly through my brain:

Did he think she was prettier than me? Did he think she was sexier than me? Was she better than me? What did I do to deserve this? What did I do wrong?

I didn't know it yet, but this betrayal had ripped open a deep emotional wound from childhood I hadn't even known existed. And soon enough, the answer to those questions I was asking myself came rushing out, bringing with it all the pain I had ever felt as a little girl:

I am not enough.

Just two days ago I had been living my dream life, dating a man I thought I'd marry, discussing how we'd raise our future children. Adam was an entrepreneur; I worked for a smaller company, and the plan was for me to stay at home after we had kids. I had stopped raising my hand for promotions at work because why bother? I wanted a flexible, easy work schedule so that I could go with Adam when he traveled for business. When I got laid off from my job, I amped up my homemaking skills. I learned how to cook lavish meals. I packed his lunch. I was the perfect CEO's girlfriend, preparing to be the perfect CEO's wife. Dating Adam gave me purpose.

I had gone from confident career woman with a perfect life plan, a designer loft, and a boyfriend to jobless, homeless, and boyfriend-less. Everything I had built my identity on—status, career, six-figure salary, relationship—all disappeared.

I wasn't just mourning the end of my relationship; I was mourning the deaths of my identity and of a beautiful future that would never come.

Too ashamed to move in with my mom, I crashed at friends' houses for months while Adam tried to win me back with flowers and overtures of remorse and care. It was clear he wanted to reconcile, but infidelity was one hard line I had drawn in our relationship. When he realized that there was no chance of us getting back together, something snapped. The man I had loved and called my best friend went from apologetic and caring to stone cold. Even though I didn't want to get back together, he was the person whom I was used to turning to for comfort. That's what the crazy thing is—you can't help but want soothing from the very person who hurt you. But Adam had had enough; he stopped answering my calls and blocked me from his life.

While intellectually I knew we were finished, I still yearned for him. I hated him but wanted him. What a mindfuck. One evening I found out he had canceled the tickets for a concert we had planned to go to together, and I just lost it. The concert was one more thing that he had "taken" from me, and it pushed me over the edge.

Blinded by sadness and defeat, I started to become anxious that I would never feel any different. This soon escalated into a panic attack. I tried to calm myself by taking a bath, and as the gasps for breath started to settle, my anguish turned into something else: apathy. Now the thoughts looping through my brain became something much darker. Maybe the only way to end the pain was to end my life. I went straight into the logistics of how I'd pull it off.

Would it be possible to die by suicide in such a way where I wouldn't traumatize someone who found my body? Well, if the house cleaner found me, it wouldn't be fair since she's a stranger. I can't let my friend who lent me her home find me—she was so gracious to let me stay.

No matter what scenario I came up with, I couldn't figure out how to do it without harming an innocent person. Who would have thought my good manners would save me?

I had clearly hit rock bottom.

The next day, I woke up asking myself these questions:

How did I get here?

Why did this happen to me?

Where do I go now?

I was at a decision point. I could keep spiraling down, or I could fight to get myself back up.

My grief transmuted into anger. I would later learn that, in the stages of grieving, moving from sadness to anger was a positive sign—it was energy moving. I decided I was done suffering. I made an action plan to get myself back on my feet, and for a while, it worked. But then some reminder of Adam would send me back spiraling, and I'd be on the floor crying again.

As time went on, the crying may have become less frequent, but acting bitter and resentful became my norm. I was walking around with an invisible sandwich board that read: THIS HEART IS CLOSED FOR BUSINESS. Friends who visited me found themselves held hostage by my one-woman self-pity show, starring me.

Determined to enter the next stage of my life, I desperately searched for a safe place where I could receive the healing I so needed. I tried everything: therapy, acupuncture, Reiki, meditation, chakra cleansing, psychic readings . . . you name it. In between the super woo-woo healers advising me to repeat positive mantras and the therapists reminding me how messed up my childhood was, I had no idea if anything was working. I went to Mexico on a yoga retreat, and while it was fun to get my om on, the moment I got home I was faced with all the same feelings I had before I left. I wasn't getting better. I was just suspending time.

One day, as I was repeating my story for the hundredth time to a friend I hadn't seen since the breakup, something shifted. I had exerted so much energy in despising Adam and trying to recruit others to do the same that I was exhausted. I watched myself casting blame and aspersions on everyone and everything, and something dawned on me:

I may not be able to change the events of my history, but I *can* choose to change the story I attach to those events.

I was choosing a story that wasn't serving me. My anger and pain kept me hyperfocused on how I had been wronged. I needed to reframe my relationship in my story. I needed to see my time with Adam as a bridge to something better, not as a destination I was now never going to reach. The only way to cross the bridge, however, was to take the energy I had wasted hating Adam and channel it into something empowering for myself.

I wanted to learn everything I could about the science, psychology, and spirituality of heartbreaks and relationships. I wanted to help others. Because if I could help another heartbroken person feel a little less alone and a little more hopeful, then maybe my pain was worth it. This work gave me a new purpose for my life.

Taking what I learned during my journey to acceptance and healing, I decided that I was going to help other women by creating for them what didn't exist for me: a breakup bootcamp so that women would not have to suffer through heartbreak alone.

In 2017, Renew Breakup Bootcamp became a reality.

Each bootcamp has a team of what I call "heart hackers"—more than a dozen experts ranging from psychologists to hypnotists and energy healers—to assist women in processing their pain in order to heal, rewire their subconscious patterns, and shift limiting beliefs. Countless women have been able to transform their lives after Renew, the very ones who were once stuck feeling "crazy," crying:

"It's like the rug has been pulled out from underneath me."

"I'm scared I won't ever find someone else."

"I gave him the best years of my life."

Within a year, this multiday retreat was featured on the front page of the *New York Times,* with segments on *Nightline, Good Morning*

America, and *The Doctors* and in articles in national publications including *Fortune, Glamour, Marie Claire,* and more.

"Breakup bootcamp is now a thing," wrote *Vogue,* noting the luxury aspect of the "relaxing weekend away." CNN focused on the digital detox aspect of the retreat, a place where "no phones are allowed," and the *New York Times* called it a "getaway for those of us who just can't get over it," highlighting the range of experts from the scientific to the metaphysical. The bootcamp was receiving international attention for its holistic approach to healing heartbreak, how every detail was intentionally designed, from the group therapy to the nutritious food to the luxurious environment in nature. I was thrilled. It meant that my hunch was right—and that other women also needed what I had been looking for.

I took my ten years of research, writing, and trial and error in my journey of creating a better version of myself to craft the ultimate curriculum to help women move through the heartbreak process. The program design is based on everything I wish had existed for me. I wanted to give my clients the luxury of a beautiful retreat setting and delicious food, and also arm them with tools so they would leave the retreat stronger, different. After a weekend at bootcamp, I wanted them to have a new story of their past, present, and future; a new plan; a new kind of inspiration. I worked with psychologists, neuroscientists, behavioral scientists, coaches, sex educators, and spiritual healers to develop every minute of programming. It worked. It is working.

Now, I am sharing everything I've learned from my clients, from experts, from research, and from my own journey with you, dear reader. This isn't your typical relationship book by any means. This isn't a dating guide. This is a living guide. This is a learning guide. This is a loving guide. This is a book on how to live better, learn more, and love yourself, so your next relationship will thrive.

YOU MAY NOT BE ABLE TO CHANGE THE EVENTS OF YOUR HISTORY, BUT YOU CAN CHOOSE TO CHANGE THE STORY YOU ATTACH TO THOSE EVENTS.

A LOVE LETTER

Here we are, two strangers connected by common experience. Heartache. Feeling disappointed in love. Exhausted from the suffering. Where do you begin when pain seems like it has permeated every single cell of your body? How do you even begin to have hope that this "happened for a reason" when you can't even see a reason to get out of bed?

Yes, it can hurt that bad.

I understand. That pain used to overwhelm me too. It followed me around like a ghost that I couldn't escape, even in my sleep where it haunted my nightmares. I used to hate that pain. I used to cry at the injustice of what had happened. I questioned karma, I questioned humanity, I questioned if I would ever feel happy again.

I'm here to tell you a secret. The pain doesn't go away.

Instead, it transforms. It alchemizes into something beautiful. It becomes a part of your depth, your compassion, your empathy to see another woman who is also suffering from heartbreak and, in one look, help her feel a little less alone. That shared humanity, that compassion that we're all perfectly imperfect humans finding our path, that connection—is love.

I'm not here to take away your pain or to heal you. I'm not going to offer a magic pill that will fast-forward a way around the hurt. Instead, I'm here to provide tried-and-true tools to help you move *through* the pain and pave a new path forward. I'm here to give you permission—to mourn, to grieve, to feel all the feels—and assure you that you don't have to adhere to a timeline to "get over it." I'm here to emphasize that this very process of falling, of getting back up and learning, *is* your power.

Strength is the practice of opening your heart, even when it hurts. Especially when it hurts. It's to confront the pain with compassion and curiosity, even when it feels much easier to avoid, distract, or suppress. Strength is to let the feelings—the good, the bad, and the ugly—

expand your emotional range. You are in the natural cycle of life, and the ending of a cycle marks the beginning of a new one.

You are not broken; you are just bruised. You are not shattered; you are just shape-shifting. This shake-up is merely a pivot for you to change the direction of your life. Trust the unfolding. Surrender to it. You are the author of your story; every choice you make is words on a page, writing your next chapter.

What story do you want to tell?

Your pain is a catalyst for change. Together, we are going to embark on an adventure to dissect the past so that we can build an empowering, inspiring future.

Are you ready to renew?

IT'S NEVER JUST ABOUT THE EX

There is nothing stronger than a broken woman who has
rebuilt herself.

Hannah Gadsby

It's never about the ex.

It's always about the recycled pain.

We often re-create the emotional experience of how we were
wounded as children. If we do not heal the original source of our
wounds, we will continue to repeat the same emotional experience—
just with different people.

The majority of people we date will not be our destination. They
were meant to be bridges; each relationship is an opportunity for us to
learn a lesson so we don't keep repeating a pattern, crossing the same
bridge over and over again. Each time we cross a bridge, we have a
chance to become a stronger, wiser version of ourselves.

Even the most painful relationships reveal critical information
about habits wired deep in our subconscious. If we don't stop to assess
the lessons, if we don't tap into the wisdom the journey was meant to
provide, we get stuck.

As we expose the core wounds, beliefs, and patterns that govern
how we show up in our intimate relationships and learn how to re-

place old habits with healthier ones, we shift our direction. One degree at a time, we eventually find ourselves at a new destination.

But here's something I've been waiting to tell you: that destination is not a happily-ever-after relationship. It comes from within.

After crossing enough bridges, we realize that the destination is actually never about another person; it's about self-love. This is the foundation needed before a healthy partnership with another is possible. But before we get there, we need to see the bridge for what it is.

And it starts one ex at a time.

One of the best guides to how to be self-loving is to give ourselves the love we are often dreaming about receiving from others. There was a time when I felt lousy about my over-forty body, saw myself as too fat, too this, or too that. Yet I fantasized about finding a lover who would give me the gift of being loved as I am. It is silly, isn't it, that I would dream of someone else offering to me the acceptance and affirmation I was withholding from myself.

bell hooks, All About Love

A DAY AT BREAKUP BOOTCAMP

"No hate-fest rabbit holes," I tell the latest group of women to come to Renew Breakup Bootcamp. "We are not here to find more reasons

THE MAJORITY OF PEOPLE
WE DATE WILL NOT BE OUR
DESTINATION. THEY WERE
MEANT TO BE BRIDGES;
EACH RELATIONSHIP IS AN
OPPORTUNITY FOR US TO
LEARN A LESSON SO WE
DON'T KEEP REPEATING A
PATTERN, CROSSING THE
SAME BRIDGE OVER AND
OVER AGAIN. EACH TIME
WE CROSS A BRIDGE,
WE HAVE A CHANCE TO
BECOME A STRONGER,
WISER VERSION OF
OURSELVES.

to bash the ex. The question we are going to explore is: Why were you drawn to this person in the first place? Did you ignore the red flags? Did you give away your power and sense of self-worth to someone else? Why?"

Each time a Renew participant exclaims what a surprise her breakup, infidelity, or separation was, when we dig deeper, we discover it was not all that shocking. There were signs. There was a gut feeling something wasn't right. There was the gradual chipping away of self-worth, the overstepping of boundaries, or a trail of red flags ignored. We can get so consumed in our relationships that we don't even realize that we are losing ourselves to them, and only when the relationship crashes do we finally get the message that something wasn't working.

Having spoken to hundreds of women about their heartaches, I've noticed that they generally fall into a handful of categories, but of course not everyone fits in a tidy little box.

The overachiever: She kills it in her career and adopted a "do more, get more" mentality when she was young. This root belief comes from "I'm not enough," often from childhood, when she learned she'd receive love or validation only if she earned it. The coping mechanism does wonders for getting high grades and promotions, but it doesn't translate into healthy romantic relationships. These women are often the hardest on themselves. When it comes to their healing, they become frustrated with themselves that they can't just do something to make the pain go away immediately. They harbor an extra layer of shame because they see their suffering as weakness that they can't get rid of.

The superhuman: With similarities to the overachiever, the superhuman is the woman who prides herself on doing it all. She demands perfection of herself and others. She is constantly fixing herself, learning all the latest techniques and methods in order to have the relationship she wants. Without realizing it, she approaches relationships the same way she approached getting a 4.0 in school. Sometimes this woman is so in her head that she's disconnected from her body. Her focus on doing has stopped her from simply being. She finds it hard to stay still. Her judgment of others who do not meet her standards of perfection mirrors her self-judgment and lack of acceptance of self. Her root belief is "I'm unlovable," and she's adapted by being useful in order to be loved.

The pleaser: She bends over backward for her relationship but, in the end, feels abandoned, unappreciated, and starved for more love and investment from her partner. Her root belief is "I'm not worthy of love." She's adapted by becoming a doormat. She prioritizes the needs of others before her own, because deep down inside, she doesn't feel that she is worthy of having her needs met. She's petrified that if she were to express her needs, she'd get rejected or abandoned.

The anxious: When she gets into a relationship, she feels most comfortable if she can completely merge with her partner and puts her relationship at the center of her world. Her life, identity, and priorities revolve around the relationship. She has a hard time with boundaries. Her root belief is "I'm not safe/okay on my own." Her partner becomes the foundation she stands on, the only person who can make her okay, and when the relationship is in turmoil or ends, she feels like the rug has been ripped out from beneath her.

The closed heart: She's been hurt so badly that she's never fully recovered from the trauma. Even if on a cognitive level she's over her ex, her subconscious still associates love with pain. Her belief is that she cannot trust and therefore it is not safe to open her heart. She either stops dating completely or dates people whom she knows she won't fall for or ever truly have to be vulnerable with. She may even date people who live in a different city/country or chase a fantasy relationship, because, subconsciously, she knows these won't ever amount to a real relationship. Her heart is locked behind a gate, and people need to prove themselves relentlessly to get her to open.

The jaded: She's been disappointed so many times that she defaults to skepticism and cynicism. Her beliefs are that there are no good men out there, she's too [insert self-criticism here] to date, and dating sucks in her city (or whatever excuse she can rationalize) to explain why she's still single. Her exterior is hard to compensate for the soft heart that was hurt, rejected, and betrayed in the past. She gives off an aggressive "don't fuck with me" energy to show how confident and untouchable she is, but inside, she feels insecure and afraid.

The addict: Unable to self-soothe, she uses validation from men as her vice. She has a belief that love is chaotic. She feels alive in the rush of lust and will create drama to keep a rush, any rush, going. She avoids true intimacy by reveling in fantasy and chasing highs, and operates in extremes.

Regardless of which category these women fall into and no matter how powerful they may appear on the outside, each and every one of them struggles with feeling disempowered in her romantic relationships.

Sitting in a circle, the participants reveal one by one what brought them here (all names and identifying details have been changed).

"I know I deserve better," says Leila, a gorgeous, newly divorced professional powerhouse who has conquered the corporate world but can't seem to rid herself of toxic relationship patterns. "We keep breaking up and getting back together. I know I deserve better, but my self-esteem is so broken. I just can't seem to let go."

She was twenty-nine when she met Mike, a charismatic venture capitalist who lived in New York. The beginning of their relationship was exhilarating. Mike courted her with grand romantic gestures and weekend getaways. As time went by, Leila planned her life around Mike, and without realizing, her personal validation had become entirely based on Mike's attention. But it was never enough. She wanted more of everything: more time, more commitment, more connection. He started to grow distant. Leila would rearrange her schedule to accommodate his and give more and more, putting her needs second, hoping her devotion would make Mike love her.

Instead, she got dumped.

"I don't feel in love anymore," his text read.

It didn't take much searching on Instagram to find out he had met someone else.

The women pour their hearts out with story after story, often apologizing for their tears. Even in the midst of their pain, many of them feel guilty, as if their emotions were a burden to the group.

Jenny was in an on-again, off-again relationship with an addict. She knew logically the relationship was unhealthy but couldn't resist getting back with him whenever he reappeared. This lasted for eight years.

Cindy's first husband physically abused her. Her next boyfriend was emotionally abusive and kept constant surveillance on her, accusing her of cheating when she was not. She kept hoping he would change, but he never did. It wasn't until he threatened to kill her that she realized he was, in fact, as dangerous as her ex-husband, if not more so.

Teresa wanted a husband and family so badly that she was willing to settle for anyone who seemed nice and stable. Because she'd get anxious dating people she liked, she settled for a boyfriend with whom she had zero chemistry, hoping attraction would grow. It never did.

Karolina was fake dating. She gave the guy she liked the girlfriend experience without him ever committing to be her boyfriend. She would keep giving and giving in hope for a commitment. It never came.

These relationships were all unhealthy, yet each of the women was devastated by her breakup. Why?

Regardless of the situation, age, or background, all of them had one thing in common. In their heads they all embraced a linear relationship model that progressed like this: date, move in, get married, have kids, stay together forever. That plan indicated "success"—at least, success in the eyes of mainstream society. They would do whatever possible to keep that plan intact, even if that meant enduring abuse and sacrificing their own needs.

After more exploration with each of the participants at Renew, it became apparent that the greatest source of the pain around their breakups was not the ex or even the relationship—it was the destruction of their sacred relationship plan.

I was no different. Any guy I liked I would analyze to see if he could be a potential boyfriend/husband/father. In conquest mode, I was never fully present, because I was always anxious about the next step in the progression of my plan. I would "fall in love" quickly before I really knew someone (I'd later learn that is textbook infatuation, not love). I would fit the person into the plan I had in my mind, never cluing the guy in, of course. Half the time I didn't even really like the actual guy; I just liked the idea of him. Fantasy can really mess with you.

Whenever my "happily ever after" fell apart, I felt devastated. Was I "broken" because I lost my Prince Charming? No, it was because my identity revolved around the relationship and the plan I vehemently held on to.

When we are tied to one plan, we don't have the flexibility to adapt—and we can break. One of the first steps to healing from a breakup is to accept that the plan you have for your life can and will change and that you have to be willing to adapt.

To help Renew participants arrive at this notion, the women are in programming from 8:30 in the morning to 11:00 at night, bootcamp style. The intensive schedule is designed to push them past the edges of comfort to create the kind of emotional shake-up needed for new ideas to implant. After all, we're dealing with decades of destructive patterns. Many of the women who come to Renew have, like me, tried everything. Renew Breakup Bootcamp is their last resort.

Because true healing requires a fully holistic approach that encompasses the mind, body, and spirit, at Renew a psychologist deep dives into emotional regulation, shifting beliefs, self-compassion, and tools using cognitive behavioral therapy. An anxiety expert teaches tried-and-true practices designed to calm the nervous system, and a dating coach explains love addiction and how to break the cycle. A hypnotist and neurolinguistic programming master leads the women on a meditative journey to access their inner child. On a somatic level, a divorce mediator uses techniques derived from sacred and secular African movement to help the women process anger and anxiety through and out of the body. A holistic doctor takes them through a series of breath work exercises to help them release stored trauma and energetic blockages in the body. A sex educator teaches movement exercises to activate their sensual energy and reconnect to their bodies. The highlight of the weekend comes on Sunday, when a professional Dominatrix teaches the psychology of power dynamics. Private sessions with energy healers, life coaches, and intuitive mediums are also offered. The bootcamp experience is thoughtfully designed to guide attendees through the process of acceptance, letting go, forgiveness, and gratitude—all important elements of closure.

While you may not be able to make it to a physical retreat, consider this book the Breakup Bootcamp bible. All the tried-and-true methods, best practices, and tools have been extracted to help you experience Breakup Bootcamp in the comfort of your own home.

And a note to all readers: While this book is written as if speaking only to a female heteronormative audience, the information applies to anyone who's ever suffered heartache and wants to rewire unhelpful patterns, regardless of gender identity or sexual orientation.

When one door closes another door opens; but we often look so long and so regretfully upon the closed door, that we do not see the ones which open for us.

Alexander Graham Bell

Before we even begin the process of moving forward, we need to properly grieve the past. In order to accomplish this, it is helpful to understand what stage of grief you are in.

STAGES OF SEPARATION

Mourning the loss of a relationship can feel much like grieving someone who has passed away.

Grief has six stages, no matter what the source of that grief. Remember, the timeline for moving through grief is not always linear. There will be days you feel like you're over the hurt and ready to embrace your new life, only to find yourself triggered and catatonic the next day. This may seem like a setback, but it's a natural part of the process. Here are the six stages of grief, or more accurately in this context, separation.

Shock: Shock occurs both on a physical and on a psychological level. Physically, a surge of adrenaline rushes through the body, which may result in you feeling jittery, dizzy, and outside your body.[1] Psychologically, you may feel lost, panicky, overwhelmed, and inundated with intense emotions. This is your body's natural protection against pain. Your body has not yet adjusted to a new reality without your partner. Once you start to process what has happened, you reach the next stage: denial.

Denial: At its core, this is a rejection of reality. The sooner you accept reality—that it's over—the sooner you start the process of healing.

Depression: The first step of healing is depression. You feel sad, apathetic, and numb. Everything reminds you of your ex and the memories you shared. In this stage, your natural inclination may be to isolate yourself, but it's important that you embrace support from loved ones at this time.

Anger: Life seems unfair and unjust. You question why this is happening to you and may resent that your ex doesn't appear to be in as much pain. Anger indicates energy is moving, which can motivate you to make proactive changes.

Bargaining: Your brain doesn't want to accept it's over and starts to strategize ways to win back your ex or how to fix the relationship. During this stage you might ruminate on what you should have done differently or "better." You might even make up excuses to see your ex. You may relapse during this stage, reconnecting with your ex only to separate again. It may take a few cycles of being on-again, off-again before you reach a tipping point and accept that the same behavior is going to keep yielding the same results. It's important during this stage to not lose sight of the reality that your relationship ended for a reason and that both people were cocreators of its ending.

Acceptance: This stage is when you embrace the reality of the situation and start to make choices to help yourself move on. Now you can minimize catastrophic statements such as "I'll never love again" and "I will always be alone." You see hope for your future and decide you are ready to close the chapter and start the next one.

It's important to recognize that to get to the acceptance stage, you need to go through the other stages. You might feel stuck in one stage longer than another, and sometimes this is our way of holding on to the relationship. Because even if you're broken up, but you're still angry at your ex, or you're still bargaining to get back together, or you're obsessing over all the details of what went wrong—you're still in a relationship with the person.

There is no one size fits all in terms of the amount of time it will take to get over a breakup, although many tend to overestimate that the pain will last much longer than it actually does.[2] Clinical psychologist Ramani Durvasula suggests that it takes about six weeks after a breakup for many people to start to adjust to life without their ex.[3] Another study published in *The Journal of Positive Psychology* found that people felt better eleven weeks after their breakup.[4] Don't beat yourself up if your timeline is unique. Trust that there is an end to the suffering, even if you can't imagine it at the time.

The women who come to Renew are all at various stages. Some are fresh in the throes of loss, having broken up just weeks prior. Some are still in an on-again, off-again relationship that they can't seem to get out of. Some have been divorced for a few years and are having a hard time moving forward, let alone dating. Some are not dealing with a breakup at all but are frustrated with their romantic lives and want to change their patterns. It's helpful for all these women to witness one another. While in different stages of the cycle, they are all there for the same reason: they want a chance to create healthy love.

HEARTBREAK IN THE BRAIN

Understanding what's happening in the brain during a breakup is key to getting past it. A roller coaster of emotions after a breakup is natural. The same flood of chemicals that causes you to be blissfully in lust during the beginning stages of love also causes you to suffer when it ends.

During the first stage of dating, these chemicals are designed to make you and your mate procreate. The exhilaration, the obsessive thoughts of your new beloved, and those butterflies-in-the-stomach feelings are all a result of the motivation system—the mating drive that is a part of the reward system in the brain. We will examine in detail the exact chemicals present during the lust phase in later chapters, but what's important to note now is that during a breakup, your brain is experiencing those exact same chemical reactions, but in reverse.

Studies show that recently broken-up singles exhibit activity in the same part of the brain as a drug user fiending for a fix.[5] The brain is literally in withdrawal. The part of the brain affected, the ventral segmental area, is associated with motivation, goal-oriented behavior, and the reward system responsible for the release of dopamine. Dopamine is that feel-good chemical that leaves you wanting more of whatever stimulus gave you the reward in the first place, whether the stimulus is cocaine, chocolate, or a loving touch from your partner.[6] Dopamine cravings give you *motivation*, encouraging you to act in the way that will get you more of whatever it is you need, and in the case of romance, that need is your beloved. The brain is expecting the reward to come (validation from a partner, return of affection, physical touch); however, after a breakup, the reward either is delayed or doesn't come at all. Though on a cognitive level you know the relationship is over, the neurons in your brain that are expecting reward do not stop firing, keeping you unconsciously "in love" and addicted to your ex to get your fix.[7]

During a relationship, you have thousands of neural circuits in the brain that are devoted to your partner. Psychologist Phillip Shaver argues that during separation, "each [neural circuit] has to be brought up and reconstructed to take into account the person's absence."[8] I think of this as your brain requiring a major remodel.

Your brain is used to getting fed doses of dopamine from interactions with your partner. After the loss of that person, your brain doesn't immediately forget the feel of that dopamine and needs to learn to live without it. This takes time, and when you make contact, look at old texts, or obsess over his social media activity, you are activating those old neural circuits and connections. This only continues your attachment to your ex. In a process called "synaptic pruning," neural connections not being used are eliminated and the brain can focus on making new ones.[9] So, if you stop having contact, through time those neural pathways start to weaken. Hallelujah for the plasticity of the brain!

EMOTIONAL ADULTING

A breakup brings up a lot of emotions. You're not only dealing with the separation and the grief that follow the coupling's end but also any unresolved, suppressed emotions lingering from the past. So, instead of adding another layer of suppressed or unexplored emotions, we are going to face them, once and for all!

We need to clear our emotional debt and start living a life where we can actively process our feelings, so we don't end up in emotional insolvency. There are many dysfunctional ways we deal with emotions, including avoiding them, inflating them, or morphing them into something socially acceptable.

THE ONLY WAY OUT IS THROUGH— FEEL YOUR FEELINGS

We live in a society where we are taught to distract ourselves from, numb, and hide our pain. In a "just get over it" culture, we often do not honor that emotions have a life cycle, and they need the chance to be felt and processed. But when we avoid our emotions, they eventually creep up on us. It just takes one disappointment, criticism, or rejection, and the emotional time bomb goes off. Suddenly you're overwhelmed with not only the feelings of abandonment from the last guy but from the guy before that and the one from high school too. It's like a domino effect of compounding trauma. Without knowing the true source of your intense hurt, it's easiest to point the finger at the person or situation at hand. But it always comes from something deeper.

Healing starts when we can face our emotions as they arise, and the first step is to pause when we feel that uncomfortable feeling. We habitually act quickly to get out of feeling uncomfortable because that's how we are culturally programmed. We label feelings as "good" or "bad" and judge ourselves for feeling, instead of accepting that we are humans having a human experience.

There's another way we avoid dealing with our emotions, and it's a behavior I've witnessed in a majority of women who attend Renew. That behavior is being the caretaker of everyone but ourselves.

Forty-one-year-old Tracy was a single mom. Two years after her divorce, she met someone new, fell madly in love, and got engaged. Her fiancé was wealthy and charming, and he courted her with romantic intensity. Along with her self-given title of supermom, after dating her new Prince Charming, Tracy fell into a role she knew how to embrace, the super-wife-to-be. She accommodated her fiancé's schedule and where he wanted to live (even when that meant uprooting her life in the town where she had lived for a decade) and tended to his needs as a busy entrepreneur. When she wasn't serving her man, she was devoting every minute to giving her daughter a perfect life. Even in times of distress when her tank was near empty, she would give her last ounce of energy to the people she loved.

"It's all I know how to do," she cried during a group session.

Tracy, just like so many women, had been conditioned to be nurturing and to tend to the needs of others since girlhood. We grow up socialized to think that giving nonstop is what makes us a great girlfriend, wife, or mother. Even when we're gasping for our last breath, we put the oxygen mask on others first. But while we're out trying to win the martyr badge of honor, we don't realize that we're just avoiding dealing with our own stuff.

You see, when you're constantly taking care of the emotions of others, you don't have to face your own. How convenient!

This is not a healthy type of giving or nurturing. It's coming from an unhealthy intention (whether you're conscious of it or not), which is to avoid sitting in the discomfort of your feelings. Taking care of others as a way of avoidance can be just as addictive as reaching for alcohol or some other substance.

You've got to feel the emotions in order to process them. It's in this process of feeling, accepting, and reflecting that you learn critical lessons that are necessary for your growth and letting go.

EXERCISE: Identify Your Emotional Reaction Go-To

The moment you feel an uncomfortable emotion—whether that be sadness, anger, longing, and so on—what do you do? How do you react to the urge? Do you self-medicate by reaching for alcohol, drugs, food, or validation from others? Do you suppress your feelings and distract yourself with work? Or perhaps you inflate the emotion with catastrophic thinking, exaggerating the negatives and minimizing the positives? List how you might currently avoid/distract yourself from feeling and processing your emotions:

_____

_____

_____

_____

DO NOT FEED YOUR EMOTIONAL MONSTER

There is a difference between feeling emotions and feeding them. The former means being present with what you're feeling, accepting it, and letting it pass. The latter requires delivering more of what the emotion wants so that it can grow bigger. The emotion wants to grow in intensity, size, and frequency. Its food of choice is your thoughts, body language, and actions. It's not your sensible self that is playing Coldplay's "Fix You" on repeat while you sob in a fetal position. Nope, that's your hungry emotional monster!

The physiological life span of an emotion in the body and brain is ninety seconds, according to research by neuroscientist Jill Bolte Taylor.[10] That's right, the adrenaline rush, the heat in the face, the tightness in the chest, the rapid heartbeat—all those sensations will naturally rise, peak, and dissipate within a minute and a half. So, what causes emotions to linger?

The story you attach.

Instead of having awareness that the sensations of emotion will naturally flush out within minutes, we identify with the feeling and get stuck on how a person or a situation that caused it is wrong and how that person or situation *should* be, rather than accepting what is. Humans have a tendency to attach stories to emotions, because from an evolutionary perspective, the stories served as alerts to dangerous threats, which helped keep our ancestors alive. On top of that, when we're predisposed to feeling negative emotions (sad, anxious, ashamed, guilty, or angry), the corresponding neural pathways become stronger, and thus it becomes easier to trigger those emotions and the correlating stories.

The emotional spiral worsens when we repeat that story over and over, walking, if not sprinting, on a vicious loop going nowhere. This is the mental trap of rumination, the story becoming a blur with no start or end.

For example, after my breakup, I often felt out of sorts after restless nights of insomnia. My body was not in a healthy state, nor was my mind, making me prone to a good emotional hijacking. One day I was feeling particularly lonely and started to look at my ex's social media. I saw a photo where my ex was at a party, smiling with his friends, drink in hand. He looked like he was having a grand ol' time. I felt a surge of anger. Suddenly my mind started racing . . .

Did he meet someone else?

How dare he be having a good time, like nothing happened! He's not feeling any pain, while here I am, alone, depressed, and suffering!

I hate him!

I then painted him as a terrible person, crafting story after story confirming how unjust my situation was. I curled my body into a ball, dropped my head down, and put my hands over my face. But I kept going, looking at more photos, the photos of his friends. I worked myself into a rage. My anxiety surged. Soon, I was experiencing shortness of breath and burst into tears. Quickly, I was in a full-blown panic attack. Instead of letting that spark of anger pass, I kept adding stories, layer upon layer, retriggering the stress response. I not only kept my mind in a negative space, but my body experienced the anger over and over. This cascade of emotional turmoil was sparked from one picture. Once the emotional monster was fed, it hijacked my entire being, and off I went on the rumination roller coaster!

The Rumination Roller Coaster

First of all, rumination is a natural human tendency, especially after breakups. So, give yourself some slack if you take a ride or two. But learning how to redirect your thoughts so you don't overdo it is an art form.

Clinical psychologist Dr. Elaina Zendegui, who specializes in cognitive behavioral therapy and dialectical behavior therapy, teaches the women at Renew that the first step of changing our ruminative thinking patterns is to identify the cycle when it's happening. You want to catch the first signs, just like feeling the first drop of rain before a thunderstorm.

According to Dr. Zendegui, "Distressing emotions (e.g., shame, sadness, anxiety) or the bodily sensations associated with them may be clues that you're ruminating. Once you catch yourself ruminating, gently pull your attention back to the present moment. Gently refocus your attention to your sensory experiences or your breath. When the cycle restarts (and it probably will), notice this and bring your attention back again. If you need more practice, as many of us do, you can begin a daily mindfulness meditation practice to build skills around awareness of ruminative patterns and drawing your attention to the present moment."

In the following sections, we will go over tried-and-true methods that can help you stop rumination in its tracks and move the emotions through and out of the body. But first, let's look at how your ruminating thoughts and stories could be retraumatizing yourself.

Are You Retraumatizing Yourself?

How many times have you told your story about the awful breakup? As you recounted the story in vivid detail, your friends and family may have tried to show their support by echoing your sentiments: *What a loser. Such a narcissist! I can't believe this happened to you!*

Your well-intentioned friends think it's empathetic to use pain as a way to connect. But the bash-the-ex rabbit hole only fuels the emotional charge. The story also begins to morph, taking a slightly different form each time it's told. Like the messages in a game of telephone, our memories are not facts and are changed ever so slightly each time they're recalled.

Research into the molecular mechanism of memory and learning reveals that whenever we recall a scene—or retrieve a memory to our conscious mind—we disrupt it, and by doing so, we alter it forever.

Amir Levine and Rachel S. F. Heller[11]

When you apply a filter of victimization, and add interpretations and assumptions to the mix, your story distorts into something much more painful. No longer is your story about your breakup, but now it's about how you gave him the best years of your life, how there's no good men out there and that you'll be alone forever. You merge fact and fiction, creating dramatic stories that haunt your present and future.

And by recounting that story over and over again, you retraumatize yourself.

Our body cannot tell the difference between events in the past, the present, and the future.[12] When we relive our story over and over again, recounting the memories in painstaking detail, our body is creating a stress response. Ever burst into tears while you're talking about something traumatic that happened years ago? That's because your body thinks the scene you're recalling is happening in real time.

EXERCISE 1: What's Your Version of the Story?

When we vilify someone, we automatically assume the role of the victim. That does not help you heal or move forward. Throughout this book, we are going to actively reframe your story. To start, grab your journal and a pen. In ten points, write your story about what happened between you and your ex. You can start anywhere you'd like, just keep it to ten points. You get to cheat on this one—you can make each point as long as you'd like. Elaborate as if you were telling the story to a friend. We will be using this ten-point story for the next exercise.

Caught in a Thinking Trap?

Your brain can be one tricky son of a bitch. After all, it was designed over two hundred thousand years ago. It was designed to make you survive the harsh conditions of the environment, and the hunter-gatherers who were the most sensitive to any risks or cues of danger had the best chance of survival. Also, social exclusion from the tribe was a matter of life or death. Even though today we don't face the same threats, our brains have yet to adapt. Our brains are still survival machines, have an innate negativity bias, and are extremely sensitive to social rejection. The reason you can get into rumination spirals of negative thinking isn't because you're crazy; it's because your brain is doing its job—trying to keep you safe.

But the same MO also can keep us in negative thinking traps! Behavioral scientist and positive change strategist Dr. Naomi Arbit explains:

"Neuroscientists have pinpointed an area of the left cerebral hemisphere, often referred to as 'the interpreter.' This part of our brain is constantly weaving narratives in order to try and help us maintain our sense of self, our personal narrative. This interpreter filters incoming information and experiences and puts its own spin on it. But the narratives fabricated by this part of the brain do not necessarily correspond with the truth. This is worsened by our tendency to believe these narratives and accept them as fact."

Our brain weaves its own narratives and that can cause us to create cognitive distortions. Also referred to as thinking traps, these are irrational ways of thinking that reinforce negative thinking, often perpetuating psychological states like depression and anxiety.[13]

EXERCISE 2: Separate Fact from Fiction

Review your ten-point story and separate fact from fiction. Start by identifying and circling any of the common thinking traps. Notice if there are any thinking traps you are more prone to. Once you've done this, write your story again, but this time use only five points and stick to the facts.

- **Filtering:** Focusing on only the negative, filtering out any positives. Also referred to as negativity bias (e.g., *The whole relationship was a lie*).

- **Catastrophizing:** Thinking in extremes and imagining the worst-case scenario (e.g., *I'll be alone forever*).

- **Overestimating:** Exaggerating and amplifying the chance that something bad will happen (e.g., *If I run into him I'll have a mental breakdown*).

- **Fortune-Telling:** Predicting the future as if it's 100 precent factual (e.g., *I'll never find love at this age*).

- **Overgeneralizing:** Making sweeping conclusions and broad assumptions based on one or a few experiences (e.g., *I was cheated on, so all men are liars*).[14]

- **Mind Reading:** Misconstruing facts and data and assuming that you know what others are thinking or feeling (e.g., *He looked at me and then said something to his friend with a chuckle, he must be making fun of me*).

- **Should Statements:** Imposing expectations on yourself or others of how things should be, which is often rooted in criticism, judgment, and arbitrary rule-making (e.g., *I should have been married by this age, I'm so stupid for wasting my best years on that guy*).[15]

- **Blaming:** Refusing to take accountability for emotions, thoughts, and actions (e.g., *It's his fault I'm so broken*).

- **Personalizing:** Making situations about you even when there's no evidence or logical reason to do so (e.g., *I must be unworthy of love because he ghosted me*).

- **Change Fallacy:** Expecting people to change in order for you to feel a certain way. Often rooted in a belief that others are responsible for your happiness (e.g., *If he put a ring on my finger, then I'd be happy and feel safe*).

- **All-or-Nothing Thinking:** Perceiving situations or people in black and white, often using words such as "always," "never," "everybody," and "nobody" (e.g., *Men never want to commit to me. This always happens to me*).

Once you've finished your five points, notice if the updated story feels a little less emotionally charged. Does it seem more neutral, lighter? We will be referring back to this updated story in the last chapter.

IF YOU WANT TO HEAL, EXPRESS YOUR ANGER

After a breakup, you're in survival mode. Emotions are at an all-time high, and not having them overwhelm you is a challenge, to say the least. This time is also a training ground for you to learn emotional regulation, a skill that, once acquired, you can apply for the rest of your life during trying moments. As you move from one stage of separation to another and back again, you'll need different tools, depending on what emotion is popping up. It's like a game of emotional whack-a-mole!

LET YOUR FREAK(-OUT) FLAG "FLOW"

> Angry people live in angry bodies.
>
> *Bessel van der Kolk*

Studies show that bereaved people who avoid grief and make an effort to suppress emotion take the longest to recover from loss.[16] When you try to repress your anger, stress skyrockets.

Anger can be broken down into two main components: the emotional component (how it feels in the body) and the behavioral component (how the anger is expressed).[17] Our goal is to express anger in a healthy way, without aggression (hurtful or harmful actions) or suppression.

The opposite of suppression is expression. We've got to process the emotional energy that is stuck in your body. Remember, the way forward is through.

Seeing Red

To help Renew participants work through anger from an energetic approach, naturopathic doctor and holistic coach Erica Matluck leads one of the first physical sessions on the first day of bootcamp. She explains how anger is rooted in the solar plexus chakra, which correlates anatomically with the abdomen. Chakras are energy centers that, when blocked, can trigger physical, emotional, and mental imbalances. Instead of letting the energy of anger build up and result in a volcanic explosion, she teaches the women to use a combination of intention and imagination to defuse it. Here's how.

EXERCISE 1: Transmute Your Anger

- Stand up tall with your feet firmly on the ground, shoulder-width apart. Close your eyes.

- Assign your anger the color red.

- Bring your attention to your solar plexus (the area around your belly button).

- Visualize the red color in this area and really feel it. Pay attention to the sensations. Notice the temperature and how the sensations move with your breath.

- Next, identify a word that is needed to heal the anger ("forgiveness," "acceptance," "compassion," etc.) and assign that word a color (blue works well for most people).

- Imagine that color pouring into your body through your abdomen and let it flood your entire body and the area around your body. Watch it change the color of your anger and flush it out completely until you are bathed in the second color.

- Take a few deep breaths here and repeat the exercise three times.

Plank a Pose!

In the second exercise, Dr. Matluck emphasizes the importance of moving the energy of the emotion through the body. Energy is meant to flow, and when it doesn't, it can cause dysfunction in the body.

She suggests that there is a strong relationship between healing anger and confronting limiting beliefs: "Fire is the element associated with this chakra, and by creating heat in the body while confronting limitations set by the mind, we can use the energy of fire to transform anger that is stored in the body."

To demonstrate this, she leads the women through an exercise where they set a timer and do a plank pose for as long as they believe they can. When they can no longer hold it, they look at the timer to note where their perceived limit is. Next, the women are advised to add thirty seconds to their previous time and repeat the plank pose. You can hear grunts in the room as they reluctantly try again.

"Watch the urge to give up and allow the heat you're creating melt your anger away," Dr. Matluck encourages as she walks among the women, burning sage as a way to cleanse the space.

As she notices some women struggling to hold their plank position, she advises them to bring their focus back to the breath, breathing slowly and deeply, and to continue pushing past their limit. When the entire room is done with the second plank, almost every single woman was able to hold her plank longer than her first time—a small but meaningful feat in pushing past a perceived limit.

EXERCISE 2: Ready to Plank?

- Create a plank position with your body. You have the option of supporting your upper body with your hands or your forearms.

- Set a timer and do the pose for as long as you can.

- When you're done with your first plank, note the amount of time you were able to hold your position—this is what you believe your limit is.

- Rest for a few minutes.

- Set your timer, adding thirty seconds to your previous time, and repeat the pose. Don't forget to breathe deeply.

- Imagine your anger melting away. If it helps, use the visualization from the first exercise, imagining your anger in a red color and it melting or fading away.

- Try to keep going, even after the time is up!

EXERCISE 3: Ready, Set, Write!

The last exercise is to reflect through journaling. By writing about how we feel and where we feel it, we start to make sense of what is happening. This is a great time to try "flow state" writing. Set a timer for fifteen minutes and make sure you turn off your phone or other distractions so that you are uninterrupted. Put an inspiring song on repeat to help you reach a state of flow. At Renew, we play Cello Suite no. 1 in G Major, by Johann Sebastian Bach, for this writing exercise. Give yourself a writing prompt and go! Here are some examples:

- What are my deepest areas of grief and frustration?

- What is my body trying to tell me?

- What can I learn?

Try not to filter or judge your thoughts; just keep the pen going. By doing a flow state exercise like this, parts of your subconscious start to come out—it's like emptying what's been stored and stuck in the mind. The act of writing is therapeutic in itself and can decrease physiological reactivity.

WHEN YOU'RE WIGGIN' THE F* OUT (AKA FEELING ANXIETY)

You couldn't help but peek at his Instagram (okay, maybe that's an understatement) and went down a rabbit hole of stalking all of his most recent likes. Ugh, what's that Instagram model got that you don't?

Whatever the trigger is, the angst starts to build, and suddenly you're feeling as if your world is collapsing. The panic is real.

Physically experiencing a sense of anxiety is a natural by-product of breakups, according to neuroscientist Jaak Panksepp, who suggests that rejection and separation from a loved one plunges us into "primal panic."[18] We are wired to connect as a species. Even though a separation is not physically dangerous, the amygdala is processing the loss of connection as a threat to survival. On top of that, the brain is in a neurochemical withdrawal, which results in a heightened state of anxiety and obsession that can permeate your emotional state for hours, even days.[19] Here are tools to help you prevent the downward spiral from happening.

Shake, Shake, Shake

When we face extreme emotion, our body is flooded with adrenaline and our heart rate skyrockets.[20] That's because our body's sympathetic nervous system, which is responsible for our ability to respond to perceived danger, gets activated.

This occurs in both animals and humans. Let's take the gazelle, for example. When a gazelle is confronted with a predator, its survival instincts take over and it will go into flight, fight, or freeze mode.[21] Once the threat is gone, it will shake its entire body as if having a convulsion. Its nervous system is physically discharging the excess energy and arousal caused by the threat. Equilibrium returns shortly thereafter.[22]

For an anxious person, a trigger that threatens her safety causes the same cascade of survival mechanisms. Next time you feel anxiety, instead of absorbing the energy, try shaking your entire body for a couple of minutes to get rid of the excess stress chemicals and restore your inner balance.

Move Your Body

If shaking isn't your preferred method of releasing excess energy, you can opt for a jog or some other physical activity that changes your biology. But if taking twenty minutes to go for a run isn't possible, do jumping jacks followed by a meditation. The key is to knock yourself out of the panicked and high-stress physical state first. By following up the activity with a calming meditation to center you, you can actually interrupt the anxiety spiral in its tracks.

During a session at Breakup Bootcamp, a participant, Lydia, who was still very much in love with the ex-boyfriend who had cheated on her, had a moment when she got to practice this. She was in the middle of a session where the topic of infidelity was being discussed, and suddenly she felt a pang of anxiety. She excused herself and walked out, and I followed her outside. She started weeping, trying to catch her breath in between sobs as she screamed how unfair her situation was. She was scared about what would happen upon returning home, and her panic started to escalate. I could tell she was about to start hyperventilating, so I had her try this practice on the spot. With my guidance, we both started to move our bodies, shaking, jumping, and flicking our hands, arms, and legs. Then we did a deep-breathing exercise together, ensuring the exhales were longer than the inhales (this has a calming effect). Lydia was able to regain an emotional equilibrium, and we had a calm conversation about what sparked the angst. At first, Lydia was embarrassed that she had to leave the session, but she was grateful that the moment happened so that she could experience how to calm herself down in real time, a tool she still uses today.

Breathe It Out, Literally

The one thing we can always count on—the miracle within every one of us—is our breath. It has two functions: (1) to nourish the body with oxygen, and (2) to cleanse the body of toxic waste.

The breath is connected to our mind and our emotions. Breathing fast and shallow creates panic, whereas breathing slowly and deeply creates calm. Take control of your breath, and you'll minimize stress, think more clearly, and naturally self-soothe.

Are you breathing through your nose or mouth? You want to start breathing in and out through your nose, as this helps filter the air, protecting the body from pollution and dust. Nose breathing also moistens the air coming in, which helps protect respiratory passageways.

Are you expanding your belly when you inhale? When you inhale, your belly should expand like it's a balloon filling up, which enables you to use the full capacity of your lungs. When you breathe out, the belly should deflate. If your belly isn't expanding and contracting, then you're breathing shallowly, which doesn't properly oxygenate your organs and can contribute to feelings of anxiety or panic.

Is your breathing fast or slow? Breathe slowly and rhythmically to expel metabolic waste products. If your exhalations are shorter than your inhalations, you're prohibiting the body's ability to rid itself of toxins.

Are your shoulders hunched or open? Keep your shoulders back and spine straight. If your shoulders are hunched, your chest is concave, restricting your ability to breathe deeply.

EXERCISE: 4-7-8 Breathing Technique

The 4-7-8 breathing sequence is based on an ancient yoga technique and was developed by Dr. Andrew Weil. It will help calm down stress and anxiety immediately.[23]

1. Place the tip of your tongue on the roof of your mouth (right behind your front teeth).

2. Breathe in through your nose for a count of four seconds.

3. Hold your breath for seven seconds.

4. Release your breath through your mouth with a whooshing sound for a count of eight seconds.

5. Without a break, repeat the entire technique four times in a row, then resume normal breathing and activity.

The 4-7-8 breathing technique is effective, because when you are feeling anxiety, your breathing tends to become very shallow and you don't get all the oxygen you need. This technique helps you increase oxygen intake, allows the oxygen to energize your cells, and expels carbon dioxide from your lungs.

QUICK TIP: *If you can't remember the count, that's okay. Just remember to make your exhale longer than your inhale, as this calms your parasympathetic nervous system. Unlike the sympathetic nervous system, which is responsible for fight or flight, the parasympathetic nervous system, often referred to as "rest and digest," is responsible for relaxing the body.*

'BOUT THAT DOPAMINE (AKA I NEED A PICK-ME-UP)

After my breakup, sides of me came out that I never knew existed.

I would stalk the social media of the woman my ex had cheated with, obsessing for hours and imagining the scene of the infidelity. I would reach out to my ex and berate him (until he eventually blocked me). I would talk nonstop about the details of the betrayal to anyone who'd listen. Oh, and the lavish revenge plans I devised could have made for an Oscar-winning horror movie.

Let's just say, I was not fun to be around during this time. No, I hadn't gone crazy (well, maybe just a little). My brain was seeking a reward in the midst of the trauma it had endured.

If I could have found some information that would solve the puzzle of my confusion, I thought I would find the relief I was seeking. Contacting my ex, even though each interaction was awful, was still providing me with a hit of dopamine.

The brain is going to do what it needs to survive, and in the case of breakups, it will seek out dopamine to provide the same reward that it received during the relationship. We can't choose whether our brain seeks out dopamine, but we can choose the source of where we get that dopamine from. If you're experiencing withdrawal symptoms such as depression, anxiety, lethargy, loss of appetite, and insomnia, here are some ways to get that dopamine hit in a healthier way.

Notice the triggering emotional need. When you get that urge to contact the ex or read old text messages, pause and take stock of what emotion is behind the urge. When you become aware of the driving emotion, you can distill the driving need behind the emotion. Are you feeling bored and need stimulation? Are you feeling lonely because you are craving human connection? Are you stressed and have a need for physical comfort?

When you pinpoint the underlying need that's not being met, you can figure out another way to satisfy that need. For example, if it's connection you're craving, then you can reach out to a friend and get your fix that way. If it's stress you're experiencing and you're craving the hugs you used to get from your partner, try getting a Swedish massage.[24] Research has shown that receiving a massage can lower the stress hormone cortisol, while increasing the mood-balancing chemical serotonin. Notice the urge when it arises and find creative ways to satisfy it that don't involve your ex.

Remove and replace. It's time to digitally detox from your ex. Delete old messages and photos, unfollow his accounts, and, even better, take a break from social media altogether. Block his number if you have to, so you don't obsess about him *not* contacting you. Your brain is primed for obsessive behavior during this time and your motivation system is in crave mode. Thus, every time you stalk his social media or text him, you are falling into a mental trap that keeps you addicted. To stop this self-sabotaging cycle, the first step is to recognize what is happening in your brain. The second is to recognize you have the choice to either let that urge control you or take control of it.

Before you stroll down memory lane and binge on old videos and photos of your romantic dates, stop and ask, "Am I being kind to myself right now?" You know the answer. Replace the urge with another behavior that forces you to be present. This may mean you go for a jog, cook a meal with a friend, or write a letter of gratitude to someone you love. The first few times you divert your behavior it will feel contrived and extremely challenging, but the more you practice replacing the self-sabotaging urge with a healthy practice, the easier it becomes.

Sure, there will be a time when you can see a reminder of your ex and not get triggered into an emotional spiral, but now is not the time to play with fire. During the early stages of separation, the attachment is still too strong and the emotional charge too high, and thus a complete detox of the ex is required. If you work together or coparent and cutting off communication isn't possible, then the goal is to keep interactions to a minimum and without any positive or negative charge. That means when you get good news and feel tempted to share it with your ex, you call your friend instead. Or when you're feeling angry, you stop yourself from picking a fight. You want to keep your interactions as neutral as possible so you're not continuing to get a "hit" of dopamine from him. And yes, even when you're picking a fight, you're still getting a hit. The emotional charge keeps you attached.

To truly cherish the things that are important to you, you must first discard those that have outlived their purpose.

Marie Kondo

Remove physical reminders. Addicts can relapse because of external triggers. The more you can decrease your exposure to tokens of your ex, the more you minimize your chances of relapse. Throw away the photos and get his things out of your sight. It also helps to change your living space. Move around your furniture, for example, to help minimize the association of your home with him. Minimize your clutter to metaphorically make space for the new to come in.

Put. Down. The. Phone. It's natural to crave contact with your ex (or scroll his feed) when you're in the withdrawal stage of a breakup. To help manage this, remind yourself that the craving is like an ocean wave that will build up to its peak state and then eventually subside.[25] Also, if your brain knows that the stimulus (in this case, a hit of dopamine from your ex) is impossible, the craving is minimized.[26] Set up a system that will help you get through the initial intensity of the craving. You can use a product like the Kitchen Safe that locks up your device with a set timer so you can literally save yourself from yourself. You can also install the app Freedom to block the internet or specific apps for a set period of time. Willpower is a finite source—set yourself up for success by putting systems in place.

Listen to music. No, not sad love songs that take you down memory lane. Choose upbeat, happy songs that can spark your inner Beyoncé. A study published in the *New York Times* found that when listening to "peak emotional moments" in music—that portion when you feel a "chill" of pleasure—dopamine is released both in anticipation and at crescendo.[27]

Thinking about a last hurrah? Think again. Near the center of the brain lies the deep limbic system. This part of the brain sets the emotional tone, promotes bonding, stores highly charged emotional memories, and modulates motivation and libido. Whenever you have sex, neurochemical changes occur in your brain that encourage limbic emotional bonding. In other words, while you may think you are just having casual sex, you are establishing an emotional bond whether you like it or not. Women have a larger limbic system than men and will typically feel more connected by sex. So, if you're trying to get over someone, literally do not get on top of or under him! Sex with the ex is prohibiting those bonds from breaking, keeping you more attached and addicted. Avoid that temptation at all costs.

Reach out. Feeling sad and out of sorts can cause you to withdraw from others and isolate yourself. It's crucial for you to override any tendency to disconnect. Instead reach out to someone who is stable and centered, because that person will have a calming effect on your nervous system. That's right, our nervous systems have evolved to be affected by the people around us in a process termed "dyadic regulation." Association with those who are grounded and centered activates our relational engagement system—a neural circuit that "uses the stability of another person's nervous system to help us stabilize our own."[28] Reach out to a friend or a professional for support, not necessarily to get answers but to feel the stability you need.

WHEN YOU NEED TO CHILL

Keep your relationship rumination at bay by practicing meditation, which will help you create distance from your thoughts and emotions and keep them from taking over. Research shows that meditation alters brain wave patterns, even if you're just starting the practice. One study revealed that those who practiced meditation for just eight weeks showed enhanced immune function and an increase in the part of the brain that creates "happy thoughts."[29]

If you already have a meditation practice, great! If not, here are some important things to know. First, science confirms that meditation is associated with decreased levels of stress, depression, anxiety, and insomnia. Research shows that it changes the brain, increasing gray matter critical for learning and memory, quality of life, connection, and compassion.[30] Think of it as a daily habit; like brushing your teeth is a practice of good oral hygiene, meditation is a practice of good mental hygiene.

You may have tried it before and thought, *I can't meditate. I can't clear my noisy mind.*

The goal of meditation is not to have zero thoughts; it's to be more mindful when the thoughts come up. This means to simply observe, without judgment, whatever thoughts arise. Imagine your thoughts are clouds floating by. Practicing mindfulness is not about resisting thoughts—this just makes them linger longer. It's training yourself to be an observer, and understand that the thoughts, just like clouds, are impermanent and eventually pass.[31] If you stick to the practice for a month, you'll start to notice subtle differences, such as improved mood and reduced reactivity. You might notice that you start to pause when something provokes you and that you don't react with the same emotional intensity. Meditation is like athletic training for your brain.

There are many different kinds of meditation: transcendental, mindfulness, mantra, Vipassana, yoga nidra, loving-kindness, tai chi, and more. Do some research, test the various forms, and see what works best for you.

But—But . . . I Don't Have Time

Good news! Meditation actually saves you time. And science backs this up. Meditation has been shown to dramatically increase your productivity and improve your sleep so much that you need less of it.

If you're meditation leery, try this hack: Set aside three minutes a day when you play your favorite song. Sit in a comfortable position, close your eyes, and do a deep-breathing exercise as the song plays.

Humans are wired to do something they look forward to, and if you look forward to hearing the song, eventually you'll start to look forward to the mental pause. After a few days to a week of breathing while listening to your favorite song, add a ten-minute meditation after the song. Consider an app like Headspace or Insight Timer, which offers guided meditations. After about two weeks, wean yourself off the music.

WHEN YOU'VE FORGOTTEN YOURSELF

One of the most challenging parts of separation is suddenly all the time, energy, and attention that were going toward your partner now have nowhere to go. There's a vacancy that can feel strange and unbearable.

Think about it. Before your relationship you probably spent a lot of your time and attention doing things for yourself, like seeing friends, going to fitness classes, learning new things, and so on. Then you met your partner. Your "you" time gradually became "we" time—dates, then sleepovers, then Sunday mornings. Eventually you settled into a relationship cadence in which your schedules were fully integrated, and the time and space that was once spent focused on your single lifestyle merged into the lifestyle of partnership. After a breakup, there's suddenly a big gap. It's no wonder you may feel discombobulated, with a schedule and lifestyle you no longer recognize.

To put into perspective just how much of our time, energy, and attention we invest in our relationships (often at the expense of developing other areas of our lives), Dr. Zendegui leads the women through a "draw your pie" exercise. On a blank sheet of paper, she instructs them to draw a circle and divide the circle as if it were a pie, each slice representing how much time and energy they devoted to an activity or priority. Within minutes, there are gasps and chuckles within the group, half ashamed, half shocked.

Dr. Zendegui asks for a volunteer: "Who wants to share?"

Cindy raises her hand. Embarrassed, she reveals how the biggest slice of pie, over 70 percent, was consumed by her relationship.

Upon further probing, Cindy admits that she misses the independent woman she once was: "I didn't realize how much of myself I lost. I had all these dreams and put them on hold. But I got so stuck I never even went back to those dreams."

This makes the perfect segue into the second part of the exercise, in which Dr. Zendegui instructs the women to draw another circle to represent their new pie moving forward. This time, they're guided to divide the slices to reflect a more balanced pie, one that includes making time for self-care, friends, and other activities that they find fulfilling.

By not filling the gap that used to be reserved for the relationship slice, the missing and aching for a love lost is going to persist. And if you don't fill it with other things that are important to you, you may just fill in that gap with rumination of your ex!

You need to fill that part of the pie with activities that feed your sense of identity and independence, and you need to make sure the next time you're in a relationship, you don't allow the majority of your

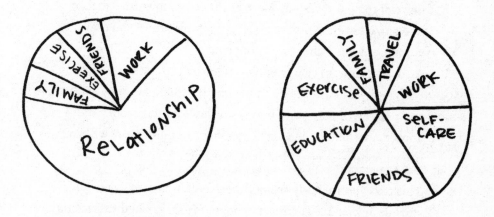

Cindy's pie before and after. On the left is how she used to spend her time and energy. The right is the new pie—how she's going to fill up her new blocks of time with new focuses, from self-care to meeting new people to taking a trip to Costa Rica she's been dreaming about for ages.

pie to merge into "we" (relationship). Balance is key, and if you devote over half your pie to an external factor—a person, a job, or a vice— eventually, when that external factor changes, you may find yourself wiped off your feet.

EXERCISE: Balance Your Pie

- Using the example on the previous page, draw two circles to represent your "pie"—your pie when you were in a relationship and your ideal balanced pie moving forward.

- Make a plan to fill up the pieces of the pie that were once consumed by "Relationship" with enriching activities that nourish you—self-care, volunteering, traveling, taking up a new hobby, or whatever else creates joy and empowerment in your life.

- Create an action item for yourself to proactively build on a specific piece of the pie. Does one piece of the pie go toward exercise? Book an additional fitness class. If it's community you crave, volunteer with a charity or nonprofit to help others in need. Also, reach out to two friends you haven't invested much time with lately and ask them out for lunch. Create tangible action steps that will help you fill up your newfound freedom and appreciate the independence in a positive light. How will you use your time, energy, and attention?

- This pie exercise is also something to refer back to when you start dating again. To prevent yourself from gradually devoting more and more of your pie to your relationship at the expense of the other things that light you up, you can use the pie to remind yourself to create discipline around how you exert your time and energy. Balance is key!

THE ADAPTATION PRINCIPLE

Do you know what winning the lottery, losing your limbs in a car accident, and a devastating breakup have in common?

While each scenario seems like it will alter your levels of happiness forever, in reality, you'll likely adapt to it. Jonathan Haidt, author of *The Happiness Hypothesis*, explains how humans tend to overestimate the intensity and duration of their emotional reactions: "Within a year, lottery winners and paraplegics have both (on average) returned most of the way to their baseline levels of happiness."[32] He notes that while humans are extremely sensitive to changes in conditions, they are not as sensitive to absolute levels. Nerve cells respond to new stimuli (a jackpot of money, a loss of limbs, or a separation) and then gradually habituate and recalibrate.

Humans are pretty bad at predicting how they'll feel in the future. During this time when you may believe there's no end in sight for the pain, remember that this simply isn't true. If we apply Haidt's theory, then it's probable that once your cells recalibrate to life without your ex, you'll eventually return to your baseline of happiness. Note: This doesn't mean that having chronic conflict with your partner doesn't affect your happiness. According to Haidt, "you never adapt to interpersonal conflict; it damages every day, even days when you don't see the other person but ruminate about the conflict nevertheless."[33] But after the shock to the system, you do eventually adapt to loss and hopefully, after reading this book, extend your range of baseline happiness.

BECOMING A HUMAN AGAIN

After a separation, your heart, mind, and body are in a state of shock. Reality can seem foggy and chaotic. Routine creates order in the chaos and is something self-made that you can count on. While in survival mode, you may feel like you don't have control over your emotions, but you do have control over your routine. So, it is time to double down on that practice.

EXERCISE: Create a Morning Ritual

Each morning, set aside time for yourself so that you can get grounded and start your day feeling inspired. Ideally, you would have an hour for this, but if you can only afford fifteen to thirty minutes, that's a good start. Begin your morning ritual before you look at your phone and allow the outside world to start dictating your mood. You're the boss here—set the tone of the day the way you want: calm, positive, and inspired.

PART 1

Meditate. If you need some assistance to start meditating, try an app like Insight Timer, Headspace, Mindful, or Calm.

PART 2

In your journal, write down one intention/goal for the day. When you write, use phrases such as "I can" and "I will" instead of "I should."

PART 3

Choose one of the following mood-enhancing exercises that you will complete during the day. If you wish, you can choose to complete more than one.

- Remind yourself to pause and notice your surroundings today. Look for three things that are beautiful. Write them down in your journal.

- Get your heart rate pumping by exercising for a minimum of thirty minutes.

- Write a letter or email of gratitude to someone you love (not your ex!) and tell them how much they mean to you.

- Do something to pamper yourself—take a long bath, buy yourself flowers, have a manicure.

- Do something that gets you in touch with your body—yoga, tantra, dance! If you can't make it to a class, play your favorite upbeat song and dance by yourself at home for five minutes.

- Spend thirty minutes with a friend. It's best to do an activity together while talking, and make it a rule to not talk about the breakup.

- Play with a dog. A study conducted by the University of Missouri showed that non–pet owners who played with a dog for just a few minutes a day had increased levels of the brain chemicals serotonin and oxytocin—both mood elevators.[34]

- Get a massage. Massage also boosts serotonin levels and reduces levels of the stress hormone cortisol.

- Force yourself to smile. Laughter helps stimulate production of the feel-good hormone serotonin. Watch a funny movie or your favorite stand-up routine on YouTube.

- Help a stranger. Be kind for no reason. Volunteer. Studies show that people who were assigned to do one random act of kindness a week for multiple weeks showed a sustained increase in happiness levels.[35] Research also shows that volunteering has a significant impact on mental health.[36] It helps shift the focus from yourself to others and helps break the cycle of negative thinking.

- Learn something new. Whether you pick up a language, an instrument, or a hobby, learning a new skill physically changes the brain. The brain builds new neural connections and strengthens the synapses in the cerebral cortex.[37] This can help improve working memory and verbal intelligence and increase levels of self-satisfaction and happiness.[38]

THE ABSOLUTE GAME CHANGER: EMBRACING GRATITUDE

Guess what the antidepressant Wellbutrin does? It boosts the neurotransmitter dopamine. You know what else does? Gratitude. Feeling grateful activates the brain stem region that produces dopamine and makes us feel happier, more connected, and positive.

Happiness researcher Shawn Achor has conducted robust studies on the correlation between gratitude and happiness. He estimates that 90 percent of our long-term happiness is not predicated on the external world but rather on how our brain processes the world.[39] Thus, if we change our way of seeing the world (through a lens of gratitude), we have the power to change our formula for happiness and success.

His research shows that you can train your brain to be more positive. Practicing gratitude for a two-minute span twenty-eight days in a row can actually rewire your brain.[40] At the end of that period, your brain begins to form a pattern of scanning the world for the positive and not the negative. Building your gratitude muscle takes work, but the more you do it the stronger the muscle becomes.

EXERCISE: Start a Daily Gratitude Practice

When you're in the throes of pain after a breakup, it can feel impossible to find positivity or gratitude. But here's the secret about gratitude: it's a state that is cultivated, not something you simply have when things are going well.

Incorporate a gratitude practice in either your morning ritual or your evening ritual. Write down three things you're grateful for today and why. Close your eyes to visualize what you've written down and feel thankful for them. Relive the moment. Put yourself back in a particular situation and smile the way you did at the time, recount what you saw, smelled, tasted, and felt that made you happy and grateful. You can re-create the feel-good chemicals by associating yourself into the memory, allowing yourself to re-experience the warm feelings of the moment.

BONUS POINTS: *Find an accountability buddy—a friend or family member—and send a screenshot of your entry every day for thirty days. Have your buddy do the same.*

Jenny

"YOU SAVED ME." Jenny hugged me in tears at the end of the retreat weekend. "No, really, you saved me," she emphasized.

Jenny, who was in a toxic relationship with an alcoholic for eight years, had gone through extensive therapy since being raped as a teenager. She found herself repeatedly in dysfunctional relationships and had reached the end of hope. She was considering taking her life, and Renew was her last resort.

Fast-forward two and a half years later, and Jenny's life has completely transformed. She has been ticking off the bucket list goals she had set for herself at Renew, including setting up a 501(c)(3) nonprofit to help rescue animals in Austin. As of the time of this writing, she has continued the gratitude journaling exercise for 908 days straight. She hasn't missed one day since Renew.

"There are days when I don't feel like doing it. Dark days.

Hard days. But I force myself to do it anyway. I also reserve Sunday nights as my journal time. It's a small gift to myself. I've learned that healing takes 150,000 steps and you have to take one step at a time. It's no one thing. There's no magic bullet. My life has transformed in a way I can't put into words. I see things differently, I feel different."

She tells me that all the steps she's taken have added up. They've helped her to stop feeling like the victim and to truly be able to see her ex with compassion. While she still wants nothing to do with him, she genuinely wishes him happiness.

"That's what closure is to me—to not have any charge toward him, not negative, not positive, just neutral."

THERE ARE NO VILLAINS HERE

When we are in pain, it's easy to point the finger at someone else. Vilifying a person can feel good for the moment, just like eating a tub of ice cream feels good in the moment. But afterward, your stomach hurts. The same goes for having a hate-fest rally with your girlfriends. At the time, taking turns bashing the ex feels liberating and maybe even falsely empowering: "Fuck men! We are independent women, hear us roar!" But this exercise only feeds your victimization. Using pain to connect with others does not heal you; it hinders you.

Partners can do terrible things. They ghost, they cheat, they lie, they abuse, they act carelessly. In no way are the hurtful actions of others excusable or justified. And you have every right to feel hurt, sad, angry, and even resentful. But if you want to move forward into a new way of living, then the goal is to focus your energy on yourself—not the person who hurt you. You're just giving that person more power, more energy, more time, by staying stuck.

Sometimes we hold on to the pain because that's the last part of the relationship we have left. Directing the pain at the person who hurt you unwittingly keeps you from having to really let go.

Every minute you spend diverting your focus in vilifying your ex, you are taking a precious minute away from creating a better future.

SOMETIMES A BREAKUP IS THE SHAKE-UP YOU NEED TO REDIRECT YOUR LIFE

> To think your hurt is special is nonsense. You have pain, I have pain. The world has stories of pain. . . . It's not your wound that makes you special. It is the light that shines through that does.
>
> *Kamal Ravikant*

The women who come to Renew all come thinking they're trying to get over their exes. But at the end of the retreat, they realize that they have unhealed wounds that have been lingering for decades, and the breakup just reopened them. Perhaps you're reliving the sense of abandonment you experienced when your parents divorced, or the jealousy sparked by not feeling as prized as your sibling, or the sorrow of not feeling good enough for your father's attention. The feelings that a breakup ignites are neither good nor bad; some are a natural part of the grieving process, and some are lessons waiting for you to learn. How did you get to a place where your pie was consumed mostly by the relationship? And how can you make sure you create balance the next time? Why did you choose this person? Why did you stay when you knew the relationship was wrong? Losing ourselves in our relationships happens to the best of us, and often it's so gradual that we barely notice until we've completely disappeared.

Chances are the emotional experience you had in your last relationship is pretty similar to the one before.

The common denominators are your patterns.

Your breakup is a shake-up, necessary for you to finally unearth all the things that have been stopping you from creating a healthy love for yourself, first and foremost. Think about it—no one person can make you feel the intensity of emotion you are feeling. If you feel worthless after your breakup, the ex didn't have the power to make you that way. There are likely layers upon layers of feelings of unworthiness going back decades. If after a breakup you feel utterly abandoned, is it possible that there were deep fears of abandonment lurking in your heart? This is what your reactions are trying to tell you. Your ex simply ripped the bandage off an old wound that's been waiting to be healed. Now is your chance.

YOUR GRIEF IS SACRED

Even if you know that there's a silver lining and that eventually you'll move on, breakups still hurt. You are totally allowed to feel those feelings; they are all natural.

I'm sure you wish there were just some magic pill you could take to make it all go away, but the reality is it is here, past your comfort zone, where growth happens.

Feeling a range of emotions, from the dark to the light, is the gift of being human. Feeling deeply expands your emotional range. Your pain is a gift. Your grief is sacred. It is in that pain where you have the chance to reconnect with yourself.

»»— 2 —→

HOW YOU ATTACH IS WHY YOU'RE UNATTACHED

You are absolutely worthy of love. You are made of love and you don't need someone to trigger you into it by their unavailability.

Damien Bohler

This book is not written to help you get rid of your pain. It's to teach you how to process it, grow from it, and even respect it. Welcome to the process of evolution: Entropy. Chaos. Order. Rebirth.

Of course, when you're in the midst of breakdown, it's not so easy to see that pain is the messenger of wisdom, as in the case of Priya:

"It's been seven hours and he still hasn't replied to my text or call!" Priya yelled into the phone as soon as I picked up.

Priya was a participant at Renew Breakup Bootcamp who had stayed on as a coaching client. I'd given her permission to call me when she felt like she was spiraling out of control. This was one of those times.

"I've been trying to connect with him and he seems so distant. He's clearly not that into me. I just don't think he can meet my needs. I can't do this anymore."

Priya is a catch in most every way—she has a successful career, owns her apartment in downtown Vancouver, and has many loving friends. For five months, Priya had been dating Sarf, who had recently gotten out of a long-term relationship and was trying to take things slow. When he took too long to text her back, Priya would work herself into a rage, creating complicated story lines in her head that would perpetuate her belief that she would be abandoned and rejected, as she had been in her last relationship. She would then punish Sarf by strategically calculating the number of hours she'd let pass before texting him back and start flirting with other guys to take the edge off.

"He's avoiding me. He's lost interest. I know it," she sobbed.

Welcome to the mind of someone with an anxious attachment style. With a deep-rooted fear of rejection and abandonment, Priya would react to any potential indicator of disinterest by lashing out. This is classic "protest behavior," a characteristic common in someone with this type of attachment style.

Our attachment system is a mechanism in our brain responsible for tracking and monitoring the safety and availability of our caregivers as children and eventually, our romantic partners as adults. Attachment theory suggests that by the age of five, we develop a primary attachment style that will define the way we romantically bond and attach to others in our adult lives.[1] Research shows that regardless of culture or geography, adults fall into one of three primary attachment styles: secure, avoidant, and anxious.

ATTACHMENT THEORY

Our brain controls the attachment system, which monitors and regulates our connection with our attachment figures (parents, children, and romantic partners). As infants, our brain grows and develops in response to our earliest love relationships, and as we get older, our brain actively works to connect/attach us to our loved ones based on our earliest responses.[2] These first interactions teach us if we can depend on loving responses from another to help us maintain our emotional balance.[3]

When parents are sensitively attuned to the needs of their baby, a secure attachment is likely to develop.[4] The child learns that her primary caregiver is available and attentive to her needs and grows up being able to attach in a healthy way with her romantic partners. Securely attached children grow up better able to regulate their emotions and tend to be more empathic and caring than those who are insecurely attached.[5] They learn to reach for closeness when needed and trust that they will be offered comfort, safety, and care. They are not consumed with worry or anxiety that their needs won't be met or that they will be ignored or abandoned.

AVOIDANT

In contrast, when parents are not attuned to their baby, or are distant, intrusive, or inconsistent in their caregiving, the child adapts by developing defensive attachment strategies and coping mechanisms in an attempt to feel safe and to modulate intense emotional states.[6] In these cases an anxious attachment style may develop, resulting in the child growing up feeling a lack of safety and a deep fear of abandonment with her romantic partners.

SECURE

Lastly, if parents enmeshed their child by putting their own needs onto the child, such as living vicariously through the child's achievements or being overly controlling or smothering, the child may develop an avoidant attachment style. The enmeshed child grows up to become fiercely independent at the expense of emotional closeness with her partner.

ANXIOUS

Attachment styles shape the mental models in how we regulate emotions and guide our expectations in love and relationships as adults. At every age, we are hardwired to habitually seek and maintain closeness both emotionally and physically with at least one person. This tendency is amplified when we feel uncertain, stressed, or anxious.

EXERCISE: Attachment Quiz

By understanding the different attachment styles, you can identify the triggers that cause you (or future partners) to feel suffocated by intimacy or deprived of it. Take this quick quiz to determine which attachment style best describes you.

Instructions:

1. Using a scale of 0 (strongly disagree) to 10 (strongly agree), rate each statement from each category below based on how you identify with it.

2. For each statement, assign points based on the value of your score. For example, assign 4 points to a statement that you rated as a 4.

3. When you have completed each category, total the scores from each statement to find your category score.

CATEGORY I

1. I'm afraid I will be abandoned or rejected.

STRONGLY DISAGREE   0 1 2 3 4 5 6 7 8 9 10   STRONGLY AGREE

2. I am usually yearning for more connection from my partner.

STRONGLY DISAGREE   0 1 2 3 4 5 6 7 8 9 10   STRONGLY AGREE

3. I start to panic when I do not hear from my partner.

STRONGLY DISAGREE   0 1 2 3 4 5 6 7 8 9 10   STRONGLY AGREE

4. I tend to disclose too much information too soon when I first
    start dating someone.

STRONGLY DISAGREE   0 1 2 3 4 5 6 7 8 9 10   STRONGLY AGREE

5. I count the hours that it takes for the person I like to text/call me.

STRONGLY DISAGREE   0 1 2 3 4 5 6 7 8 9 10   STRONGLY AGREE

6. When the person I like doesn't reply to me quickly enough, I
    want to punish him.

STRONGLY DISAGREE   0 1 2 3 4 5 6 7 8 9 10   STRONGLY AGREE

7. I'm constantly thinking about a romantic partner, pining over
    him, fantasizing about him, or obsessing over him.

STRONGLY DISAGREE   0 1 2 3 4 5 6 7 8 9 10   STRONGLY AGREE

8. I tend to act clingy or needy with my romantic partner.

STRONGLY DISAGREE   0 1 2 3 4 5 6 7 8 9 10   STRONGLY AGREE

9. I tend to base my self-worth and identity on my partner's validation of me.

STRONGLY DISAGREE   0 1 2 3 4 5 6 7 8 9 10   STRONGLY AGREE

10. I get completely devastated after a breakup, even if the relationship was short.

STRONGLY DISAGREE   0 1 2 3 4 5 6 7 8 9 10   STRONGLY AGREE

Category I points: _____

CATEGORY II

1. I'm afraid that too much intimacy will take away my freedom and independence.

STRONGLY DISAGREE   0 1 2 3 4 5 6 7 8 9 10   STRONGLY AGREE

2. I feel easily smothered by romantic partners.

STRONGLY DISAGREE   0 1 2 3 4 5 6 7 8 9 10   STRONGLY AGREE

3. I have a hard time being in touch with/talking about my feelings.

STRONGLY DISAGREE   0 1 2 3 4 5 6 7 8 9 10   STRONGLY AGREE

4. I have a hard time being vulnerable and opening up to others.

STRONGLY DISAGREE   0 1 2 3 4 5 6 7 8 9 10   STRONGLY AGREE

5. Having to depend on others makes me feel uncomfortable.

STRONGLY DISAGREE   0 1 2 3 4 5 6 7 8 9 10   STRONGLY AGREE

6. If a partner tries to push for commitment, I feel pressure and want to withdraw.

STRONGLY DISAGREE   0 1 2 3 4 5 6 7 8 9 10   STRONGLY AGREE

7. I tend to focus on the imperfections of a new partner within the first few months of dating and usually end it.

STRONGLY DISAGREE   0 1 2 3 4 5 6 7 8 9 10   STRONGLY AGREE

8. I tend to feel suffocated in relationships.

STRONGLY DISAGREE   0 1 2 3 4 5 6 7 8 9 10   STRONGLY AGREE

9. I tend to chase people with an impossible future.

STRONGLY DISAGREE   0 1 2 3 4 5 6 7 8 9 10   STRONGLY AGREE

10. I need a lot of alone time and time away from my partner.

STRONGLY DISAGREE   0 1 2 3 4 5 6 7 8 9 10   STRONGLY AGREE

Category II points: _____

CATEGORY III

1. I'm comfortable with emotional intimacy.

STRONGLY DISAGREE   0 1 2 3 4 5 6 7 8 9 10   STRONGLY AGREE

2. I feel comfortable giving and receiving love.

STRONGLY DISAGREE   0 1 2 3 4 5 6 7 8 9 10   STRONGLY AGREE

3. I trust that I can count on others and others can count on me.

STRONGLY DISAGREE   0 1 2 3 4 5 6 7 8 9 10   STRONGLY AGREE

4. When a conflict with my partner arises, I communicate and work through the problem.

STRONGLY DISAGREE   0 1 2 3 4 5 6 7 8 9 10   STRONGLY AGREE

5. I feel comfortable expressing my needs.

STRONGLY DISAGREE   0 1 2 3 4 5 6 7 8 9 10   STRONGLY AGREE

6. I feel comfortable communicating my boundaries.

STRONGLY DISAGREE   0 1 2 3 4 5 6 7 8 9 10   STRONGLY AGREE

7. I respect my partner's privacy and boundaries.

STRONGLY DISAGREE   0 1 2 3 4 5 6 7 8 9 10   STRONGLY AGREE

8. I tend to trust my partner and my partner's feelings for me.

STRONGLY DISAGREE   0 1 2 3 4 5 6 7 8 9 10   STRONGLY AGREE

9. I'm comfortable with commitment.

STRONGLY DISAGREE   0 1 2 3 4 5 6 7 8 9 10   STRONGLY AGREE

10. When I'm upset, I am able to self-soothe and get myself back to equilibrium relatively easily.

STRONGLY DISAGREE   0 1 2 3 4 5 6 7 8 9 10   STRONGLY AGREE

Category III points: _____

Total Points

Category I: _____   **Category II:** _____   **Category III:** _____

If you scored highest in Category I, your attachment type is _anxious_.

If you scored highest in Category II, your attachment type is _avoidant_.

If you scored highest in Category III, your attachment type is _secure_.

SECURE ATTACHMENT

About half the population has a secure attachment style, meaning they are comfortable with intimacy but are not codependent. These are people who had consistent caregiving and soothing as children, which helps a young, developing brain and nervous system form in a way that enables them to function during times of stress. The child grows up to be a secure, functional adult who can self-soothe—the hallmark of a securely attached adult.[7] People who feel secure as children grow up more likely to feel secure with their romantic partners as adults.

The securely attached do not define their identity or self-esteem on their lover's reinforcement. They don't have major abandonment issues, know inherently that they are worthy of love, and can give and receive care comfortably. The securely attached aren't as sensitive to the negative cues of the world and can keep an even emotional keel in the face of a threat with more ease than those with insecure attachment styles. During a fight they don't feel the need to act defensively or punish their partner. Also, the securely attached are not threatened by criticism and are willing to reconsider their ways and compromise. Research suggests that the best predictor of happiness in a relationship is a secure attachment style. Two secure partners have the most stable relationship and are more likely to live happily together even if they endure significant life stress.

AVOIDANT ATTACHMENT

An avoidant attachment is characterized by a desire for a high degree of independence to avoid getting too intimate with another. Emotional intimacy triggers feelings of discomfort and often suffocation, so avoidants find it hard to trust and frequently suppress and deny their feelings. Often avoidants associate "love" with duty or work. They subconsciously suppress their attachment system and create situations to leave or sabotage close relationships. They have a pattern of connecting and then pulling away as soon as the relationship feels too intense.

A significant amount of research suggests that an avoidant attachment is the outcome of emotionally unavailable, chaotic, or unresponsive parents. Here are some common scenarios that can result in a child developing an avoidant attachment:

- Parents expect premature independence from their children, discouraging crying and emotional expression. The child learns to cope by suppressing her natural desire to seek out a parent for comfort when in pain, frightened, or hurt, out of a fear of rejection, disappointment, or punishment.

- Parents shame the child into silence as a way of diminishing their own emotional chaos and stress, thereby disempowering the child.

- Parents reverse the roles and expect the child to become the caretaker or therapist, thereby falsely empowering the child and causing her to grow up seeing intimacy as a job.

- Parents are overly smothering and are mis-attuned to their child's needs, possibly because they too have an insecure attachment style and are misreading their child's cues.

- Parents do not have personal boundaries and unconsciously (or consciously) rely on the child to fulfill their needs. The child feels "responsible" for her caregiver's happiness and, in some cases, survival. In this scenario, the child loses all sense of self and starts to believe that self-esteem is directly related to how much she takes care of other people.

As adults, avoidants subconsciously equate intimacy with a loss of independence. They idealize self-sufficiency and feel pressured easily. It is challenging for avoidants to be aware of their own feelings, and they have a tendency to move away instead of through their feelings of discomfort and fear. Consequently, they may start to pull away from or leave their partners instead of discussing their emotions.

Avoidants are quick to think negatively about their partners, seeing them as needy and overly dependent. They tend to feel deep-rooted aloneness, even when in a relationship. When someone gets too close, avoidants subconsciously turn to "deactivating strategies"—tactics used to squelch intimacy. Examples include:

- Choosing to not get involved in a close relationship because of a subconscious fear of rejection.

- Pulling away when things are going well (e.g., not calling for several days after an intimate date or a trip).

- Keeping things in the gray area to avoid commitment and maintain feelings of independence.

- Avoiding physical closeness or withholding affection such as hugging, kissing, or holding hands.

- Focusing on small imperfections in their partner.

- Forming relationships that have an impossible future (e.g., with someone already in a relationship or who is emotionally unavailable).

- Waiting for the perfect "one" or reminiscing about their single days or a past idealized relationship.

- During an argument, instead of disclosing feelings, becoming distant and aloof.

- Rationalizing their way out of commitment and/or intimacy.

Avoidant attachment makes up approximately 25 percent of the population.[8] Out of the three attachment types, avoidants tend to end their relationships more frequently and divorce more. In romantic relationships, they score the lowest on every measure of closeness.[9]

Avoidants have a challenging time being in touch with how they feel and disassociate from their emotions after a breakup. This causes them to move on quickly and not spend the time to process the breakup. That's likely why it's rare for an avoidant to attend Renew, because she tends not to feel the sharpness of the pain in the same way as an anxiously attached person. But after the same patterns keep repeating, sometimes an avoidantly attached person will make the effort to become more secure as she realizes she has an ongoing issue with creating and sustaining intimacy.

ANXIOUS ATTACHMENT

An anxious attachment is characterized by a deep-rooted fear of rejection and abandonment. Whereas the avoidant seeks to be independent from her partner, the anxious is codependent on her partner. Anxiously attached types crave intimacy and become preoccupied with their relationship, worrying about their partner's ability to love them back. They feel doubtful of their own worth and seek constant approval and reassurance from others. The angst that results from the fear of abandonment drives them to act clingy and needy of their partner, resulting in them being emotionally desperate in their relationships.[10] Ninety percent of the women who come to Renew Breakup Bootcamp have an anxious attachment style. This comes as no surprise, since the anxiously attached have the hardest time letting go after a breakup.

This was the case for Mandy, a twenty-four-year-old overachieving psychology major who attended two Renew Breakup Bootcamps. Her first time was to get over her first love. Her second was a year later, when she was in a new relationship that she didn't want to "mess up" and wanted to build on the knowledge she had gained in her first bootcamp.

Mandy had a need for constant contact with her partner. Frequent calls and texts throughout the day let her know that "we're okay." But when her new boyfriend went on a vacation and didn't contact her, she descended into an anxiety spiral.

"I hadn't heard from him and he didn't open my Snapchat message to him. But he posted on Instagram. Ugh, I hate living in the digital age!"

She was driving from San Francisco to Los Angeles, and during the entire trip she played out various scenarios. *Is he with someone else? Why is he not contacting me?*

"I missed him, but I was also angry and full of angst. I felt like I was being abandoned."

After rehearsing yelling at him out loud during her drive, she decided to call him.

"He answered the phone in his typical cheerful manner. Everything was fine. And suddenly all that dread and anxious charge just melted away. I got reassurance that we were okay and felt normal again."

Mandy's reaction is not her fault. Her anxious attachment system, which stems from childhood, felt threatened, and she reacted with a survival response.

Attachment researchers describe the common scenarios that result in a child developing an anxious attachment:

- Parents are inconsistent in their responsiveness to the needs of their child. They are sometimes nurturing and respond effectively to their child's distress, while at other times they are intrusive, insensitive, or emotionally unavailable. When parents vacillate between these two very different responses, their child becomes confused and insecure, unable to predict if her needs will be met.[11]

- Early abandonment, whether that be emotional abandonment or physical (one or both parents left, died, or were absent), causes the child to not feel whole. The child grows up thinking she is not enough or unlovable, which often leads to a need for excessive reassurance from others. She needs romantic partners to validate and reassure her that she is special and lovable. Also, the anxiously attached can tend to be so desperate for love that they will latch on to just a few crumbs of someone's attention to temporarily soothe their feelings of inadequacy.[12]

- Trauma, whether through sexual, physical, and/or emotional abuse, can cause extremely low self-esteem and result in the child acquiring an inherent belief that she is worthless or unlovable. The child develops an unhealthy idea of love after witnessing her parent(s) in toxic patterns.[13]

- A history of neglect and/or abandonment, including a lack of nurturing, positive attention or love while growing up, gives the child an inherent fear of rejection.

Owing to the inconsistent availability of their parents, anxious types are "rejection-sensitive." They anticipate rejection or abandonment and are constantly on the lookout for signs that their partner is losing interest.[14] They are inclined to worry that they will be disappointed and habitually need proof that they are loved. Studies show that people with an anxious attachment style are more sensitive and quicker to perceive offset emotions—a unique ability to sense when their relationship is being threatened. Even a slight hint that something is wrong will activate their attachment system, and once triggered these types can't calm down until they get a clear indication from their partner that the relationship is safe.

When an anxiously attached person is triggered, she will react with protest behavior—actions that attempt to get attention from her partner to reestablish contact/connection. Examples include:

- Excessive attempts to reestablish contact (e.g., repeatedly texting and/or calling)

- Withdrawing (e.g., ignoring, not taking calls, etc.)

- Keeping score (e.g., calculating how long it takes for the partner to return contact and then waiting the same amount of time to respond)

- Acting hostile (e.g., eye rolling, walking away, leaving the room)

- Threatening to leave (e.g., making comments such as "I can't do this anymore" and threatening to break up while really wanting the person to beg her to stay; testing the person to see if he'll fight for her)

- Manipulation (e.g., saying they have plans when they don't, not answering calls, playing games)

- Provoking jealousy (e.g., flirting with others, seeing an ex, etc.)

- Punishing to exact revenge (e.g., withholding love or acting out in a destructive manner to hurt their partner)

The anxiously attached tend to bond quickly, often rushing into relationships without taking the time to assess whether their partner can or wants to meet their needs. They tend to idealize their partner and overlook red flags and issues.

WE MAY NOT EXHIBIT ALL the behaviors associated with an attachment style, but we generally fall into one of the attachment categories. Attachment style is a spectrum, and where one is on that continuum may fluctuate based on life situation, partner, and context. It's not impossible to date someone with a different attachment style, but the question is more about where both people fall on the anxious-avoidant spectrum and how far away each person is from a secure center.

LIKE ANXIOUS MOTHS TO AN AVOIDANT FLAME

The anxiously attached desperately grasp for that which is unavailable, while the avoidant runs from that which is too available and together they paint a painful portrait of passionate despair that can go on for years and years.

Damien Bohler

The anxiously attached and avoidants are drawn to each other because both types "enforce each other's world view."[15]

For anxious types, the high-high-low-low of an insecure attachment is enlivening and familiar, even though it's painful. They often equate an activated attachment system to passion and falsely associate people who are securely attached with boredom. But in reality, the anxious among us are unconsciously addicted to the manic nature of being with someone who keeps them guessing all the time. They confuse their longing and anxiety for love, and subconsciously, emotional unavailability becomes a turn-on, when it should be a deterrent. This relationship dynamic validates their abandonment fears and beliefs about not being lovable enough.

Avoidants are drawn to anxious types because the needy and smothering nature of the anxiously attached reinforces avoidants' beliefs that they will be smothered and that intimacy will take away their independence. They cannot date another avoidant because there is no glue that keeps them together.

Avoidants and the anxiously attached tend to become defensive during arguments, escalating conflict by withdrawing or attacking. Through the chase, conflict, or compulsive behavior, both avoidant and anxious types are able to relive the pain of their early attachments—while dysfunctional, it's oddly comfortable because it's so familiar.

There is always a push-pull dynamic where one person wants more emotional closeness (the anxiously attached) and one wants more independence and freedom (the avoidant). The dysfunctional dynamic continues, regardless of whom each of these people date, unless both work to become more secure.

But there's hope!

Thanks to neuroplasticity, the attachment style developed as a child can change. In a longitudinal study of people's attachment styles, psychologists Lee A. Kirkpatrick and Cindy Hazan found that 30 percent of people had undergone changes in their attachment style.[16] The goal is to become more secure in your attachment, and the first step is awareness and learning how to stop unhealthy intimacy patterns in its tracks.

WHAT TO DO IF YOU HAVE AN ANXIOUS ATTACHMENT STYLE

If you have an anxious attachment style, understand you may have a predisposed draw toward avoidants. While it feels "natural" and probably quite comfortable to be in a manic push-pull with your partner, know that dating an avoidant will only exacerbate your anxious attachment.

Do not let chaos be your measure of chemistry. Do not confuse a lack of tension with a lack of passion.

Recognize when you are mistaking feelings of anxiety, insecurity, and extreme emotional highs and lows for passion. Your brain may be tricking you. Chances are you are not in love at all.

The anxiously attached need to focus on the missing ingredient to becoming secure: an internal knowing that they are safe. People who are securely attached feel inherently safe and trusting of themselves and their relationships with others.

To become more secure means to first start shifting old neural pathways that immediately go to a place of disconnection and strengthening the neural pathways for healthy connection.

Safety Meditation

The core belief that the anxiously attached have is that they are not safe. To start rewiring this belief, try this meditation to start embodying feelings of safety.

Close your eyes, breathe in deeply through your nose for four seconds, hold your breath for another four, and then release through your mouth as if you're sighing out all the anxiety and frustration. Repeat ten times. Next, imagine yourself as a little girl. How old are you? What are you wearing? Imagine yourself doing something you love. Perhaps you're painting. Dancing. Playing on a beach. Now imagine your family or people you love around you, forming a circle. You are in the middle. Take a moment to really embrace that support. Say to yourself, "I am safe. I have all the resources I need." Repeat that a few times as you bask in the gratitude, care, and support that is around you. Now, imagine that little girl grown up, as your present-day self. Think about yourself now, doing something you love. If you're in a relationship, then, just as before, imagine your partner along with the people who love you, surrounding you in a circle, beaming devotion and support in your direction. Say to yourself, "I am safe. I have all the resources I need." Repeat this mantra three times and let yourself feel how much love and support you have.

Relabel, Refocus, and Remember

Visualization is a powerful tool that can release oxytocin in our brains. When you're feeling anxious, take ten deep breaths so that you can give your brain the oxygen it needs. Jeffrey Schwartz, a psychiatrist at UCLA who specializes in neuroplasticity, suggests a method to relabel and refocus. Create separation from your experience of angst and stress by noting that this is just your overactive sympathetic nervous system sending faulty messages. This might seem silly at first, but when you're in the midst of a stress response, being able to change your inner dialogue from *I'm going crazy! I can't handle this! I feel like dying!* to *This feeling of anxiety is my brain playing a trick on me* will allow "the cognitive part of your brain to come online and begin to modulate the agitation."[17]

Next, refocus your attention using what former instructor of psychiatry at Harvard Medical School Dr. Amy Banks calls a "positive relational moment" (PRM).[18] Think back to a memory where you felt safe and happy in the presence of someone you trust. Close your eyes so you can recall the memory in detail and play out the scene. Were you laughing? Smiling? Copy the same facial expression you had in the PRM as if you were reliving the moment now. If you can really summon up the memory and relive the feel-good feelings from it, you'll calm down your sympathetic nervous system and also stimulate dopamine.

The key is to repeat this process over and over again, because you'll eventually weaken your old neural pathways of feeling anxious and disconnected and strengthen your neural pathways for feeling safe and connected.

Resist "Bombing" Your Partner

Anxiously attached types often feel comfortable with intensity. The angst of chasing someone for love and connection becomes addictive,

DO NOT LET
CHAOS BE YOUR
MEASURE OF
CHEMISTRY. DO
NOT CONFUSE
A LACK OF
TENSION WITH
A LACK OF
PASSION.

and when that toxic intensity isn't there, it can feel uncomfortable and unfamiliar. You may feel an urge to use an "anger bomb" on your ex or current partner—picking a fight in order to emotionally reconnect. Or you may attempt to use a "seduction bomb" in order to get the person to respond, even if the connection is toxic.[19] Part of your self-soothing practice needs to be to resist these urges and tolerate the silence. When you feel the urge, practice your breathing and meditation exercises. Know that the intensity will eventually calm if you give it the time and the space.

Avoid Avoidants

If you continue dating avoidants, you will stay stuck in the push-pull dynamic that confirms your negative beliefs and fears of abandonment. Your chances of growing into a more securely attached partner are much higher if you choose a securely attached partner. Obvious, right? So, before you invest your heart into someone, take the time to find out if he is avoidantly attached. Save yourself from the emotional gymnastics later on by doing the work up front first.

Connie: AN ANXIOUS MASQUERADING AS AN AVOIDANT

"I THINK I'M both avoidant and anxious," said Connie, a thirty-three-year-old public relations manager, during a group exercise to determine our attachment styles. "I'm so afraid of being anxious that I cut people off completely. If they do something that disappoints me, I delete them off everything. They're dead to me."

On the outside, Connie's distancing behavior would pass as avoidant attachment; however, upon closer inspection, it became clear that Connie feared being hurt and rejected, and she created walls and protective mechanisms to ensure that nobody would get the chance. She was indeed an anxiously attached type masquerading as an avoidant.

The key thing to consider when evaluating your attachment style is what your primary fear is. If it's a fear of being abandoned or rejected, that's indicative of an anxious attachment. If it's a fear of losing your freedom, that's indicative of an avoidant attachment. Sometimes we develop coping mechanisms to deal with the unpleasant feelings of our attachment style and engage in the opposite behavior. This can cause confusion, so remember to dig deep and find your primary fear.

Another clue that signifies a lack of secure attachment is acting out in extremes. In Connie's case, her only way of handling the anxiety of someone potentially disappointing her was to cut them out completely. She would not let her guard down and was slow to trust—not out of a place of love, but out of a place of fear. Speaking to Connie a year after Breakup Bootcamp, she said her greatest takeaway was learning how to open up her heart and let people in—both romantically and platonically. She started making a conscious effort to open up more when meeting new people and being vulnerable in sharing her history, her stories, and her feelings. When she dated someone and he didn't communicate at the frequency she liked, she'd make it a point to practice compassion and give the person the benefit of the doubt, versus jumping to negative conclusions and withdrawing.

WHAT TO DO IF YOU HAVE AN AVOIDANT ATTACHMENT STYLE

If you have an avoidant attachment style, you may cycle through people, having many short-lived relationships, rationalizing that you just haven't met "the one." But if you continue squelching intimacy, even the most perfect person wouldn't stand a chance with you. You might even say you want a relationship and actively pursue one, but your indirect strategies for avoiding true intimacy don't enable love to develop past the stage of infatuation.

The problem with people with an avoidant attachment style is they generally don't know when they have a problem. This was the case for Serina, a forty-year-old financial advisor from New York, who came to Renew after breaking it off with yet another boyfriend.

Serina loved her independent life and was perfectly content seeing her boyfriend once a week. She had always been like this and often had long-distance relationships with no concern over the distance or time apart from her partner.

When her boyfriend (now ex) wanted her to move to the Upper West Side, she freaked out. Her commitment alarm bells started to ring as she saw her future suffocating her: "I started to feel the future. First Upper West Side, next the suburbs! It was all too much."

Since learning about attachment styles and realizing that she had avoidant tendencies, Serina has been much more aware of the role she plays in connecting or disconnecting from people.

During our call a year after her attendance at Renew, she shared a story of a man she had recently dated who asked why she didn't reply to his text messages. She generally takes a day to reply to a message (whether it's from a romantic interest, family, or a friend) and didn't realize that he expected a response within an hour or so.

"That was insightful information for me. I had no awareness. I just have a different relationship with time. I don't need to know what someone is doing all the time and thought everyone else was like that too. Now I force myself to communicate more. When I start dating someone, I directly ask what their expectation for communication response time is."

Understanding how her lack of communication was taking a toll on the people she cared about and making a concerted effort to improve this was a critical first step for Serina.

If you find that your avoidant behaviors are not giving you the relationship outcomes that you want, here are a few different areas that you can start working on.

Practice Labeling and Writing Down Your Feelings

Avoidants often have a hard time being aware of their feelings. They feel the symptoms of their feelings—increased heart rate, anxiety, stress, rage, and so on—but cannot identify the emotion at the root. Developing this awareness is key to becoming more secure and also having meaningful dialogue around feelings when conflict arises with your partner.

A study conducted by UCLA professor Matthew D. Lieberman revealed that putting feelings into words makes sadness, anger, and pain less intense.[20] For example, anger shows up as increased activity in the amygdala, the part of the brain that monitors fear and sets off a series of biological alarms and responses to protect the body from danger. When the angry feeling is labeled, Lieberman and his team of researchers noted a decreased response in the amygdala and increased activity in the right ventrolateral prefrontal cortex—the part of the brain that processes emotions and inhibits behavior.[21]

Build Boundaries, Not Walls

As an avoidant, you may not expect that your partner can fulfill your needs or heed your boundaries, and as a result, you have become accustomed to suppressing them. By not expressing your needs and limits to your partner, you set him up for failure, which triggers your natural instinct for creating distance. To avoid reaching this point, it's important that you communicate clearly. If your partner is demanding more time and attention from you, see if you can have a noncharged conversation to negotiate where both you and your partner feel like your needs are being met. Remember, having healthy boundaries means that you not only set them but also keep them. For instance, if you decide that Sundays are reserved for "me" time, but then cave when your partner asks you out, you are communicating, "Don't take my boundaries seriously." You train people how to interact with you.

Express a Need a Day

Since avoidants tend to disassociate from having needs and do not feel safe counting on others to meet their needs, you can build your comfort for getting needs met by expressing a need a day. Start small. For example, ask your partner to help you with a favor, or if you're feeling overwhelmed with work, communicate to your partner that you'll be focusing on your project and won't be able to talk until the evening. By intentionally asking for what you need and experiencing someone following through without negative consequences, you'll gradually build up your comfort in relying on others.

Set a Time Frame Before You Consider Ending It

With the awareness that your avoidant attachment causes you to find reasons to push someone away, set an actual time frame where you commit to staying in the relationship. (Of course, this doesn't apply if the relationship is toxic or unhealthy.) For example, instead of second-guessing the relationship on a regular basis, commit to staying in it for three months and only after then reassessing if you want to stay or not. During that time frame, do not engage in hemming and hawing about your decision; simply enjoy the time with the other person. This pushes you to move through the uncomfortable feelings that will inevitably rise and gives you a chance to experience the discomfort settling or even dissipating completely, if given the luxury of time.

Avoid Anxious Types

Dating a secure partner will help you become more secure. A secure partner will be more likely to tolerate your periodic withdrawals, as he will not take your need for space as a personal dig against him or your relationship. An anxious partner, on the other hand, will react to your need for space by trying to push harder for your time and attention in order to feel reassured. Also, a secure partner has the emotional keel to deal with conflict and come up with resolutions, versus catastrophizing them. A secure partner can model how to be present and how to communicate in a healthy way, helping you grow.

YOUR ATTACHMENT STYLE IS NOT STATIC

The tips I've shared above can help you create a healthier connection with a partner and move you toward a more secure style. Our styles are not static and evolve as a function of the people we are with and the choices we make about how we behave. The more you practice communicating and connecting in a healthy way, the more you can rewire and renew. You are not held prisoner by the way you grew up forever.

Even the most secure among us will at times react to triggers in ways that harm connection. Whether you're secure, anxious, or avoidant in your attachment style, use the following exercise to determine what your key triggers are and take stock of your past reactions to triggering events in order to strategize a healthier response. This can also be helpful when you are dating someone, for it provides a framework for you to have an open discussion on your triggers and how your partner can best support you and vice versa.

EXERCISE: Replace Your Reactions

By first recognizing the patterns of your reactions, you can then identify alternative ways of responding and practice honoring your boundaries and the boundaries of others without hurting the connection.

In the first column of the worksheet on page 88, write down what triggers you. If you identify as anxious, you may find most of your triggers result in protest behavior; if you identify as avoidant, you may find most of your triggers cause you to create distance. You may veer more secure and find yourself having triggers in both categories.

Once you've identified your key triggers, in the second column write down how you have typically reacted in the past. Next, in the third column, brainstorm a healthier response. The objective is to create a strategy for replacing your old reaction with a healthier response while you're in a nonactivated state (that is, not upset or emotionally charged) and to have a plan of action the next time your nervous system is sending you panic signals.

If you are in a relationship or starting to date someone, you can use the last section to identify the triggers of your partner and how you have reacted in the past. Now that you understand the different attachment styles, use compassion in coming up with a healthier way to respond to and support your partner.

Example: Anxious

Trigger: The person I'm dating takes hours to reply to my text.

Past Reaction: I keep texting and texting, which makes me more angry and desperate.

Healthy Response: I won't jump to conclusions when I don't hear back and will use self-soothing exercises to manage the feelings of anxiety. Instead of texting multiple times to get validation, I will journal or call a friend and commit to not sending another message until I've calmed down.

Example: Avoidant

Trigger: When the person I'm dating keeps wanting to hang out and I need time for myself.

Past Reaction: I get overwhelmed and don't return any calls or texts, or I see the person out of guilt and end up feeling resentful.

Healthy Response: Communicate clearly that I need some time for myself, that my taking time for myself doesn't mean I feel differently, and that once I've had some space I'll reach out to find a time that works for the both of us.

Example: Supporting your partner when he is triggered

Partner's Trigger: He feels suffocated and resentful when he doesn't have enough free time.

Your Past Reaction: I would make assumptions that when he wanted space this meant he was losing interest. I would get upset and guilt him into spending time with me.

Healthy Response: Now that I understand that time apart is healthy and not a threat to the relationship, I can welcome his need for space without guilting him and ensure each week I have designated days where I too am seeing friends and doing activities that light me up.

ANXIOUS

Trigger	Past Reaction	Healthy Response

AVOIDANT

Trigger	Past Reaction	Healthy Response

YOUR PARTNER

Trigger	Past Reaction	Healthy Response

IS YOUR CHEMISTRY COMPASS BROKEN?

Our ability to love intimately and sexually unfolds in stages, starting with our attachment with our parents. Our early patterns of relating and attaching to others get "wired" in our brains in childhood and then repeated in adulthood. If childhood patterns are problematic, we then grow up with a chemistry compass that's broken, and we are pointed toward those who embody the worst emotional characteristics of our primary caregiver(s). Our psyche tries to re-create the scene of the original crime (how we were wounded as children), hoping that we can save ourselves by changing its ending.

Psychologist Ken Page describes this as an "attraction of deprivation," when "our conscious self is drawn to the positive qualities we yearn for, but our unconscious draws us to the qualities which hurt us the most as children."[22] Basically, we try to get our unmet childhood needs met by our romantic partner. We're often attracted to a man for qualities we dislike and then want him to get rid of the exact things we were first drawn to. This is where the loop from childhood plays out in adulthood. Our partner doesn't fulfill the need we lacked growing up, which leads to the same familiar conflict and suffering we experienced before.

Remember Mandy, the one who rehearsed her I-hate-you speech for hours when her boyfriend didn't reply to her Snapchat message? During the session at Breakup Bootcamp when she did an exercise to discover her attractions of deprivation, she had an aha moment.

Mandy realized that she needed a lot of validation from men and finally understood the root of why. After exploring her reactions when a man she liked didn't give her attention, she was able to make the connection to her wound from childhood: a lack of affection from her father. She secretly yearned for her father's approval, for physical affection, for encouraging words of support. But instead he had a cold demeanor and rewarded her with praise only if she achieved academically. Mandy became accustomed to earning love, and when she didn't get validation, she would feel anxiety. In her romantic relationships, this was a familiar dynamic, and she was drawn to types who fit the emotionally unavailable role once held by her dad.

We develop instincts that become our chemistry compass, pointing us in the direction of those whom we find attractive or repulsive. So, if growing up you didn't have a positive model of what a healthy partnership looked like, it can be challenging to know what love feels like. The right person may be right in front of you, but you don't notice because you're too preoccupied chasing the bad boy, the unavailable workaholic, or the guy who fits a superficial checklist. Human beings like what feels familiar, and if inconsistency, fighting for love and attention, or enduring emotional abuse was your norm growing up, then subconsciously, you're going to keep choosing partners who make you feel the same way. This is often referred to as the "familiarity principle of attraction."

With a broken chemistry compass, even if you do date someone who can meet your needs, because it's so unfamiliar, you might self-sabotage or try to change the person to mirror your parents.

HAVE I MET YOU BEFORE? OH, HI, DAD.

My kryptonite: DJs.

In my twenties, I would beeline straight for the DJ booth, because behind those decks was where I'd meet my soul mate, obvi.

Dates in my twenties consisted of DJs, club promoters, and the ultimate double whammy—a DJ who was a club owner. DEAD.

These men were always the king of the room, had social clout, were charismatic (and often alcoholics), and I. Loved. Them. Of course, they loved me too, at like three A.M. when the club shut down, after I'd fought off other groupies clamoring for their attention. These men were unavailable and not invested in building a relationship with me; they sometimes gave me attention and most of the time did not. Then in my thirties, this "type" morphed into a more age-appropriate version. My new target: CEOs of tech start-ups.

These were visionaries dedicating their life and most of their waking hours to building their world-changing app! I felt lucky to get a sliver of their time. There's no pattern here, right? HA!

While the professions of the men I chose were vastly different, the emotional experience was exactly the same as my dynamic with my father.

When I was growing up, my father was neither physically nor emotionally available. My mother was in a constant state of anger, resentment, and misery, doing everything around the house and for the family business. But no matter what she did, my father never appreciated her. My mother was trying to earn her husband's love, and I was trying to earn my father's love—it was one big chase with no prize in sight.

The two things I yearned for the most from my parents were safety and connection.

I subconsciously picked men who were unable to meet either of those needs, feeling the same angst, inconsistency, and lack of safety over and over again. I would be constantly disappointed in the unavailable men I dated when they didn't change to meet my needs, and I pushed away the available ones who could love me in a healthy way because that felt foreign. Once I realized I was attracting the experiences in my adult relationships that could evoke the same emotions I felt as a child, I had a starting point for change. Instead of wasting years on a hamster wheel of dysfunction, I took a peek to see what was on the other side. The preview was enough for me to choose to avoid that wheel forever. Hold the applause—this awareness took me about three decades to figure out. I'm writing this book so you don't have to spend such a long time to come to this conclusion.

IT TAKES A VILLAGE

Now that you have a framework for managing your triggers in a healthier way, the next step of becoming more secure is to start surrounding yourself with relationships that foster trust and a sense of safety.

Regardless of your attachment style, it's important to address not only the romantic relationships in your life but all relationships. Our brain is influenced and molded by what it is repeatedly exposed to. This means if you feel unsafe, judged, and energetically depleted by the majority of people you're surrounded with, you're not going to build those necessary neural pathways associated with healthy connections. To start building our neural pathways of feeling connected, we need to surround ourselves with a village of safe relationships.

EXERCISE: Who's in Your Village?

Conduct an inventory of the five adult people you spend the most time with. This can include your friends and family, but may also include people you might not necessarily feel close to but spend a lot of time with, such as work colleagues, roommates, and neighbors. The objective is to assess who is in your village and if those are high-safety or low-safety relationships.

For each person, answer the statements below regarding how you generally feel around him or her on a scale of 1 (never) to 10 (always). Don't think too hard and go with your gut.

STATEMENT	#1 (NAME)	#2 (NAME)	#3 (NAME)	#4 (NAME)	#5 (NAME)
I feel safe and secure when I'm around this person.					
After I leave an interaction with this person, I feel positive energy.					
I trust this person.					
I feel respected by this person.					
I know I can count on this person.					
I feel supported in this relationship.					
I feel a sense of connection and belonging when I'm around this person.					
I feel that I can share my feelings with this person without being judged or criticized.					
I feel there is an equal exchange of give and take in this relationship.					
This person respects my boundaries.					
TRUST SCORE:					

SCORING

The chart gives you an idea of the relationships that are shaping your brain and central nervous system.[23]

Low-Safety Relationship (0–35)

These may be abusive or high-conflict relationships. If you're surrounded by people who score low on trust, you likely find yourself feeling on edge, anxious, or depleted from your relationships. There may be an uneven power dynamic, where you feel subordinate or disrespected. Because you're not getting healthy dopamine from your closest relationships, you may have a tendency to seek a dopamine fix from other sources—for example, indulging in food, alcohol, shopping, or other addictive vices. If the majority of your relationships are low safety, it will be difficult for you to feel relaxed and calm because your sympathetic nervous system is on constant high alert. It's in your best interest to try to decrease the amount of time you spend with these people. If a relationship is physically or emotionally abusive, it's of the utmost priority to get out of the relationship, which may mean you seek professional help to support you.

Medium-Safety Relationship (35–65)

If most of the people you spend time with are in this category, you may find yourself feeling apathetic about your relationships. Relationships may not feel rewarding or stimulating. You may want to try to grow the relationship by changing the current dynamic, setting limits, and/or communicating what you need in order for the relationship to be a positive value exchange.

High-Safety Relationship (65–100)

If most of your relationships are in the high-safety category, that's great news! This means your life is filled with relationships that foster growth. Since you're spending a significant portion of time with these people, not only are you getting a healthy dose of dopamine, but you're also feeling connected, trusting, and safe.

IT'S A TALL ORDER TO suddenly remove unsafe relationships from your life, especially if you coparent, live, or work with these people. Start off by gradually reducing your exposure to these people and increasing your exposure to safe relationships. Also, you can change the existing dynamic of these unsafe relationships by setting new terms.

Set New Terms of Engagement

For the "unsafe" people who are still in your life, you can start to change the dynamic by communicating boundaries and providing constructive feedback to express what you need in order for the relationship to feel mutually positive. If they engage in behavior that makes you feel emotionally or physically threatened, end the interaction altogether. If someone is not honoring your needs and boundaries after you've clearly communicated them, they are not respecting you. If disrespect is a pattern regardless of your attempts to shift the dynamic, you need to decide if you take space from the relationship or ultimately get out of it.

For example, I had to change the terms of relating when I spoke on the phone with my mom, who would typically launch into complaints and insults about my father. Because I now recognize this as classic enmeshment (where instead of treating me like a daughter, she uses me as her therapist), I kindly but firmly told her that I no longer want to hear complaints about my dad. I told her that at the end of the day, he's still my father and it hurts me to hear such negative things said about him. I offered that I'd be glad to hear about how she was feeling and brainstorm solutions, but if she launched into any more hate-fests about my dad, I would get off the phone. It took my telling this to her many times for her to finally get it, and she eventually stopped insulting him to me. I still need to remind her occasionally, but over time, we've shifted the dynamic.

It is perfectly normal and okay to reassess your relationships from time to time and evaluate if they're nourishing you or harming you. We change, other people change, and just because you have a history with someone doesn't automatically give them a spot in your present and future. This doesn't mean you need to stop caring for them. You can love and care for these people all you want, but that doesn't mean they need to be a part of your immediate peer group. And if you really want to keep spending time with someone but find that the interactions are negative or one-sided, you can communicate in a loving way that the dynamic needs to change along with your new terms. Note that people who have known you the longest may have trouble with this in the beginning. They may be used to a relationship with you where you are the brunt of the jokes, the pushover, or the one who constantly nurtures and gives more—but keep standing your ground. Keep communicating your new terms of engagement with both your words and your actions, and as you hold your integrity, you'll find that people start to respect your standards. Here's a template you can use as a starting point and customize to your situation.

- **Lead with something positive and create connection:** "I love you and value you in my life."

- **Communicate what isn't working and how it makes you feel:** "When I share my experiences and feelings and I'm met with criticism and anger, I feel unsafe to open up and sad that we can't connect."

- **Set a tone of compassion that you understand they're not ill-intentioned and may not realize how you're affected, and then state your preference:** "I know you love me and also value constructive and positive communication. Would you be open to listening to what I have to say without interruption, and afterward, sharing what you're feeling and asking me questions to better understand my perspective? I'll do the same for you."

- **Practice! It's possible you'll be met with resistance, but if you can, try to redirect the conversation and set the new tone, right then and there:** "Let's start over. Can I share what happened at work today? I'd love your feedback on this new manager."

You train people how to treat you. Each time you lower your standards, justify abusive behavior, or allow someone to breach your boundaries, you set a precedent for how much disrespect you'll tolerate.

Becoming more securely attached is a process that is influenced by your environment, family, community, and partner choices. Your attachment style won't change overnight, but you now have a deeper understanding of how and why you react to intimacy the way you do, and how to become more secure.

Your relationship outcomes are the result of your patterns, which are the result of your beliefs. Do you know what beliefs are ruling your love life? In the next chapter, we'll find out.

CHANGE YOUR BELIEFS, CHANGE YOUR LIFE

Whatever you hold in your mind on a consistent basis is exactly what you will experience in your life.

Tony Robbins

To get a clear picture of how beliefs shape our behavior, let's examine elephants in India. Let's say you are an elephant keeper. How would you keep a ten-thousand-pound elephant from running away? Perhaps with a massive steel cage? Or electric fences with barbed wire?

What if I told you the secret to keeping a ten-thousand-pound elephant from escaping is a piece of rope and a small wooden peg?

This might not make sense, because a rope is no match for the strength of an elephant. But the rope does not serve a physical purpose but a psychological one.

You see, when a baby elephant is born, the keeper ties its leg with a rope to a peg. At that point, the rope is strong enough to keep the elephant from roaming away. At first, the baby elephant will try to use all its strength to break free from the rope. But after multiple failed attempts, it learns that trying to escape the rope is futile. As the elephant grows and becomes stronger, the rope becomes too weak to retain the animal. However, the elephant no longer tries to escape.

After so many failed attempts when it was a baby, it's accepted that it has no choice but to stay in place. Once the elephant is fully grown, a peg doesn't even need to be used anymore; just having the rope on the elephant's leg keeps the animal in check. The elephant's belief that it is impossible to escape the rope has become ingrained, and for the rest of its life, it will never again try to escape.[1]

Learned helplessness. It affects humans just as much as it affects elephants.

We often form beliefs that are relevant to a situation or time of life, but even when that situation no longer applies, the belief becomes so ingrained that we never challenge it. Beliefs that were developed long ago that might have been useful once may hold us back later in life as we accept those beliefs as the complete truth.[2]

The good news is humans have a much greater rationalizing capability than animals, and we can choose to change our predisposed beliefs. We do not need to be prisoners of imaginary confines; we can choose to challenge old beliefs that hold us down. In this chapter, we are going to learn how to untie the ropes of the false beliefs and limitations of our past.

THE LEVELS OF CHANGE

How many times have you tried to diet, stop eating sugar, or minimize your addiction to social media, only to give up in defeat? Join the club. It can feel frustrating when you desire change in your life, but things seem to stay the same no matter how hard you try. Don't despair, it's not because you don't have the capability or the strength; it's just that you haven't learned the right approach. Often, we think that willpower is the way to enforce new behavior, but then fall back into old ways after a period of time. Relying on willpower alone is not an efficient way to create lasting change. In order to stick, change must come in levels and it starts at the nucleus.

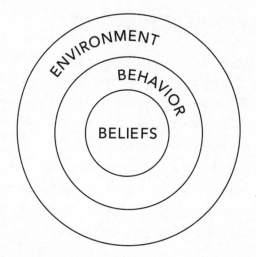

If we change at the outermost level—our environment—little else changes. For example, perhaps you think dating sucks in your city, so you decide to move to another city. But soon you fall into the same patterns and face the same intimacy issues as in the original city. Or, if one dating app isn't providing enough quality leads, you add more dating apps to the mix to broaden your "environment."

Or we try to change our behavior. For example, you want to appear all cool about your latest crush, so you strategize time delays before replying to texts (even if inside you're counting the minutes to responding). You manipulate your behavior to appear a certain way, instead of reflecting on the reason you feel the need to play games in the first place. You can fake behaviors for only so long, and while it's possible to effect some change this way, it's often unsustainable.

A more effective way of creating change is to get to the core—your beliefs. Once you shift your beliefs, there's an automatic ripple effect to the outer rings of behavior and environment.

We need to first get at the subconscious beliefs that are ruling our behavior and outcomes. Then, by intentionally working on shifting the beliefs and practicing new habits, dramatic changes will occur. The results might not be palpable in a week or a month, but consistent practice over time can lead to significant transformation.

YOU ARE THE SUM OF YOUR BELIEFS

You are the sum of the beliefs that you've collected throughout your life. Beliefs are stored in the subconscious, often beyond our conscious recollection. This is why, most of the time, people are perplexed and frustrated that they cannot change an unwanted behavior. That is because it's run by underlying programs, old beliefs.[3]

Most beliefs start early in life, because between the ages of one and seven, we are like sponges, soaking up everything others tell us, accepting much of what is said. Our brains are not fully developed yet and lack the cognitive ability to reason or think critically and logically.[4]

Medical hypnotist Susan Spiegel Solovay, who provides one-on-one sessions with Renew participants, says, "Once you understand that life is not about what happens to us—instead, it's about *the beliefs we have about what happened*—then you can go to the deeper mind to find and change unhelpful beliefs."

She explains that a belief such as "I am not good enough" can be deeply implanted from a childhood experience of being harshly criticized by a teacher, a peer, a sibling, or a parent. Even if the event was seemingly harmless, it's made an imprint. It will run like a river underneath many thoughts and cause a person to continue to prove "I am not good enough" because that is that person's inner belief. Eventually the incident during which that belief was implanted is forgotten in the conscious mind, but it remains the underlying programming of one's thoughts, feelings, and behavior.

Many studies have been conducted showing that children who believed they were not smart, not good at math or bad at spelling, would subconsciously make poor grades to live up to that idea. By working with the children to adjust their limiting beliefs, researchers concluded that in almost every case, poor grades were a result of their beliefs, not aptitude.[5]

We act like the person who we perceive ourselves to be. We literally can't behave otherwise, regardless of our willpower and efforts. From the student who thinks she's dumb to the woman who perceives herself as unlovable, we will invariably create circumstances that confirm our ideas about ourselves and find evidence that continues to prove these ideas to be true.[6] Our beliefs are the foundation upon which our personality, behavior, and circumstances are built. Ideas that are inconsistent with our inherent beliefs will be rejected and not acted upon.

OUR BRAINS ARE MEANING-MAKING MACHINES

Your brain is constantly trying to make meaning of the events, environment, and people around you. It doesn't like gray areas, it doesn't like unfinished business, and it certainly doesn't like questions left unanswered. Instead, it wants to file information into a folder and label that folder as "good" or "bad." If it doesn't have meaning for something that has happened, it will make meaning by accessing all the other neatly filed-away folders from the past, mixing assumptions, biases, and projections to come up with a story. It will keep looking for information or distorting information to prove that the old existing beliefs are true.

Master neurolinguistic programming (NLP) practitioner and author of *Neuropathways to Love* Cinthia Dennis has spent over a decade helping hundreds of clients recognize the beliefs that are getting in the way of creating the relationships they want. She is trained in NLP, an approach that uses language and pattern identification to help create change in one's thoughts and behavior.

"Beliefs are our filters on the world," she tells the participants at Renew. She holds up a pair of blue-tinted glasses and puts them on. "When I put on the glasses, I can see that you are all here, but you're all tinted blue. That is how beliefs work. The beliefs are the blue tint. We see the world and reality based on what we already believe. Reality is not neutral for us. I'd like to think all the things happening out there are mutual, but what we make them mean is our personal spin on them. The brain is designed to be efficient but not necessarily accurate. It will generalize and distort information so that it fits into what we already believe. Our beliefs cause us to feel a certain way, which affects how we behave and ultimately what we experience."

Cinthia shares the example of Audrey, a Renew participant who continued to work with her after attending bootcamp a year ago. Audrey is beautiful and charismatic and has no issue getting dates. But every time she dated someone it would end up the same way. The men were always unavailable—they were either not around, married to their work, or the player types who had no intention of committing.

"What we uncovered during our sessions was that deep down, Audrey had a core belief that she was unlovable. The only way she felt lovable was if she was useful. So she would behave in ways to earn love and eventually act in ways that would get these guys to push her away. Her brain also wouldn't let her pick anyone else. When an available guy liked her, she thought there was something wrong with him because he was choosing her."

Audrey kept repeating her experience, and each time, it would strengthen the belief that she was unlovable. Cinthia helped Audrey first to identify unavailable partners before she chose to date them and second to recognize her behaviors that were reaffirming her core belief.

Together, we are going to explore your beliefs and learn how to rewire the ones that no longer serve you.

THE EVOLVING LADDER OF BELIEFS

It's Saturday morning, and Dr. Zendegui is leading a session on changing old beliefs. After an exercise where the women identify their current beliefs about love and relationships, she asks for a volunteer from the group to share. Karen, a thirty-eight-year-old divorcée from San Francisco, reads one of the beliefs from her list: "There are no good men left."

Dr. Zendegui asks, "Is this assumption absolutely one hundred percent true?"

"Well, I suppose not absolutely. But if there are good guys, I sure haven't met them," Karen replies.

"So, is the belief one hundred percent true one hundred percent of the time?"

"No, I guess not."

"You mentioned earlier that you want to fall in love again. Do you feel this belief is helpful in getting you where you want to go?"

Karen sighs. "No, no, it isn't. But I don't know how to trust again."

Dr. Zendegui uses Karen's example to explain to the group: "Making a new belief isn't about having blinding, unrealistic optimism. The ideal new thought is not 'I'll meet someone amazing tomorrow' or 'Ryan Gosling will be mine.' Creating a new thought might mean softening the old thought or making it less extreme. Softening thoughts is often more accurate and takes the emotional sting out of the negative narratives we often tell ourselves. For Karen's belief, she might change 'There are no good men left' to 'While I've been hurt by some men in the past, there are still loving men out there whom I may have not yet met.' For those of you struggling with your separation, you might change 'I can't handle this breakup' to 'This breakup is really hard, and I know it will get easier over time.' For many, softening an extreme or black-and-white thought will cool the emotional temperature of the thought, which opens up more space for coping. Changing a thought could also mean totally changing the script. You might change 'I have to get pregnant by thirty-five' to 'If I don't get pregnant, I can explore adopting.'"

The way we shift our beliefs is to first identify the limiting belief and then create a more helpful belief. The approach is like climbing a ladder, one rung at a time, each rung representing a truer, more helpful belief. To see the full evolution, we'll look at Karen's evolving ladder of beliefs:

- **Bottom of the ladder:** "There are no good men left."

- **Next rung:** "While I've been hurt by some men in the past, I'm open to believing there are still loving men out there whom I may have not yet met."

- **Final rung:** "There are many different types of men out there, and I'm open to meeting someone who is the right match for me."

The evolving belief on each rung is a little more honest, more positive, and more helpful than the rung below. Going from the bottom of the ladder to the top instantly would be too dramatic a change for your brain, so the change in mindset has to be done gradually.

If you just state a new belief that is the complete polar opposite of your old one, your brain will simply reject it because you inherently don't think it's true. It takes shifting a few degrees to get yourself comfortable with a slightly evolved belief and, once you have a new baseline, going back again and again. Remember, you're climbing a ladder.

EXERCISE: Create Your Ladder

Examine the list on the next two pages and circle any of the beliefs that apply to you. Feel free to add beliefs that aren't on the list in the blank spaces.

Me

I'm worthless.

I'll always be alone.

It's my fault.

I'm not pretty enough/good enough/skinny enough.

I should have known. I should have done something sooner.

If only I were X, it would have worked out.

No one will ever love me.

I have to find someone to be happy.

I should be over it by now.

I shouldn't be so upset.

I can't live without my ex.

I can't handle this.

I'll never meet anyone else.

I can't be alone.

I can't ever trust anyone else.

I'm unlovable.

I'm not enough.

I'm too much.

I will be abandoned.

I will be rejected.

I have no time.

I am not safe.

_____

_____

_____

Others/The World

I can't rely on anyone.

People always let you down.

Dating is impossible in X place/at X age/in my circumstances.

All the good men are taken.

He will take away my freedom.

I can't trust men.

I'm never a priority to others.

Love is painful.

_____

_____

_____

The Future

I'll never find anyone.   _____

It never works out.   _____

I'll never get over this.   _____

I'll always be alone.

Review all the beliefs that you've circled. Choose one to work on for this exercise and create a ladder for that belief. Turn the idea from hurtful to helpful.

1. In the first rung, write down your old, unhelpful belief. Ask yourself: Is this belief 100 percent true 100 percent of the time? Chances are the belief isn't absolutely true. It's important you realize this on your own so you can see that the assumption is not a hard fact, and what you used to believe can now change.

2. In the second rung, update your belief with an assumption that is more honest and helpful. Think of a few examples of how this updated belief is true (either find evidence that perhaps you've overlooked in the past or think of scenarios where this might prove true in the future). Your updated belief should be one that pushes you just outside of your comfort zone, but not so far that you don't believe it.

3. In the third rung, write down your goal—what you aspire to believe so that you can ultimately create the life and love you want. You may not be there now, and perhaps you can't even fathom how you'll get there, and that's okay. You're writing this down so you have something to work toward. You can also add rungs in between to get you more and more ready to reach the top of the ladder.

Rung 3:
_____
_____
_____

Rung 2:
_____
_____
_____

Rung 1:
_____
_____
_____

Rung 1: What I used to believe (your old belief).

Rung 2: What I believe now (your updated belief).

Rung 3: What I aspire to believe (your goal).

Post this new, updated belief somewhere where you can see it often. Make it your phone screensaver, put it on a sticky note on your bathroom mirror, or repeat it as a daily mantra. Seek out examples of it being true. When you start to experience change, there's a positive feedback loop, which starts the process of rewiring.

Dr. Zendegui emphasizes that "thoughts not only impact what we feel, they also impact how we act. What we tell ourselves and the narrative we form about difficult situations can greatly impact how we cope, and saying unhelpful things to ourselves on repeat can impact our mood, behavior, and self-concept over time."

At the end of the changing beliefs session, Dr. Zendegui leads the women outside to wrap up the exercise. Feet on the grass, so they can feel grounded on the earth, the women form a circle. Each woman takes a turn standing in the center and states her new belief.

It's Karen's turn: "There are many different types of men out there, and I'm open to meeting someone who is the right match for me."

The group then echoes her new belief to her in unison: "There are many different types of men out there, and you're open to meeting someone who is the right match for you."

Karen looks around at the women smiling at her, silently cheering her on with loving glances. There's something about hearing her new affirmation repeated to her by the supportive women of the group that's undeniably soothing. There's a tear in her eye. "Thank you," she says as she nods her head in acknowledgment and returns to her spot in the circle, ready to support the woman up next.

Nancy: FROM "I AM NOT ENOUGH" TO "I PRIORITIZE MY OWN NEEDS FIRST"

NANCY WAS A BAWSS BABE. A marketing executive at a national hospitality company, she had moved to New York City from Seattle for her husband, who worked in finance. Standing at five foot ten inches tall, with long brown hair and sparkling green eyes, she was beautiful and dressed like she had just stepped out of a Diane von Furstenberg ad. Since she was a little girl, Nancy excelled in everything she put her mind to. She was an achiever, a make-it-happener; she would do whatever it took to make everything perfect.

Nancy had a pattern of overcompensating. She was always the one doing, while her partner would sit back without lifting a finger. This dynamic came to an abrupt halt when her father was diagnosed with terminal cancer. She could no longer act as Mrs. Perfect who kept it all together. Her husband couldn't handle the change. Instead of supporting her through a rough time, he asked her, "When are you going to get back to normal?"

That was the beginning of the end of their marriage.

Nancy came to Renew to learn about her patterns so that she wouldn't keep finding herself in relationships where she was the only one showing up. Upon digging into her subconscious beliefs, she uncovered that her limiting belief was "I am not enough." That belief was the root of why, whether professionally or romantically, she would take on the role of doing all the work, overcompensating for the lack of effort from others and attempting to create perfection.

Through the shifting beliefs exercise, Nancy realized that her needs were just as important as the needs of others, and her practice was to begin honoring her own needs. Her updated, more honest, more helpful belief became "I prioritize my own needs first."

I had a call with Nancy six months after she came to Renew to see how things were going. She told me that since she'd left the retreat, her new belief had become a mantra that she'd repeat daily. She put her new belief on the screensaver of her phone and on a Post-it note on her mirror, and she would remind herself when she went on dates that her needs came first.

She also shared with me a story about a man she'd recently dated:

"We had chemistry and he was such a nice guy. But he made it clear he was just looking for fun and loved the bachelor life in New York.

"Typically, I would have kept dating him, put his needs first in hopes that he would change and come around to wanting what I wanted—a relationship. But as much as I liked him, I told him that I was looking for someone interested in building a relationship, and if that wasn't where he was at, that there were no hard feelings, but there'd be no point continuing dating."

Nancy was disappointed that it didn't work out but was proud of herself for recognizing her needs and walking away from a situation that wasn't set up to fulfill them. Whereas before she would have kept trying to make it work with this man (as she had done in her first two marriages), she walked away before investing in another dead-end relationship.

POSITIVE AFFIRMATIONS ALONE DON'T WORK

Change can only happen when thoughts are in alignment with the emotional state of the body.

Dr. Joe Dispenza [7]

How many times have you been told to just "think positive" or to chant positive affirmations and you'll manifest what you want? And . . . how many times has this actually worked?

Affirmations are not a strategy for change. They only work for people who already believe them to be true. For those who have low self-esteem, repeating positive affirmations may make them feel worse.[8] Your belief creates thoughts that in turn create an emotion. The belief is the cause agent that creates a ripple effect. It works like this.

Belief → Thoughts → Chemical reactions → Emotions → Energy → Actions → How the world responds to your energy → Outcome

If you're constantly in a scarcity mindset—never feeling like you have enough—and feeling unworthy of love, you can repeat "I'm so lovable!" until you lose your voice, but the idea will not make it past your brain stem.

But guess what? There's a trick. You can actually outsmart your body by using visualization techniques to change your emotions.

TURNING YOUR BELIEF INTO EXPERIENCE

When we recount memories in an associated way—by reliving the memory in detail as if it's happening again—our bodies can re-create the same stress hormones they did when the situation happened the first time. Yep, that's why when we recount that terrible fight we had two years ago, our bodies re-create the same spikes of cortisol as if we're fighting right here, right now.

On a chemical level, our brain and body cannot distinguish between when we are remembering the past, experiencing the present, or imagining the future. Research has shown that the human nervous system "cannot tell the difference between an 'actual' experience and an experience imagined vividly and in detail."[9]

The bad news is if you keep recounting the negatives of the past over and over again, you can retraumatize yourself. But the good news is that you can also use your mind to trick your body into thinking something positive is happening, simply by using visualization.

Research by bestselling author and scientist Dr. Joe Dispenza explores the intersection of neuroscience, epigenetics, and quantum physics to educate people on how to heal themselves of illnesses and even chronic conditions through shifting beliefs. His teachings suggest that we can use visualization to imagine a desired future experience as if it were already an accomplished fact, and the brain will accept it as if it were a real experience. Say what?!

Let's review a study that demonstrates this. A team of researchers from Harvard took a group and divided it in half. The first group practiced a five-finger piano exercise for two hours a day over a period of five days. The members of the second group did the same thing, but only in their minds, meaning they just imagined themselves doing the five-finger piano exercise for two hours a day over a period of five days. When the researchers scanned the brains of both groups after the exercise, the results showed all participants had created a significant number of new neural circuits and neurological programming in the part of the brain that controls finger movements. Let that sink in. The members of the second group that only imagined playing the piano also showed changes in the brain, even though they never lifted a finger![10]

If you were to put that group in front of a piano after five days of visualization, most would be able to play the exercise they imagined, all because by practicing visualization, they installed the neurobiological hardware in preparation for the experience.

Your nervous system cannot tell the difference between an *imagined experience* and a "real" experience. . . . Your nervous system reacts appropriately to what "you" *think* or *imagine* to be *true*.

Maxwell Maltz[11]

EXERCISE: Visualize Your New Belief

Let's use visualization techniques to shift our beliefs about our relationships. The intention of this exercise is to imagine yourself with the updated belief you created in the ladder exercise and visualize how you feel and act differently in your environment. For example, if your belief started at "I am always rejected" and evolved to "I'm open to meeting new people and will lead with curiosity in my interactions," you might imagine yourself talking to someone at a party, asking questions, smiling, and experiencing the positive feelings of building rapport. Or if your belief changed from "I can't trust anyone" to "There are some people I can trust some of the time," summon the feelings of warmth when you are with someone you know you can count on. Perhaps instead of your arms crossed, you have more relaxed and open body language. Whatever your updated belief, this is a practice of playing with possibility and visualizing how your experience changes.

Take the new updated belief you created in the ladder exercise.

Next, find a quiet spot and get grounded by doing deep breathing. Close your eyes and imagine yourself walking into a room with your updated belief. How are you standing? What is your facial expression?

Visualize the entire scene. Who's there with you? What's the expression on their face? How are people responding to your energy differently? What are the colors, the smells, the sounds? Run though the scenario as if it's happening right now and you are experiencing it firsthand. Now, check in with how you feel. What are the emotions coming up? Don't forget to smile. Feel gratitude for this moment. Really let it soak in, along with the feelings associated with this new belief. Feel in your body that without a doubt this is your reality. When you're completely immersed, slowly open your eyes.

According to Dr. Dispenza, once we immerse ourselves in the scene of what we want to create, using imagination to evoke how we would feel as if we're experiencing it in real time, changes begin to take place in our brain.[12]

Each time we do this, we're laying down new neurological tracks (in the present moment) that literally change our brain to look like the brain of our future. In other words, the brain starts to look like the future we want to create has already happened.

Dr. Joe Dispenza

By visualizing and mentally rehearsing how you'd engage differently with your updated belief, you've created new neural pathways in your brain. Now, the more you repeat and practice, the more you strengthen that new pathway.

OOPS, I DID IT AGAIN

When cleaning a room, it gets more messy before it gets orderly. The same is true of cleaning your mind. Often, as you begin the healing process, you will begin feeling the pain or shame that your dysfunctional behavior was protecting you from. But if you can tolerate those raw feelings and process them in a healthy way this time, then you will no longer need the dysfunctional behavior. It won't have a purpose because there's no longer any toxic shame or pain to avoid. At other times, a behavior or belief that you thought you defeated may rear its head again. Don't get frustrated. Think of self-improvement as climbing a mountain. Sometimes you'll feel like you're in the same place you started, but the truth is that you've climbed higher and you're just looking at the same view.

Neil Strauss

Change is a process that requires gradual steps of progression, repeated and practiced, with room for error in between. Relapses are an inevitable part of that process. This is the sneaky li'l guy that can strike during any behavior change. When you have a relapse—perhaps you call your ex, see your ex, or hook up with you ex—you might freak out and think nothing has changed and you're back at square one. You may experience feelings of disappointment, shame, and frustration. Don't fret! Know that this is a part of the process, and instead of letting the relapse hijack your self-confidence, use self-compassion to get yourself back on your feet.

You are not broken, nor do you need fixing! You're just *optimizing*. Growth happens in the valleys. A positive attitude of resilience and perseverance is required so that we do not get discouraged and abandon our efforts during the process.

Author Linda Graham, who is an expert on the neuroscience of human relationships, notes: "It almost doesn't matter at first how small the increment of change is. What's important is that we choose practices that catalyze positive change and that we persevere."[13]

Resilience is not about perfecting each step; it's about choosing to persevere even when you feel like you've fallen back a step.

Change can happen in an instant. Results can take time to show up. In the moments when you feel overwhelmed, take a moment to reframe. Don't focus on the end point, and instead, take stock of all the actions you've taken and the next attainable action you can take next. This helps you get process focused versus destination obsessed. If this next stage requires one hundred steps, remember that you can't go from zero to a hundred. Just focus on the next step and then the next step after that. Even if you fall down or have days when you're not making any movement at all, it doesn't negate all the steps you've taken prior to this. Eventually the steps add up.

Cindy

CINDY HAD LEFT an abusive husband, and as a single mom at age twenty-eight, she had grand plans to go back to school and rebuild herself into the confident, adventurous woman she once was. But then she met Martin, a man who promised her the world. He promised he would take care of her and her son, and after a whirlwind romance, he moved in. But as months went by, Martin's true character started to surface. She found out that he was a drug dealer. He became increasingly controlling, setting up a video camera in her living room, claiming it was for security reasons. He'd show up unexpectedly at her school to "drop off food," when really he was monitoring her whereabouts. When she'd confront him on his controlling behavior, he'd turn things around and convince her that she was the one acting crazy. They kept breaking up and getting back together.

Then he proposed.

He shared his aspirations of starting a business, of starting a family. He promised a new life and that he was going to get his act together.

"I thought maybe if we had a family it would change him."

But things didn't change.

"We were fighting a lot. I knew it wasn't a healthy relationship. I knew, but I was trapped. I felt lost. I really loved this person. He became my social work project. And then I came across Renew. I knew that would be the time I could finally break things off. Before I left for the retreat, I told him to move out.

"When I was at Renew, I had hopes that it was the final push that could help me finally get out of this thing."

When Cindy showed up at the bootcamp, she was slouched over, avoided eye contact, and hardly spoke. One of the coaches pulled me aside and told me she was really worried about her. We didn't know if she was retaining any information, because her eyes looked glazed over and she didn't speak. Per Renew protocol, the retreat is tech-free, and Cindy had her phone off the entire time. Upon the retreat's end, she turned on her phone to dozens of messages from Martin:

"You told me you were going to a retreat and I know you're whoring yourself out."

"I'm going to kill you."

One after another the texts came in. Cindy was literally shaking.

RESILIENCE IS NOT
ABOUT PERFECTING
EACH STEP; IT'S
ABOUT CHOOSING
TO PERSEVERE
EVEN WHEN YOU
FEEL LIKE YOU'VE
FALLEN BACK A
STEP.

Cindy went home with one of the coaches, and together they put a plan in action to ensure her safety. She told her landlord what had happened and asked him to change the locks to keep Martin away. She asked her mom to come and stay with her. She blocked his number.

"I knew I had to have no contact. Because I knew me—and if I opened the door of communication and thought we could be friends, I'd fall back into it again."

After her first divorce, she had made a plan to get her life back on track, but she had lost herself in another abusive relationship. She was ashamed of how she got into this toxic relationship that could have had dangerous consequences for both her and her son. It happened gradually, until she was so deep in it that she couldn't even recognize herself anymore.

A year later, Cindy flew to San Francisco to attend the first Renew alumni retreat. When she walked through the door, I thought I was seeing a different person: confident, with her head up high, laughing and vivacious. Cindy had gotten her life back together. She had taken self-defense classes since Breakup Bootcamp, had a steady job, and had started hiking and dancing again, two hobbies she loved. She was focused on getting her degree and had stopped dating completely to focus on herself. She took the tools she learned seriously and implemented change right away. She was proud of how far she'd come.

But it wasn't easy, and many times when she missed her ex, the thought of opening up the door did cross her mind. She recounted a time, eight months after the breakup, when she was walking across the Brooklyn Bridge during a visit to New York. A flood of memories came rushing back, since this was something she and Martin often did together. She was overwhelmed with emotions—she still loved Martin and missed him terribly. She started to cry, feeling ashamed for still having such strong feelings for him and for her desire to see him again.

"I had to fight every urge in my body to not contact him. I missed him. I wanted to see him. But I knew if I reached out, I'd get sucked back into drama." Her awareness of her patterns gave her the ability to pause and not react to her craving. She didn't contact him that day, and at the time of this writing, she is still Martin-free.

You've now looked at your old, unhelpful beliefs and have a framework on how to update them, one rung at a time. You understand that along the way there will be bumps and detours, and that this is a natural part of the process of change. Our final step is to access the bigger picture of where you want to go. Just as we have challenged old beliefs, let's challenge what we think we should be chasing.

SEEKING HAPPINESS

Let's discuss a trendy topic in today's culture: the pursuit of happiness.

Popular media, literature, and self-help books are all marketing the hell out of happiness right now. Happiness is a big business—a $10 billion business, that is, according to a report by Research and Markets.[14] It's designed to sell you the book, the course, the app that will give you the cure—to fix you from being broken. It underscores the idea that we should be happy all the time and leaves no room for the entire range of emotions that makes us human. This approach is fundamentally flawed because it sets us up for a never-ending cycle—happiness is an elusive object, and the minute you get your hands on it, it slips from your grasp. What you don't realize is that you're playing a game that's designed to keep you suffering.

When you see happiness as something you can buy, achieve, or find outside of yourself, you create suffering. When you see happiness as an absence of pain, you create suffering. When you believe that you should be happy all the time, you set yourself up for suffering.

Here's the thing: you actually don't want to be happy all the time.

In fact, being constantly happy can be detrimental for your health and growth!

Our emotions exist for a reason and help us navigate life. Emotions lead us toward and away from decisions that are necessary for our survival and well-being. Also, a great misconception is that the road to happiness means an absence of pain.

Pain is not good or bad. It's a messenger. Pain is telling you that something is out of balance, that something needs attention, that there is change or growth waiting for you. This applies to both physical and emotional pain.

Pain is not your enemy—it's energy, tapping you on the shoulder and whispering, "Notice me." Ignore it long enough and the whispers get louder and louder, until you've given it no choice but to scream, *"Notice me!"* The pain grows. It becomes more intense and more unbearable, begging you to finally give it the attention it needs.

When you experience a life-shattering breakup, when you feel like your world is falling apart, this is often pain that has been ignored for a long time, until it finally had to break you apart so that you'd actually notice and take action.

If you are hell-bent on being happy, what happens when you experience darker emotions? You will think something is wrong with you or become disappointed in yourself. That shame might beget more self-loathing, causing you to feel even worse. Resisting the emotions you perceive as negative will only intensify them. You can also feel contradictory emotions at the same time. Life is not black and white. What if instead you embrace the light and dark, positive and negative, happy and sad, and all the emotions in between as part of the human condition? The wide emotional range indicates a fully lived life, each peak and valley necessary for growth.

Think about some of the greatest singers in the world, from Adele to Celine Dion to Mariah Carey to Lady Gaga. What do they all have in common? Range. It's the breadth and depth of range that make them masterful vocalists. Imagine your life as if you're singing your own opera. Would you really want an opera in only one key, with a simple melody, with no range?

So Feeling Bad Isn't Bad?

What if you replaced your goal of happiness with the intention of acceptance?

Acceptance is being aware of the present moment without judgment. Author Jon Kabat-Zinn describes acceptance beautifully:

Acceptance doesn't, by any stretch of the imagination, mean passive resignation. Quite the opposite. It takes a huge amount of fortitude and motivation to accept what is—especially when you don't like it—and then work wisely and effectively as best you possibly can with the circumstances you find yourself in and with the resources at your disposal, both inner and outer, to mitigate, heal, redirect, and change what can be changed.[15]

With acceptance in mind, when you feel uncomfortable emotions, accept them and give yourself the permission to feel them, process them, and learn from them. The ironic thing is the more you accept what is, the happier you'll be.

Cautionary note: There's a big difference between the functional sides of emotions that help you and the dysfunctional sides, which usually come from overattachment. For example, functional sadness enables pause and reflection; dysfunctional sadness can turn into depression. Functional anger can compel someone to be assertive; dysfunctional anger is rage. If you veer more on the dysfunctional sides of emotions where they are putting you and others in danger, it's crucial that you immediately seek professional help for support in transitioning them into a manageable, functional range.[16]

Having < Doing < Being

Look, I'm not saying happiness is to be avoided. Feeling positive and joyful in life is a state that is satisfying and rewarding. I just want you to challenge the misconceptions of constant happiness, and I also want to encourage you to accept the other emotions that come along with being a human being. When I feel sad, I say to myself, "Oh, I'm stretching my emotional range right now. I'm growing my capacity to feel." Because guess what? If you numb your ability to feel the bad, you also numb your ability to feel the good. You cannot suppress one side of the emotional spectrum without affecting the other.

This brings me to another important concept on the emotional plane. It's a big one: inner peace.

When I was in my relationship with the man I thought I was going to marry, I thought I had it all. I had the high-status job, the salary, the apartment, the boyfriend, the life plan. #WINNING.

But when I lost every element that I based my "happiness" upon, I was miserable. Not just your basic kind of miserable, but the can't-get-out-of-bed-my-life-is-over kind of miserable. I learned a critical lesson after I came out the other side, one that has forever changed the way I approach life. You see, my former approach consisted of me basing my happiness, peace, and identity on all the external factors to which I was attached. As long as those were in order, then I was "happy." But they could never bring me true happiness or peace, because they were completely dependent on things outside of my control.

Now, I see myself as the center of my universe. And all these incredible things—the career, the relationship, the status—they are orbiting around me. If one gets plucked out, I may lose my balance momentarily, but I won't be completely knocked off my center.

Serenity is not finding calmer seas, it's building a better boat.

Ryan Soave

I'm far from monk status, where I'm unaffected by my environment and external circumstances. But I am working to look within myself to be my own source of love, joy, happiness, and peace. I hope to continue evolving to the point where I can feel peaceful even if my external world is weathering a storm. To me, that is true inner peace.

So, my question for you is: What are you striving for? Is it something external? Is it only after you've achieved the job, the salary, the relationship, the house, and the family that you will finally be happy and truly at peace? Or would it be more fulfilling if you shifted your intention inward—to accept, to be peaceful, regardless of the external? Which path would be more helpful in the long run?

BREAKING THROUGH

Each woman who has come to Renew Breakup Bootcamp came feeling broken. They arrive hunched over, their eyes dull, their faces and bodies tense. By the time they leave the retreat, they have all come to the same realization: it's not about the guy, it never was. Nope, it's not about the ex, the relationship, or what he did or didn't do.

It's about relearning how to love themselves, whether single or coupled, and regain their worth, identity, and power. The breakup was not the ending; it was merely the spark to catapult them into transformation, to break free and break through into the women they were meant to become—empowered, inspired, awake.

So many women who've come to Renew have been living asleep, shackled by limiting beliefs of gender roles, what love should look like, what they are worthy and not worthy of . . . Without the traumatizing breakup to snap them out of their trance, they would have never stopped to question if the path they'd been walking on was the path they actually wanted.

Some of the women who come to Renew have since launched new careers and explored a journey of healing and spirituality, and many are now in loving, healthy relationships they never dreamed were possible. Some have even joined the Renew team, making it their mission to help others through heartbreak too. Sometimes a breakup is the shake-up we need to redirect our life.

FEELINGS AREN'T FACTS (WHEN IT HURTS SO GOOD)

Pain is inevitable; suffering is optional.

Unknown

Have you ever googled pictures of Amy Winehouse before and after drugs? It's legitimately terrifying, right?

Cocaine, speed, alcohol—we all know how bad these things are for us. Watch any "Faces of Meth" YouTube compilation and it's the stuff of nightmares. It scares most people away from drugs forever. But you know what doesn't exist and really should? A "Faces of Emotional Addicts" YouTube compilation.

I'm only half kidding here. The fact is "emotional addiction" is a very real phenomenon that affects an untold number of highly sensitive individuals. And it takes a toll on their hearts, minds, and bodies.

Ever wonder why people keep creating drama in their personal lives?

Well, just like the drug addict who is always craving more, the emotional addict can't get enough either. We may not be snorting white powder like Al Pacino in *Scarface,* but we are junkies all the same. In fact, the substances that get us high—even though they may not be illicit—are involved with emotional addiction too.

Everybody's heard about endorphins, right? Those incredible mood-lifting chemicals that are released during sex and long-distance running. But few people understand how they actually work.

In fact, it was only as recently as the 1970s that endorphins were discovered by scientists who were trying to figure out how heroin works in the body. What they discovered instead: endorphins are this amazing personal narcotic that we all have inside of us that works similarly to morphine. No dealer required.

But what many people don't realize is that these endorphins are created from both pleasure *and* pain. The emotional addict doesn't even realize that she has become fully addicted to her *negative* emotions.

Neuroscientist and author Dr. John Montgomery notes that when "cutters" intentionally hurt themselves, endorphins are released that can initially feel like a high dose of morphine. "When people who are chronically depressed think sad, painful thoughts—such as recalling a painful romantic breakup—the *pain thought itself* will instantly trigger the release of endorphin in their brains."[1]

WHEN YOUR HOMEOSTASIS IS ONE OF CHAOS

Our body does not like change because its job is to maintain a state of equilibrium, known as "homeostasis." We are wired to stay in balance with what is familiar, because what is familiar is comfortable.

You may have heard the expression that neurons that "fire together, wire together." When a circuit keeps firing, it can become the default setting, making the same response likely to occur in the future.[2] So, if we've felt safe and loved since we were young, our brain becomes really good at play, cooperation, and trust. If we felt unwanted, afraid, and abandoned as children, the associated chemicals have stuck around for decades too, resulting in us specializing in anxiety and shame as adults.

The brain wants to preserve the chemical state it's accustomed to. One of its primary biological functions is homeostasis, and it will do anything possible to maintain that chemical continuity. Cells eventually become chemically desensitized (resistant to the stimulus) and need more stimulus to create a reaction. Over time, more worry, more anger, or more anxiety is needed to turn on the brain.

All our feelings and attitudes—ones we believe are caused by outside forces—are a result of how we perceive reality based on our belief systems and also how addicted we are to particular emotions. You perceive the environment in a way that reinforces how you feel. When you leave a situation that was a source of negative emotions, whether it's by exiting a relationship, ending a friendship, or leaving behind the people, places, and things associated with bad feelings, you may find that even though you've changed the circumstances, the feelings still persist. When our cells are no longer getting their usual chemical fix, we then recall memories to do the job. When we are in the midst of change, the memories are working their hardest. If we are not careful, we will likely choose a new mate who will create the same negative feelings, because this allows us to maintain the chemical state we have become conditioned to feel as our homeostasis.

Emotions are the chemical residue of experience. If you're addicted to the emotions of shame, you might use your critical boyfriend to reaffirm your addiction to judgment. You might use your parents to reaffirm your addiction to guilt. You might use Instagram to reaffirm your addiction to insecurity. If you're addicted to feeling victimized, you might create stories about how you were wronged and how everyone else is to blame. You may repeat a story over and over again to anyone who will listen to "what happened to you."

BUT . . . IT'S COMFY HERE

Homeostasis is helpful in the sense that it maintains our bodies' natural body temperature, metabolism, and other functions necessary for survival. However, since your body is primarily concerned with keeping things the way they are, when you introduce something new, its first reaction is to resist. For example, say you rarely exercise. One day you decide that you should start working out, so you decide to go for a run, but after a few blocks, you start to feel dizzy and nauseated, gasping for air. What do you do? You could stop running and walk home in defeat. But that might be an overreaction, because your brain was just receiving signals that detected measurable changes in heart rate and respiration. Your typical homeostasis was disrupted, so your system sent alarm bells to your body to stop what it was doing immediately! If you didn't know about homeostasis, you might interpret those signals as a threat. Now you know that it is natural for your body to resist change—the status quo is just more comfortable. Keep running, or, in this context, keep pushing yourself past your comfort zone.

There are biological factors that try to keep you in homeostasis, but also social and cultural ones as well. Sometimes it's the people who've known you the longest who are most resistant to your change. They've put you in a box that's comfortable for them. They too have a homeostasis of how and who you are and a familiar way of interacting with you as that person. They know where they stand in relation to you, with the labels and roles that they have assigned you.

When you change, some people in your life may be uncomfortable with your change simply because the shift is too shocking to handle. Some may envy you, and some may be more comfortable with the old you simply because it's what they're accustomed to. It's important that you are aware of these outside factors that can limit your evolution.

EXERCISE: Name It to Tame It

In this exercise we are going to determine to which emotions you may be addicted. Once we understand this, we can bring awareness to the past experiences that imprinted these emotions and learn how to hack the loop.

PART 1

Reflect on your last few relationships. If you've had only one relationship, you can stick to that one. Write down the three emotions you felt consistently in your past relationships. For example, if you were constantly overgiving and not receiving anything back, you might have felt resentful. If you found yourself chasing for more time, more commitment, you might have felt desperate. If you had a lot of fun in your last relationship, perhaps you felt playful. The list doesn't have to just be negative emotions; if you experienced consistent positive emotions, you can include those too. The point of this exercise is to take stock of the patterns of your past emotional experiences.

Three main emotions you felt with ex #1

_____

_____

_____

Three main emotions you felt with ex #2

_____

_____

_____

Three main emotions you felt with ex #3

_____

_____

_____

Reflect on the words—are any repeating? Ask yourself what emotional states you might be addicted to feeling. How might you be participating in creating situations that enable you to keep feeling those emotions? The words that keep coming up are the emotions you are addicted to, dear reader.

PART 2

Circle any unhelpful or negative emotions that repeated throughout your relationships, and choose one to work with. If each relationship brought up different emotions, you can focus on the emotional experience of your most recent relationship.

Using the sentence stem below, write down how you contributed to the emotional experience. In the second sentence, identify how you can stop the emotional experience from repeating in the future. Repeat this sentence stem multiple times to get a full picture of all the ways you're accountable for your emotional experience and the choices you can make to stop the pattern from repeating.

For example:

Repeated feeling: **resentful**

I felt _resentful_ when _I kept paying for everything, did all the housework, and kept giving my time and energy without any reciprocation._

To prevent this from happening in the future, _I will stop automatically paying for everything and have a conversation about money and boundaries up front._

Your turn:

I felt _____ when _____

_____.

To prevent this from happening in the future, _____

_____.

I felt _____ when _____

_____.

To prevent this from happening in the future, _____

_____.

I felt _____ when _____

_____.

To prevent this from happening in the future _____

_____.

WHAT YOUR TRIGGERS REVEAL

Our relationships provide insight on what our needs are. If you can meet your own basic survival and emotional needs, you will likely engage in relationships, experiences, and opportunities that are complementary and supportive of where you are. You can vocalize and communicate your needs and boundaries and take appropriate action if your boundaries are crossed. You treat yourself with love, compassion, care, and respect and do not accept less from others.

However, if you experienced neglect, trauma, abuse, or enmeshment as a child, you may have a dysfunctional relationship with your needs. As a reaction to not having your needs met, you might feel anger or entitlement. Like a child throwing a tantrum to get attention, you could resort to drama, passive aggression, or manipulation to get your needs temporarily fulfilled.

Or you may have developed coping mechanisms to train yourself out of having needs. Instead of honoring your needs, you silence them, forget about them, or give up altogether. This manifests as:

- People pleasing

- Overachieving

- Caretaking

- Underachieving

- Rebelling

- Controlling

- Submitting

I learned in childhood that the way to survive was by tending to my own needs. I would proudly state that I had no needs, as if it were a badge of honor. But my unmet needs became the basis of repeated fights, passive-aggressive jabs, chronic tension, and a state of anxiety in my relationships. I would argue with my exes about their lack of texting and tried to enforce rules of frequency in communication. Or I'd pick a fight about the lack of romantic gestures and demand more date nights and flowers. Even when the men I dated obliged, I was only temporarily relieved of my frustration and resentment. The same pain would always resurface.

This was a recurring problem, and in retrospect, it was never about the amount of flowers or frequency of calls or texts. Behind my complaints, demands, and criticism of what my partners weren't doing was a deep, unmet need for connection. I could try troubleshooting the symptoms all I wanted, but without dealing with the root, I would never be addressing the real issue. My real issue. Instead of putting Band-Aids on the problem, I had to have an honest and vulnerable conversation about my need for connection and safety. While I can share what my needs are, ultimately, I am responsible for meeting my own emotional needs.

We all have needs, and each person's needs are personal and based on their history. Before we begin to address the core needs we each have in relationships, we must first:

1. Understand what our needs are and have compassion for the needs of others (this does not mean sacrificing our own).

2. Acknowledge needs by showing/voicing them with honesty (instead of hiding or suppressing them until you explode).

3. Take responsibility that you are your own primary caregiver and must meet your own needs as much as you are able. You do this through self-care and loving treatment of yourself, having strong boundaries, and surrounding yourself with people who respect your needs. This way you connect with others from a place of wholeness, not starvation and lack.

4. Understand that your needs are fluid and may shift depending on your life stage, situation, and partner, and that doing regular check-ins with your needs is important.

And remember, your frustration about what others are not giving you is an indicator of what you first need to give to yourself.

Zahra: "I DON'T FEEL SAFE"

ZAHRA WAS A child of a messy divorce. She was ten when her mom found out that her dad was having an affair. After that, her life became unstable, as she was in the middle of a nasty custody battle. When Zahra grew up, she immersed herself in her career and made a lot of money. Financial security was one of the ways that she could create safety for herself. But while she excelled in her corporate life, her relationships were a mess. She was cheated on in two of her relationships and had major trust issues. No matter how much financial success she had, Zahra didn't feel safe and would keep getting herself into relationships that would reaffirm her safety and trust issues.

When she was at Renew, she was four months into a new, healthy relationship with a secure man. He was showing her in both his actions and words that he was committed and wanted to keep exploring building a partnership with her. But Zahra was traumatized from her past. She felt insecure when her boyfriend didn't reply to her text messages immediately or call her enough times in a day. She would get mad, and her boyfriend would change his behavior to appease her, only for her to get mad at him again the next week for something else.

Zahra clearly had a need for safety and blamed her boyfriend for not giving it to her.

"He doesn't make me feel safe," she confided to the group.

Zahra's way of coping was to try to control and micromanage her boyfriend. If he obliged to her demands, she would feel "safe" temporarily, until the next issue came up. Her tight grip on control and rigid rules were just putting Band-Aids on the root issue—that she inherently did not feel safe.

Can you relate? Have you tasked other people with making you feel safe, loved, or happy? Our relationships—whether they be romantic, platonic, or professional—can help support us in meeting our needs, but ultimately nobody can give you something that you must feel on your own, even if they do give in to your demands. In the case of Zahra, although her boyfriend abided by all her rules so that she could feel "safe," eventually she'd focus on the next thing for him to do. Her hunger for safety and her approach to looking outside herself to get it were an insatiable pit that could never be filled.

If you don't feel safe, you can share that with the people in your life and even provide tips on how they can best support you. They can choose to be compassionate about your need, but at the end of the day, it's your responsibility to feel inherently safe. The expectation that one person can make you feel safe or loved when you haven't felt that in decades is unrealistic and a tall order for someone else to take on.

EXERCISE: Name Your Needs

Go through the list below and on the next page and circle all the needs you did NOT receive growing up or felt you had to suppress. This can provide insight on the needs that you are more sensitive to and need more of as an adult.

Common Emotional Needs

Connection:

acceptance	consistency	security
affection	cooperation	stability
appreciation	empathy	support
belonging	inclusion	to be understood
closeness	intimacy	to know and be known
communication	love	to see and be seen
community	mutuality	trust
companionship	nurturing	warmth
compassion	respect/self-respect	
consideration	safety	

Physical Well-Being:
  food
  movement/exercise
  rest/sleep
  safety
  sexual expression
  shelter
  touch

Honesty:
  authenticity
  integrity
  presence

Play:
  humor
  joy

Peace:
  beauty
  communion
  ease
  equality
  harmony
  inspiration
  order

Autonomy:
  choice
  freedom
  independence
  space
  spontaneity

Meaning:
  awareness
  celebration of life
  challenge
  clarity
  competence
  consciousness
  contribution
  creativity
  discovery
  effectiveness
  efficacy
  growth
  hope
  learning
  mourning
  participation
  purpose
  self-expression
  stimulation
  to matter
  understanding

Next, in your journal, use the following prompts to evaluate your current or most recent relationship in light of those needs.

- How did you react as a child to having these unmet needs met?

- Reflect on your last romantic relationship(s). Write down all the needs your ex(es) did not fulfill. What actions did you take to get these unmet needs met?

- What are the parallels? What are the contradictions? How have the unmet needs of your childhood affected your adult relationships?

- How are you attempting to get your needs met now? How do you react when they aren't met? Is this serving you?

For every unmet need that is causing pain or discomfort today, list ways you can meet those needs yourself. This does not mean you must have all your needs met in isolation. Brainstorm different sources where you can start meeting your needs. For example, if connection is an important need for you, the following action items are examples of how to create a sense of connection within yourself:

For example:

Need: **connection**

I can get my need for _connection_ met by _incorporating a daily guided meditation on self-compassion and abundance_ (connection with self).

I can get my need for _connection_ met by _having dinner with girlfriends once a week_ (connection with friends).

I can get my need for _connection_ met by _doing one act of random kindness each day_ (connection with humanity).

I can get my need for _connection_ met by _signing up for a dance class with friends even though it's out of my comfort zone_ (connection with self and community).

I can get my need for _connection_ met by _joining a women's group or book club_ (connection with community).

Your turn:

I can get my need for _____ met by _____
_____.

I can get my need for _____ met by _____
_____.

I can get my need for _____ met by _____
_____.

I can get my need for _____ met by _____
_____.

I can get my need for _____ met by _____
_____.

Being responsible for meeting your needs doesn't mean that you can't or won't be in a relationship where you and your partner mutually support, respect, and honor each other's needs. Whether you're single, coupled, or anything in between, ultimately, you're responsible for communicating your needs, limits, and boundaries. Next we're going to learn how to do this in a healthy way.

When "Little You" Wreaks Havoc

If you're hysterical, it's historical.

AA maxim

It's the undertone of trauma that causes us to react when people or situations trigger us. For some, this may be obvious trauma, like experiencing abuse or neglect. For others, the trauma may be more subtle and chronic, experienced as being criticized, pressured to be "perfect," or taking on the role of caretaker. When we're children, we do not have the capacity to comprehend or communicate our emotions, which is why we turn to the only way we know how to express them, putting them visually on display through screaming, crying, pouting, or hiding. To survive, we adopt coping mechanisms to protect ourselves, and through time, the repeated behavior becomes ingrained. Perhaps you became the mood-boosting mascot in your family and use humor to avoid vulnerability. Or you played the hero and now find yourself always saving someone. Maybe you were validated for being "good" only if you got top grades and adapted to become an overachiever, obsessing over perfection in order to feel enough. These adaptations then become so normalized that their root becomes invisible.

But these mutations and coping mechanisms often don't serve us as adults and get in the way of creating the relationships we want with ourselves and with others. And when we get hurt, we often "age regress."

Pia Mellody, author of *Facing Codependence*, explains that when we are emotionally overwhelmed, we can default into a childhood state, as either a wounded child or an adaptive adolescent. This happens especially in our romantic relationships because we are so emotionally connected and they are where we are most vulnerable.[3]

If you react by feeling inferior and going into a self-flagellating shame hole, you are age regressing to your wounded child. If you react by acting superior, with a "fuck you" mentality, you are regressing to your adapted adolescent. The adapted adolescent is trying to protect the wounded child, having developed defensive behaviors to survive. For instance, she may get angry and fight or shut down completely to create distance from others and protect her vulnerability. She is reacting to a perceived threat in an attempt to cover up her hurt.

If you respond with clear communication, accountability for your emotions, and healthy boundaries, then you're responding like a functional adult. This doesn't mean you don't ever get hurt or feel emotions, but rather you have the skills to regulate your feelings and self-soothe.

WOUNDED CHILD (AGES 0–5)	ADAPTED ADOLESCENT (AGES 6–18)	FUNCTIONING ADULT
Feels less than (inferior)	Feels more than (superior)	Feels equal to others (people are not more or less than)
Has no boundaries	Puts up walls	Sets limits and healthy boundaries
Acts needy	Acts needless	Communicates needs
"I am bad"	Reacts by criticizing, attacking, or indulging	Fully present and responsible in reality
	"You are bad"	Accepts imperfections

If you notice that you react with defensive or hurtful behaviors when you're in pain, you can now identify that this is your wounded inner child coming out. In a process called "reparenting," you can practice giving yourself what you needed as a child.

The question to ask yourself each time you're feeling reactive is: "What age am I being right now?" If you are in the middle of a conflict with someone, and you find either one or both of you are age regressing, the best thing to do is to give each other space to process. You cannot communicate in a constructive manner if there are two hurt children going at it with boxing gloves. Take a walk, take a bath, go into another room and ground yourself—do something to get yourself in an environment where you can calm down and start the process of reparenting.

If you see that it's your wounded child reacting, focus on trying to calm her down and ask her what she needs. It might seem silly at first, but imagine the reactive part of yourself as the hurt child inside you. She's freaking out and needs attention. It may help to visualize her—is she four or five years old? Is she having a tantrum, frozen in fear, or looking down in shame? You can look into a mirror and talk to her with compassionate words. What would you say to a scared girl who's confused and hurting? You'd probably tell her she's okay, that you love her, that she's loved. Use positive self-talk to counter the negative inner critic that whispers, "I'm bad, I'm worthless." Remember that our emotions are like a wave, and they will come, rise, and, after its peak, eventually pass. You start to train yourself how to tolerate extreme emotional energy without needing to act out in order to expel it. The key here is to nurture yourself using your tools for self-care. Don't forget to take deep breaths!

If you find yourself being defensive, distorting reality, catastrophizing, or intellectualizing to disassociate from feeling, this is indicative that your adapted adolescent is coming out. It may be challenging to realize this, because your defensive mechanisms can cause you to blame or attack someone else. If you notice that you're thinking and acting in extremes, or self-indulging by doing something that's ultimately unhealthy for you, this is a sign to pause and look inward. What is the anger masking? Is it feelings of inadequacy, helplessness, sadness, or fear? Inside every defensive adult is a wounded inner child. How old is she? What is she trying to protect? Talk to her with curiosity. Ask her what hurts. When you can extract the real emotion behind the defensiveness, you have a starting point to access what needs are not being met and to find solutions to start meeting them. When you're feeling calm and grounded, you can have a conversation with the person who pressed your buttons and share how old insecurities came up.

Reparent Yourself Using Healthy Communication

We have default patterns of reacting to conflict. But every conflict is an opportunity for us to reparent ourselves and become a healthy, functional adult. Our reactive patterns will follow us from relationship to relationship until we learn how to change them. Effective communication is a fundamental skill for all areas of life, and it takes practice.

When a disagreement spirals out of control, it's because one or both people are defensive. Instead of taking a collaborative approach to hear each other out and see each other's perspective, the boxing gloves are on, and you're in a vicious cycle of offense and defense. When you're defensive, your nervous system is activated and you're in survival mode.

Ideally, both people in the conflict have calmed down before a conversation is initiated. Of course, this isn't always possible, and by being skillful in your approach, you can change the course of the conversation into a more collaborative and peaceful one.

Those Are Fighting Words, Dear

Trish Barillas is a life coach who specializes in anxiety and breakups and is the author of the book *A Face of Anxiety,* a memoir of her journey living with anxiety/panic disorder. She leads a session on healthy

INSIDE EVERY DEFENSIVE ADULT IS A WOUNDED INNER CHILD.

communication at Renew and teaches the women that the first step in managing conflict with another person is to disarm them.

"When you're in a fight, most of the hard work is done up front—which is disarming yourself and the other person so that you're both able to have a rational conversation. One effective way of doing this is to validate what the other person is saying through active listening and reflection." Coach Trish advises that the best way to do this is to use verbal reflection to "complete a cycle" of communication.

Using verbal reflection means you restate and validate what the other person has said, to confirm that you understand and empathize. Reflection doesn't mean you're saying the other person is right; it's a tool to connect and shift the energy into one of collaboration versus defensiveness.

Trish asks for a volunteer from the group to demonstrate reflection in action.

Mandy volunteers and recalls a fight she had with a guy she's been recently dating. Trish pretends to be the guy and asks Mandy to speak to her exactly like she did in the fight.

MANDY: You're so inconsiderate to not text me sooner and let me know you couldn't make our plans. You always do this to me. You could've texted but you don't care. I'm pissed!

COACH TRISH: It seems like you're frustrated with me for not calling you the minute I heard I had to work late. And you want me to text you earlier next time?

MANDY: You could have at least texted! I was waiting on you.

COACH TRISH: I understand that you didn't make other plans because you thought we had plans. And you're feeling frustrated with how I handled it, right?

MANDY: Yeah.

Reflecting and validating the person's experience (again, this doesn't mean you're right/wrong) de-escalates the emotional intensity and charge. It helps the other person feel that you're approaching him with an intention to understand, not to fight.

CHECK YOURSELF

When you're in a disagreement or conflict, ask yourself the following questions:

Boxing gloves or handshake? What is the tone you're setting? If you enter a conversation using blame or trying to prove the other person wrong, you're setting up the conversation to be a fight. You're walking into the ring with boxing gloves. However, if you make the intention to approach with curiosity, you're taking the handshake approach; you're starting off the conversation with an energy of collaboration and compassion.

Are you using fighting words? Catch yourself when you're using "you" statements, which automatically blame and put the person on defense. Instead, use "I" statements.

Example:

"You" statement: "You're so selfish when you don't text back about our plans. You make me feel insecure."

"I" statement: "I feel anxious when I don't hear back from you about our plans, and because I value our quality time together, I'd love it if you could keep me in the loop about when we're meeting."

Are you making a clear request? As much as we know people aren't mind readers, in practice, we often expect people to know what we want without us ever telling them! Learning how to ask for what you want and also what you don't want is a key skill of communicating like a healthy, functional adult.

Making a request is not the same as making a demand or giving an ultimatum. You want to invite the other person with your request, not guilt or scare him into obliging. Your request should be phrased in the positive; it should be specific and flexible.

Example:

Negative: "Don't talk to me that way!"

Clear request: "Would you be willing to lower your voice? Or we can take a break and cool off and pick this back up later."

When you're making a request, you want to—in the words of the founder of the Center for Nonviolent Communication Marshall Rosenberg—"ask others to meet your needs like flowers for your table, not air for your lungs."

Example:

Air for your lungs: "I need more time together. When are we going out again?"

Flowers for your table: "I feel so connected when we have quality time together. Could we look at our calendars and see when we can schedule another date?"

USE THE NONVIOLENT COMMUNICATION FRAMEWORK

Nonviolent communication (NVC) is an approach for supporting partnership and resolving conflict between people, within relationships, and in society that was developed in the 1960s by Marshall Rosenberg. The method is rooted in the belief that all humans share the same universal needs: to be heard, understood, valued, and respected. Conflicts arise when words are perceived as threats, which then escalate into power struggles.

Remember, when making requests, you're not *forcing* the person to comply. That would be a demand. When people hear a demand, they see no way out of a power struggle, their only options being submission or rebellion. The point should be open for discussion and there can't be judgment or punishment because the person does not agree. You want to inspire action, not coerce with threats or intimidation.

You can use the NVC framework as a starting point and adjust it to fit your style so it feels more authentic to you. It's helpful to write down what you want to say using the NVC method before you have the actual conversation so that you can sort out what you are perceiving, feeling, and wanting.

Nirmala Raniga, founder of the Chopra Addiction and Wellness Center, has summarized the four main steps of nonviolent communication:[4]

1. **Describe the situation without judgment.** Take a mental step back and observe the facts without judgment, evaluation, or labeling what the other person did or didn't do. State what you see but not what you think: "When I see/hear . . ."

2. **Identify your feelings.** Observe what emotions are coming up for you because of the current situation. Label the emotions, and

avoid using judgmental language that puts you in the role of a victim. For example, words like "betrayed," "abandoned," and "disregarded" are not accurately describing emotions; rather, they are accusations that judge the other's actions: "I feel . . ."

3. **Assess what needs you are not receiving.** Very often, we expect other people to innately know what we need, as if they should be able to read our mind. Raniga suggests that this is a residual feeling from infancy, when our parents or other caregivers responded to our every need without our articulating them. As adults, it is important that we identify what we need and be clear and direct in our request. Doing so minimizes misunderstanding, and we will have a greater chance of having our needs met. But it is key to realize that needs and requests are different. Needs are the missing pieces. Requests are what you use to acquire your needs. Frame your request with the underlying need that you value: "Because I value connection . . ."

4. **Make a clear request.** The emotions we experience when we're upset are connected to an unmet need. Rosenberg found that human needs universally fall into one of a handful of categories: connection, honesty, peace, play, physical well-being, a sense of meaning, and autonomy. Connect your need with the correct category so you can fully understand it and the feelings attached to it. Articulate what it is you need to move forward. Try to let go of any attachment you have to the other person responding in a particular way. Both people need to feel they have the freedom to say yes or no to requests without being judged, attacked, or forced. Ask for concrete actions that would help satisfy a need. The best way to accomplish this is to build flexibility and freedom into your ask. One example is to phrase your request this way: "Would you be willing to . . . ?" or "Are you open to . . . ?"

In the case of Mandy, instead of accusing her boyfriend of being inconsiderate, she could use the NVC method to make a request.

Mandy's old way of communicating: "You're so inconsiderate to not text me sooner and let me know you couldn't make our plans. You always do this to me. You could've texted but you don't care. I'm pissed!"

Mandy using NVC: "When I've made plans for us and am not told we're not meeting until minutes before, I feel frustrated and sad. I value our quality time together and understand you're very busy at work and things come up. Would you be willing to give me at least two hours' notice when you think you'll be staying late at work? Or we can try to keep our dates to the weekend?"

WHAT IF THE ANSWER IS NO?

Using NVC helps us replace our automated habits of reacting with a more thoughtful, conscious approach to expression. But what happens if you make a request with the most "woke" vocabulary you can muster and get a no? Maybe the person shuts down and walks away from the conversation completely, or straight-out tells you that he's not willing to consider your request.

You can't change how the person reacts; you only have control of your own intentions, words, and actions. Healthy communication starts with the intention behind it. If your original goal was to force or guilt someone into giving you what you want, that is manipulation, not healthy communication.

There may come a point when you feel that your relationship with someone is one-sided and there is not a mutual respect for each other's needs. In this case, you need to reassess if the relationship is still working for you.

LOVING YOURSELF IS TAKING RESPONSIBILITY for your emotions and accepting that it's your job to feel all the things you've wanted to outsource to a partner. This means you are your own source of fulfillment, peace, safety, validation, and stability. And if you feel like you're lacking in these areas, loving yourself means doing the work to get there too. When you love from a place of wholeness, with the understanding that nobody has the power to complete you, you realize that your partner's role is not to manage your emotions, complete you, or fulfill you. Your romantic partners aren't here to make you happy. They're here to make you conscious.

5 →

BREAKING THE SHACKLES OF SHAME

The truth will set you free, but first it will piss you off.

Gloria Steinem

You have it. I have it. Everyone experiences it (except for psychopaths). Can you guess what I'm referring to?

Shame.

Shame can be toxic, painful, and even deadly. Bestselling author and shame expert Brené Brown describes this emotion as "the intensely painful feeling or experience of believing that we are flawed and therefore unworthy of love and belonging—something we've experienced, done, or failed to do makes us unworthy of connection."[1]

Among the women who come to Renew, shame is a central theme of their suffering. There is shame around the breakup itself, shame around choosing the wrong person, shame for staying and trying to make it work, shame for not being able to make it work, shame for feeling sad, shame for feeling angry, shame for feeling lonely, shame for feeling shame!

Shame can exist on a spectrum, with healthy shame at one end and toxic shame at the other. Brown describes healthy shame as guilt: "I did something bad." Whereas toxic shame is: "I am bad." When someone experiences toxic shame, she automatically assumes, "Something is wrong with me. I'm flawed."

Shame is a normal human condition and can be useful to help us learn. It's when shame is internalized as a constant reminder of rejection and unworthiness that it starts to overregulate our behavior in destructive ways.[2] This level of paralyzing shame can be physically and mentally lethal. Studies have been conducted around the connection between toxic levels of shame and eating disorders, addiction, feelings of isolation, and various other social issues.[3]

THE DARK SIDE OF SHAME

After a breakup, common defense mechanisms that people use to deal with the shame are withdrawal, avoidance, and attack (either themselves or others).[4]

- Withdrawal is when we draw into ourselves—sleeping all day, refusing to leave home, or binge-watching television. Withdrawal is used to hide our shame from others.

- Avoidance is when we hide shame from ourselves. This is when we distract ourselves with stimulating activities, such as substance abuse, overeating, or "retail therapy."

- Attacking the self is when we engage in psychological or physical self-harm. This can take the form of self-blame, negative self-talk, cutting, or even suicide. Attacking others shows up as blaming, aggressive interactions, overtures of revenge, or vindictiveness.

Studies have found that men are more likely to turn their shame into anger and blame others, while women are more likely to turn their shame into sadness and depression, blaming themselves.[5]

SHINE LIGHT ON YOUR SHAME AND YOU TAKE AWAY ITS POWER

The more we hide our shame, the bigger it grows. It will continue lurking in the shadows, becoming chronic and more and more debilitating. Bit by bit, the shame will cause more disconnection from the self and with others. But the more you discuss it and confront it, the smaller it gets. The shame cycle is a vicious one, and the only way to interrupt it is to address it with empathy. By empathy here, I mean understanding toward ourselves. We are all imperfect beings. Admit that you are feeling shame. Dig deep into why. Have compassion for yourself instead of self-punishing. Then share your feelings with someone you trust.

> Talking about our feelings of shame and naming them often diminishes their power. In fact, verbalizing our shame actually makes us resilient to it.
>
> *Brené Brown, Daring Greatly*

Sometimes we don't even know that it's shame that's the root of our defense mechanisms, and some uncovering is required where you need to reverse engineer the behavioral symptoms to discover the source.

As someone labeled a "relationship expert," there are times when I feel bad about myself for having relationship challenges. There's a sense of shame that I feel, as if I should have the love puzzle all figured out. I'm a thought leader on this subject—I shouldn't feel pain! It wasn't until I began researching the notion of shame for this book that my own hidden shame surfaced. In fact, that shame crept up when I started dating a new guy named Sammy.

Our romance started off strong: we had been sitting next to each other at a coworking space and kept talking off and on in between attempting to work. After five hours, I realized that I wanted to keep spending time with him and asked him to grab dinner. He canceled his plans, and voilà—we went on our first date. The next few weeks were filled with epic dates, make-out sessions, and daily communication. But then . . . he didn't initiate making plans with me over one weekend—my biggest trigger!

I felt angst and could observe myself launching into my habit of making up stories: *Maybe he's lost interest. Maybe I set a precedent by asking him out first, and now I'll always have to initiate. Oh no, so now I'm the pursuer . . .*

I felt needy, and I hated that about myself. Enter self-loathing. It was a big shame sandwich with anxiety and self-pity smeared on top. It tasted awful.

Despite employing all my self-soothing techniques, angst and insecurity persisted. I started to feel sad, and then angry, and then ashamed that I felt these emotions. I decided to journal about what feelings were coming up for me and what my reactive brain was telling me to do:

Withdraw: Don't contact him, shut down.

Punish: When he finally gets in touch, act aloof and lie about being too busy to see him.

Sabotage: Reach out to another guy for validation to displace my angst.

Attack: Get angry with him for not taking more initiative and threaten to break up.

Reject: Avoid hypothetical rejection by rejecting him first.

I saw that all my reactions were defense mechanisms that had been in place long before I met Sammy, and what was coming up had nothing to do with him and everything to do with me. My unmet need is connection, and a lack of communication or set plans evoked angst over a lack of safety. To work through my shame around having needs, I needed to acknowledge that I have needs, which does not mean I am needy. And even if I was feeling needy, I needed to allow that this was okay too. Growing up with parents who were "too busy" to parent me, I adapted to the neglect by becoming overly independent. I developed a belief that depending on others or needing someone was (1) "needy" and "weak," and (2) going to lead to disappointment anyway. Now I could trace back the root of why I felt so upset when I had a need.

I called a few of my closest friends and shared. What was different this time was that I opened up not just about the rejection but also about the shame I felt for being a relationship expert who couldn't seem to create the relationship I wanted. I had self-imposed pressure that I should have "gotten it" by now. I was afraid that my credibility would be questioned because another guy had come in and out of my life. My friends, who would usually look to me for advice, gladly stepped into that role. They listened with compassion. They made me feel safe, allowed me to ugly cry and even feel sorry for myself, and gave me permission to act as a human being, not as some all-knowing relationship expert. This was a moment where I learned that I am not Amy the brand, but I'm Amy, an imperfect human on an ongoing journey of growth, complete with mistakes, struggles, and moments of shame.

Sammy did reach out to make plans with me, then because of work reasons had to cancel . . . twice. I was disappointed and frustrated, and when I expressed via text that I was triggered and needed to process my emotions, he responded that he couldn't be in a relationship with someone using the words "trigger" and "process." Apparently, I triggered something in Sammy by being triggered!

I realized that part of my journey is to embrace that it's okay for me to have needs, and this does not mean I am weak. It's also a practice for me to build my muscle of relying on others, and that in doing so I will be vulnerable to pain and disappointment, but will also have the opportunity to deepen intimacy and connection. And ultimately I can share these emotions with the right partner in an open and vulnerable way.

This is self-love in action, embracing all parts of myself—the shadow and the light, not a front that projects perfection. And if someone rejects me because of this, well, then he wasn't meant to be in my life. See ya, Sammy!

EXERCISE: Tame the Shame

Moving through shame is a process of sharing with others and experiencing empathy. When we have difficult experiences that leave us feeling flawed or unworthy, we need the support and empathy of others most. Studies show that empathy decreases stress levels and improves physical and mental health.[6] The following exercise provides steps on how to move through shame in positive ways.

1. Notice what brings up your feelings of shame. This can be challenging at first because our feelings might be buried under layers of coping mechanisms. You can start by looking at your reactions to shame—what are the behaviors and urges that come up when you feel this uncomfortable emotion? Do you isolate? Withdraw? Attack? Blame? Write these down so you can identify your tendencies. Recognize that we use blame to discharge discomfort, anger, and pain.

2. How does shame feel in the body? There is a physiological response to every emotion. Bring attention to your body and simply observe any numbness or sensation. You don't need to do anything with it, just observe and be.

3. Use introspection to start uncovering what you feel shame around and the stories you've created that cause your shame. Evaluate how you judge others, as there's often key information about what we disown or dislike about ourselves by looking at what we judge others for.

4. Practice self-compassion. Start by recognizing that you are not your shame and that many of your shame-inducing experiences happened when you were a child. Feelings of insignificance and unworthiness appeared before you had any "choices" in the matter. Shame was your natural response. You cannot deny or escape your shame experiences, but to move through shame means to face the feelings, own them, and incorporate them into yourself.

5. In your journal, write down a current situation that you feel shame around. Write in detail and don't hold back. This is your chance to get it out of your system and onto paper as a way of release. Set the story of shame free.

6. Who is someone you can trust to share what you're feeling? Choose someone who you know will not reject you for sharing your vulnerability. Then ask this person if she will hold space for you to share something you've felt shame around and want to release. Offer some parameters to the person on how to best support you while you do this exercise. Remind her that you're not seeking advice; you just need someone to listen with compassion and without judgment. If nobody comes to mind, consider empathetic settings such as twelve-step support meetings or women's groups, or seek out a therapist or coach. Sharing the issues you feel shame around with someone that you know won't reject you is a crucial step for reducing shame's power.

THE ANTIDOTE FOR SHAME: SELF-COMPASSION

You know what shame hates? Self-compassion. Self-compassion is empathy directed inward. It is the antidote for shame. Neuroscience research shows that self-compassion strengthens the parts of our brains that make us happier, more resilient, and more attuned to others.[7]

One of the pioneering psychologists on self-compassion, Kristin Neff, defines this notion as "the ability to be kind and understanding toward oneself when faced with personal inadequacies or difficult situations." Her research also shows that self-compassion is a good predictor of healthy romantic relationships.[8]

Simply put, self-compassion involves treating ourselves the way we would treat a beloved friend. There are three main components of self-compassion:

1. **Self-kindness versus self-judgment.** Accept that we make mistakes and that disappointments are a natural part of being a human. We don't demand perfection of ourselves, and we forgive ourselves when we fall short. We accept that it's *normal* to be imperfect, rather than blaming or criticizing ourselves for not measuring up.

2. **Common humanity.** When things in life don't go as planned, too often we get frustrated and feel isolated or alone in our frustration. Common humanity reminds us that every single person on this planet also endures disappointments and failures. With this view, we are no longer isolated by our suffering, and we can find ourselves in greater connection with others because of it.

3. **Mindfulness versus overidentification.** In order to respond to our difficulties with self-compassion, we need to *notice* that we are having a difficult experience in the first place. Mindfulness enables us to see our internal experience but not become victimized

by it. Overidentification is when we get swallowed up by our feelings and lose objectivity.

Behavioral scientist and positive change strategist Dr. Naomi Arbit has helped countless women at Renew learn how to use self-compassion as a way to self-soothe instead of self-shame. She explains that one of the primary emotional circuits in the brain is the "care circuit," and every time we bond with others and feel warmth and love, we activate it and our brains release the powerful bonding and stress-reduction hormone oxytocin, as well as endogenous opiates (translation: you feel good!).[9]

Dr. Arbit shares the great news that we can actually activate the care circuit ourselves for ourselves, with soothing words and touch. Our brain registers this as almost identical to being nurtured and cared for by someone else. Go ahead, give yourself a hug, literally!

Activate Self-Compassion

We are going to try an experiment to activate our care circuit. Bring to mind a beloved friend or family member, someone with whom you have an easy, uncomplicated relationship and who is easy to love. Now imagine this person calling you at the end of the day completely beside herself because her partner left her. She is deeply worried about her future, feeling lost and hopeless. What would you say to this person, whom you love, in response to her suffering?

People typically respond by telling their beloved that everything will be fine, it's normal to go through breakups, that life has its ups and downs. They tell them not to worry. They tell them they'll recover and find love again. They assure them that they are loved and supported.

Now imagine it was *you* who experienced this same heart-wrenching pain. What would you say to yourself?

When Dr. Arbit conducts this exercise at Renew, this question typically has the room audibly chuckling. Why? Because most of us say cruel things to ourselves that we'd never dream of saying aloud to someone else. In fact, it's very likely that if we treated others the way we treat ourselves in such moments, we wouldn't have any friends at all!

Dr. Arbit asks the women at Renew, "When you're consoling someone you love who's going through pain, what words of support do you offer?"

One by one the women raise their hand and offer variations on the same loving themes.

"I love you. I'm here for you."

"Don't be so hard on yourself."

"You're going to be okay."

She then asks the attendees why they can so easily find consoling and compassionate phrases to offer to someone else but can't do the same for themselves. It's an important question. When we are supporting someone we love, we have the perspective and wisdom to know that their feelings are only temporary but can't seem to find the same compassion for the one person we need to love the most, ourselves.

Research shows that 80 percent of Americans find it far easier to be compassionate toward others than themselves.[10] While the impact of this self-critical tendency may seem clear, it has pervasive and long-term effects on our well-being and resilience.

Why do we speak to ourselves in such a harsh, critical language that we would never use toward a friend? When you catch yourself judging yourself, try to acknowledge that this is your inner self-critic at play. Just like we learned in chapter one how to not feed our emotional monster, the same applies here. Don't feed the shame; don't feed the judgment. This might be as simple as catching the thought and choosing not to put more energy behind it by vocalizing it. Start there.

Self-compassion is a practice of generating good intentions for ourselves. It is *not* a practice of generating good feelings, or avoiding difficult feelings and replacing them with good feelings. Self-compassion is about bringing love and care to yourself, rather than entering some predefined emotional state. And the beautiful thing is that when you generate these intentions, your suffering can transform.

When you first practice loving kindness and self-compassion, it can feel unnatural. If you expect to generate strong feelings of warmth right off the bat, you may set yourself up for disappointment. It's critical to know this in advance, because many people have an expectation that their mood will shift immediately. When it doesn't, they assume the practice doesn't work for them and often give up. But pay attention: if you find that you have trouble generating positive feelings of warmth for yourself, this indicates you need *more* practice, not less! It is *not* a sign that the practice isn't working; it's a sign that you have to persevere. If you went to the gym and tried to deadlift a hundred pounds right away but couldn't, that doesn't mean that weight lifting isn't a good exercise. It means you need to adjust your expectations and start with a lighter weight, working your way up.

You may notice that pain initially increases with self-compassion practice. When you start to give yourself unconditional love, all the ways in which you never received this type of love become painfully apparent. You may have gone decades without ever having the experience of unconditional love and compassion—and that can be enormously painful to acknowledge.

Kristin Neff advises that if we feel overwhelmed with emotions,

> the most self-compassionate response may be to pull back temporarily—focus on the breath, the sensation of the soles of our feet on the ground, or engage in ordinary, behavioral acts of self-care such as having a cup of tea or petting the cat. By doing so we reinforce the habit of self-compassion—giving ourselves what we need in the moment—planting seeds that will eventually blossom and grow.[11]

FROM SHAMING TO BLAMING TO REFRAMING

"So, Amy, is this story serving you?" my friend Dennis asked.

I hadn't seen Dennis for over a year and was catching him up on the infidelity and betrayal of my ex Adam.

"Uh, no," I stammered, surprised at his lack of pity.

"Can you think of some times when he was kind? Honest? Tell me about those times," Dennis probed.

"Well, sure, there was this time when we . . ." I started to list off all these happy and fun memories. Soon I was smiling and laughing as I recounted them. And then it hit me.

After the breakup, I vilified my ex. In my darkness, I had tunnel vision and could only see the negative. I couldn't remember any of the positive, nor appreciate the good things that happened in my life after the breakup. I couldn't see them because I wasn't looking.

I was at a choice point. I could continue painting a picture of how awful Adam and the relationship was, or I could paint a new one that explored the meaning in what happened and choose gratitude. It was time to choose the latter.

I went home that day, and on beautiful pink stationery, I wrote my ex a letter. In that letter, I acknowledged the facts of what occurred, and I took accountability for my part in what went wrong in the relationship. I acknowledged that we were both just doing the best we knew how at the time. I reflected on all the wonderful things that were now happening in my life—I was moving out of the country and embarking on a new career path. I told him how grateful I was for all that had happened between us—the good, the bad, and the ugly. In that letter I forgave him. In that letter I let go. In that letter I thanked him.

I sent him that letter. He never responded. It didn't matter; it wasn't for him, it was for me. From that moment on, I have never again felt an ounce of anger or resentment toward Adam. It was in truly accepting and forgiving that I finally let go. It was in letting go that I was free.

This is the power of reframing—a critical tool of building resilience. Reframing involves coming up with a different interpretation, looking for the silver lining, and finding the lesson for growth amid the hardship. It helps you switch from being powerless in victimization to feeling empowered. The first step is being accountable yourself.

BLAMING VERSUS ACCOUNTABILITY

"Accountability? He cheated on me and left me with nothing! Why would I be accountable when he did this to me? I gave him everything." Megan, a fifty-five-year-old mother of three boys, couldn't grasp the concept of reframing. Her husband of twenty-nine years told her he wasn't in love with her anymore and wanted a divorce. Megan internalized that as something being wrong with her. She even went on a new diet, hoping that by getting fit she'd be sexually attractive to her husband again. It wasn't until she told him she was going to initiate a deposition that he finally came clean that he had been having an affair and was leaving her for someone else.

Megan had done everything a "good wife" should do. She sacrificed for her family, supported her husband's business, and put her career aside so she could raise the children. She gave and gave. And after three decades of giving, she felt blindsided and bitter when her husband left her. Two years after the divorce, she found herself at Renew, hoping she could find an end to her pain.

She couldn't forgive. She refused to.

With compassion, I offered some feedback: "Megan, the lying and betrayal that occurred at the end of the relationship are inexcusable. I'm not taking away how painful that must feel, and you have every right to feel that. But you've suffered long enough, and blaming him does not make the pain go away, nor does it relieve you from it continuing to haunt you."

THE EMOTIONAL CHARGE KEEPS YOU ATTACHED

If you're still blaming your ex, analyzing your ex, or hoping for your ex to change, you are still in a relationship with your ex. When you blame, you are shackled to the person who hurt you, giving that person the keys to your emotional freedom. Blaming keeps your recovery dependent on the actions of another person—something that you ultimately cannot control. This powerlessness keeps you in a state of suffering.

When we outsource our recovery or closure to someone else, we fail to recognize that nobody can give us the healing we yearn for. Blaming keeps us in victimization mode, waiting for something external to change in order for us to feel better. But it doesn't come, and months, years, or even decades can go by.

Accountability means we acknowledge what happened, we take steps to protect ourselves from letting it happen again, and we focus on recovery. It also enables us to regain a sense of internal control in the face of what feels like chaos.

BUT WHAT ABOUT THE PLAN?

One of the hardest parts of a breakup is the investment you made in a plan . . . that fell apart. Not only are you mourning the relationship,

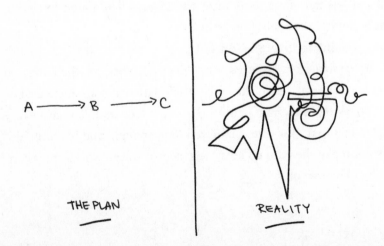

THE PLAN   REALITY

WHEN YOU BLAME, YOU ARE SHACKLED TO THE PERSON WHO HURT YOU, GIVING THAT PERSON THE KEYS TO YOUR EMOTIONAL FREEDOM. BLAMING KEEPS YOUR RECOVERY DEPENDENT ON THE ACTIONS OF ANOTHER PERSON—SOMETHING THAT YOU ULTIMATELY CANNOT CONTROL. THIS POWERLESSNESS KEEPS YOU IN A STATE OF SUFFERING.

but you're mourning the future that never got a chance to happen. The problem is mainstream society doesn't show us that there are many different paths out there, and one is not better or worse—it's just different.

I get it, the pressure is real. Out of the group of friends I grew up with, I'm the only one who is not married with kids. I went to five weddings last summer alone!

Date, get married, have kids—all by age thirty-five. That was supposed to be my plan too, until it got derailed and I had to reevaluate. And when I started doing some digging, I realized how much of my life was on autopilot. As I asked more questions, the more I realized that my default plan was not even one that I had come up with. It was absorbed through osmosis by witnessing my parents, my friends, and the media's representation of what relationships should look like, through socialization and cultural norms.

Maybe my future isn't meant to end up in a nuclear family, or maybe it is. Maybe I will decide to adopt or be in an open relationship or be monogamous. Maybe my legacy will be to not have children at all, but instead to devote myself to helping others. Or growing a garden.

The point is, I don't know for sure what my plan is. The plan can change, and if we don't have buoyancy to flow with the ups and downs, we can break. Most important is a willingness to question the beliefs we vehemently hold on to, reflect on where the roots of those beliefs came from, and ask if those beliefs serve us—not the other way around.

Do not become a slave to your plan. Own your story, or you'll constantly be living someone else's.

EXERCISE: Connect the Dots

Think about a time in your life when something didn't go according to plan and, as a result, something even better happened. Perhaps it was being let go from a job only to find a higher-paying, more fulfilling one. Or maybe it was the horrible breakup that helped you learn key lessons about yourself and finally gave you the courage to move out of your hometown. Write down three unexpected "plot twists" that ultimately resulted in something positive.

1. _____

2. _____

3. _____

> You can't connect the dots looking forward; you can only connect them looking backward. So, you have to trust that the dots will somehow connect in your future. You have to trust in something—your gut, destiny, life, karma, whatever.
>
> *Steve Jobs*

IT HAPPENED *FOR* ME

After my big breakup, if you had told me that the heartbreak, debilitating depression, and thoughts of suicide would be the basis of my starting a company, I would've called you batshit crazy. But that's exactly what happened. You are reading this book because of that breakup. In retrospect, I can now see how the heartbreak didn't happen *to* me, it happened *for* me.

I have looked back and found enough evidence to know now that when something doesn't go according to plan, it's because I'm being protected. There's something else in store. I practice reframing and building that muscle of optimism—because that's helpful for my present and future.

It's time to stop dwelling on the dreams that were not meant to be and celebrate the possibility of what's in store. If I had been able to do this exercise back when I was incessantly ruminating on how unjust life was, I would have saved a lot of time and energy.

In the previous exercise you found evidence that there have been times in your life when something that didn't go according to plan only worked out for the better. Now let's identify how this current plot twist can turn out to be something even better in your future.

EXERCISE: Play with Possibility

In this exercise, identify what didn't go according to plan and brainstorm how this might open up another door for you in the future. Imagine yourself five years from today, looking back at how one thing didn't go according to plan only for something else to work out. We are playing with possibility here, so fast-forward to future you and connect the dots.

For example, if your plan was to get married by age X, think about future you, five years from now. Perhaps she's in a healthy relationship with an amazing human. Perhaps she also started a coaching practice to help women through heartbreak. Here's mine, as an example:

My plan was _to get married to Adam_. Instead, _I started a company to help people with their heartbreaks, published a book, and am now in a loving, healthy relationship_.

Use your imagination here! Even if you have no idea how that would happen, or it seems unrealistic right now, just play with possibility. Be creative and get wild; don't hold back!

My plan was _____.

Instead, _____.

My plan was _____.

Instead, _____.

My plan was _____.

Instead, _____.

Exercising your mind to see the possibilities of your new future is part of the practice of letting go. It helps you get unstuck from the past and redirect your focus to future possibilities. This practice helps you in your process of creating closure.

TO FORGIVE, OR NOT TO FORGIVE?

Maybe you were cheated on. Betrayed. Lied to. Maybe the person you thought would never let you down blindsided you. When you're seething with anger, the idea of forgiveness may seem impossible. A part of you feels like you're selling out your emotions, and sometimes that rage is the last piece of the relationship you've got left.

We are bombarded with messages that we need to forgive, and that by not forgiving we're poisoning ourselves. I get it—the message rings true and makes for a good Instagram quote—but depending on which stage of hurt you're in, sometimes you're just not ready. And no amount of cognitive reasoning or mantras is going to get you there.

Forgiveness is a process, not a destination. It's an intense yet beautiful journey. Some people are able to make this journey in a shorter time than others, and some might not ever get there, despite their attempts. When someone in pain is advised to just forgive, it's like saying, "Just get over it"—it's shaming and reeks of an air of superiority. It's not helpful.

A more helpful goal is to build compassion, starting with self-compassion. The more you practice self-compassion, the more you build up the reserve. It's yours for the making, step by step. This is important because it gives you a sense of control over your outcome. You don't need to go from zero to a hundred. Just focus on going from zero to one, then one to two. Reaching forgiveness, however, can seem much more binary—either you forgive or you don't. Zero to a hundred. Self-compassion, on the other hand, is cultivated little by little, degree by degree.

Until we can direct love and kindness inward, it's going to be pretty challenging to direct it outward. The goal of forgiveness might be too big and overwhelming to handle right now, and that's okay. Start with practices that cultivate your self-compassion. Write a list of self-care activities and do one a day. Start a five-minute meditation practice. Experiment with different mindfulness techniques. As you keep building your inner reserve of self-love and care, you might find that you naturally get to a place where forgiveness doesn't seem as impossible anymore.

LETTING GO

There is a clear turning point for the women at Renew that happens on Saturday night. While Friday is focused on addressing the pain, uncovering the wounds, and processing the emotions, Saturday is about rewiring patterns and shifting beliefs. The exercises and practices all build up to a pinnacle moment: a letter-writing exercise to let go of the past, so we can welcome the future.

It's ten P.M., and the women are all given blank pieces of paper. They are instructed to write a letter to the person they are letting go of. For the women who are not quite ready to write a letter to their ex, they are encouraged to choose someone else in their life they want to create closure with, be it a family member, the ex before the ex . . .

With the song "Immunity," by Jon Hopkins, playing in the background, the women fall silent as they focus on their writing. You hear sniffles and even sobs; there's a somber, yet cathartic, feeling in the air. After each person is finished, we all go outside where a bonfire is waiting. We form a circle around the fire and I lead the final part of the exercise:

"Here we are, together, to witness each other in our rite of passage, to let go of the past, so that we can make space to welcome the new. One by one, we will put our letters into the fire and witness them burn."

More tears. Some are tears of sorrow, as their pain exits their bodies. Some of the tears are of power and pride. All these women are ready to let go, to start the next phase of life.

Now, it's your turn.

EXERCISE: The Letting Go Letter

Write a letter to someone who you want to let go of. You might not be ready to write a letter to your ex right now, and that's okay. You can choose someone with whom you've had unfinished business. This is an exercise you can repeat and work yourself up to writing a letter to your ex. Accept, find the lesson, forgive, generate gratitude. *Just let go.*

Choose some stationery and your favorite pen. Find somewhere quiet and play music in the background that feels inspiring. Follow the prompts below to write your letter.

And when you're finished, rip up that letter or set it on fire.

- **"This is what happened."** Describe the facts of the situation. Be accurate, recounting both the positives and negatives without embellishment, interpretation, or judgment.

- **"This is how I felt/feel."** Without accusatory language, be honest about how you felt/feel. Your feelings are not right or wrong; they are simply your experience.

- **"This is what I take accountability for."** Even if it seems like the other person was at fault completely, the fact is every relationship takes two people. Victimization does not help you. Take accountability for your part in the situation.

- **"This is what I forgive."** Even if it hurts, forgive. Find compassion that your ex was trying the best he knew how at the time. Forgiveness is a gift you give yourself.

- **"This is what I let go."** The pain, the regret, the negative charge, the blame—let it go. You're done ruminating on the past and committing to letting go of what no longer serves you.

- **"This is what I learned."** Illuminate your personal power. See the strength and courage you've gained from the situation and that while you may have been bruised, you're not broken.

- **"This is what I'm grateful for."** Give thanks to the person or the situation for providing the chance for you to grow.

Closure is not something you attain; it's the compound effect of a process that encompasses grieving, acceptance, accountability, letting go, forgiveness, and gratitude.

Jenny's CLOSURE

"I USED TO get so angry I'd start to cry. I would hold on to the grudge and internalize the pain. Over and over, I'd beat myself up. Putting all that raw emotion on paper and getting it out of my system and burning it was cathartic. To be honest, I've done it a number of times. It's helped me be a better person, a better employer, a better daughter, a better friend. But most of all, it's been a valuable tool in creating my own closure. I used to think that closure would come if he changed, if he stopped bothering me, if he was kinder . . . but I realize that closure isn't about what he does or does not do.

"To me, closure is not wanting revenge. It's not feeling sad, not feeling anything toward him, really. I hope one day he gets his life together and is happy, but I don't think about him.

"Closure doesn't happen overnight. There are a hundred steps, and if you miss a step you'll keep going backward. There's no way around it, you have to go through it. I've recognized that there's so much I've learned from that loss, and that's what helped me let go.

"Every day is a renewal of the person I want to be and the person I want to evolve into."

THE END MARKS THE BEGINNING

Things come and go; there's impermanence even in the things we think will last forever. Because life.

The person you thought would never let you down does. The company you thought valued you lays you off. A pandemic hits, forcing you to create a new normal and recognize how precious life really is.

And as much as you try to plan, control, and perfect, the reality is there's only so much you can do to prepare for the spontaneity that is life. The sooner you can accept and even excel in uncertainty, the sooner you experience freedom. This is resilience.

So here we are. The plan you thought you knew for sure has changed. When you're in the thick of it, you can't see what's coming next, and this can be incredibly scary! You can embrace everything you've learned so far, but there's one other ingredient in the secret sauce of some of the most successful, happiest, fulfilled people I know.

Trust.

Trust is cultivating the patience to let things unfold. It requires a surrender of your ego's grip on control and your attachment to what should have been. Trust is tapping into your inner knowing, having faith that something bigger is at play. Just because your relationship didn't go according to plan doesn't make it a failure.

There is no such thing as failure in love. Relationships end, but they don't fail. Love is only a failure when you don't learn from the experience and you don't try again.

>>> — 6 —>

FANTASY WILL F*CK YOU (YOUR BRAIN ON LOVE)

Desperate needs bring about a hallucination of their
solution: Thirst hallucinates water, the need for love
hallucinates the ideal man or woman.

Alain de Botton

Do you know what Snow White and Carrie Bradshaw have in common?

They're liars.

I waited. I pined. As a young girl I dreamed about my Prince Charming. But the prince never came, let alone saved me. As I grew up, my hope of finding a dashing prince evolved into a fantasy of finding my Mr. Big (for you Gen Z-ers out there, I'm referring to the suave, charming finance mogul who was the on-again, off-again love interest of Carrie Bradshaw in the popular sitcom *Sex and the City*). And yet, with disappointment after disappointment, that fantasy of a man swooping me off my feet and changing my life held strong.

Here's what those fairy tales, romantic movies, and love songs create: a culture of women shattered by love. We have unrealistic expectations of what it is to love and be loved. For most people, what we call "love" today can be categorized as variations upon certain themes we experience as adolescents: intense lust and longing, attraction to novelty and excitement, the desire to "possess" and idealize, and the hope of feeling special when chosen.

So yeah, Snow White, Cinderella, Carrie Bradshaw, and the rest of the taffeta-gowned gang, although entertaining, have reinforced a dysfunctional way of approaching romance. The women attending Renew have generally put the same amount of stock in fairy tales as me. Many had convinced themselves they were with a Mr. Big in the making or a Bradley Cooper in need of some taming. Most of them were dating the guy with potential. Of course, he just needed more time, more work, more love.

Let's learn a valuable lesson that all those fairy tales failed to mention: they're all tales. We live in a society where we've been bombarded by fantasy ideals since childhood, brainwashed into unrealistic expectations of love. While the princess ideal is still kicking around, today we have other variations of tales running wild. The modern woman may not have the desire to be saved, but she sure as hell is pressured to have it all, be it all, and do it all. She's the trailblazing supermom, wearing a power suit when she's running her company and Agent Provocateur when she's the sexual goddess at home. She has the perfect life, the perfect relationship, and a slick Instagram feed that documents her romantic vacations. She may have exchanged her glass slippers for Louboutins, but the modern-day fairy tale still creates unrealistic expectations about love.

GREAT AT FALLING IN LOVE, LOUSY AT STAYING IN IT

It wasn't always like this. Before the 1750s, there was a more pragmatic approach to relationships. Marriages were often strategic transactions between families involving matters of power, wealth, status, land, and religion. The idea of marrying for love and passion was considered absurd, if not downright irresponsible. Romanticism emerged partially as a reaction to the Industrial Revolution and the Age of Enlightenment.[1] The movement was popularized in Europe in the mid-eighteenth century by poets, painters, and artists alike and has continued to permeate culture ever since.

Philosopher and bestselling author Alain de Botton warns that such Romantic ideals create unrealistic expectations for long-term relationships: *"Romanticism has been a disaster for our relationships. It is an intellectual and spiritual movement which has had a devastating impact on the ability of ordinary people to lead successful emotional lives."*[2]

Romanticism tells us that the excitement and euphoria characteristic at the beginning of a relationship should continue throughout a lifetime, that choosing a partner should be guided by feelings, that we don't need to be educated in how to love, and that our partners should understand us intuitively. Likewise, what once took a village should now be the responsibility of our partner: he must be our lover, our bedrock of safety, our best friend, our accountant, our keeper of secrets, all while being stable and intriguingly exciting and sexy at the same time. Romanticism equated sex with love and love with sex. And that sex must be mind-blowing until death do us part.

Romanticism sets up the scene for a love story's introduction, but it fails to take us through the middle and end. Oh, you know, that pesky thing called reality. Romanticism has created a population of hopefuls who become really good at falling in love but terrible at staying in it.

Now, I'm not advocating that we go back to the notion of marriages as strategic alliances; however, I think we have swung the pendulum so far that romance trumps practicality, and that is setting us up for suffering. If we are looking to create relationships that last, we need to have a balanced perspective that unites both mindsets.

Romantic ideals pump through our veins and often go unquestioned. We become so obsessed with chasing butterflies that we rule out suitable potential partners or exit relationships as soon as the sparks fade. We blame our partners and we blame ourselves, but we don't question if the very thing we're searching for is illusory.

If there's one important point for you to remember from this chapter, it is this: the intense passion that burns at the start of a relationship is scientifically and statistically unlikely to last longer than twelve to twenty-four months.[3] If you are looking for a long-term partnership and basing your decision on how you feel when in a heightened state of lust that has an inevitable expiration date, you're going to be sorely disappointed.

You don't want to fall in love. You want to stand in love.

To create a successful relationship, we need to examine our definition of love and replace the fantasy of "falling in love" with standing in love. The former is an easy, fleeting feeling; the latter is a practice. The former you have no control over—you are a victim to the passionate throes of emotions—but the latter, you choose. The words of Jerry Maguire, "You complete me," while swoon-worthy, are actually dysfunctional, codependent, and potentially borderline evidence of love addiction (more on this later).

We must question the belief systems that do not serve us and the plans we form that are based on our upbringing and cultural norms, and then we must create the type of relationship that we need, taking into account where we are now and where we want to go. And to do that, the first thing that we need to do is dismantle one of those age-old beliefs still kicking around: the idea of a soul mate.

BURSTING THE SOUL MATE BUBBLE

Do you believe in soul mates?

Ah, the soul mate—the perpetuating romantic myth that's still chugging along against all odds. Literally. If you haven't met your "soul mate" yet, don't blame your luck, your charm, or a blip in your destiny. Blame it on numerical probability. According to a January 2011 Marist poll, a whopping 73 percent of Americans believe that they are destined to find their one true soul mate. Assuming your soul mate is set at birth, is roughly in the same age bracket, and is recognizable at first sight, mathematical estimates indicate that your chances of finding your soul mate is only 1 in 10,000 (0.01 percent).[4] That figure doesn't take into account the fact that 9,891 of those people likely live in a place you will never conceivably go. The numbers just aren't on your side. It's time to stop placing your bets on finding a soul mate and playing a more realistic hand instead.

When you develop an image of what your ideal type—or soul mate—is, you are creating a story. This story consists of yearning for the feeling of being "in love," which amplifies the desire for an idealized lover, particularly when the apple of your eye is elusive or unavailable. Pining for that unattainable ideal becomes an enthrallment of the experience of the intense emotions of being in love rather than a reality-based interest in the potential partner. The never-ending chase to find one's soul mate is no different from searching for a pot of gold at the end of a rainbow, which we all know is impossible, as rainbows are nothing but an optical illusion. Soul mate shopping is a surefire way to stay single, avoid true intimacy, and habitually walk away from relationships the moment sparks fade.

Research shows that people who hold a strong belief in destiny are prone to lose interest in their partner much faster and are likely to give up much more easily when a relationship starts to go through hardships.[5] Whether you are soul mate shopping, projecting your fantasies onto someone, or putting potential partners on a pedestal, it's a function of the same behavior: avoiding reality when it comes to love.

Say you finally meet a person who fits the hopes and dreams that you've been clinging to your whole life. You lock eyes. The connection is fast, furious, and filled with passion and intensity. Your mind then tricks you, omitting the non–soul mate qualities this person might possess, amplifying your similarities and all the things that appear perfect about that person. This is confirmation bias at play.

Confirmation bias occurs when we are motivated by the desire that a certain idea needs to be true. Instead of seeing facts, or someone's true self, we only see evidence that supports our initial belief. You want to find your soul mate? Well, your brain is going to try its hardest to help you find that person, but once the infatuation phase is over, that idealized person becomes just another normal, flawed human being.

When I look back at the times when I fell hard for someone, only to be sorely disappointed later by how he treated me or how the relationship didn't progress, it's clear I wasn't basing my feelings on reality. I was high on my own fantasy. I would have an image of who my perfect person was, I'd meet someone who sort of resembled that picture, and suddenly, my soul mate alarm bells would go off. And guess what? That image was really just my ego projecting into the future.

Creating a false story about someone can cause us to develop ideas around a connection that isn't real or may amplify a spark into something more than what it really is. This is especially true if you're hungry for a relationship or in a state of desperation to meet "the one." Even if there is an authentic connection or spark, when your mind races to create a fantasy future, you are no longer present. Instead, your mind is focusing on the next step of your goal, which objectifies the person to fill a void. You start latching on to the person to make you feel a certain way, and this is where the connection morphs from a mutual exchange to a needy attachment.

Perhaps if I had learned this lesson a little sooner, I wouldn't have spent years pining for my soul mate, John.

DON'T GO CHASING UNICORNS

When I first met John, I felt *all* the things. He felt strangely familiar. My mystical side liked to think we were two souls who had previously been together in another lifetime, reconnecting in this plane. I've tried hard to squash that hopeless romantic in me, but it rears its heart-bedecked head every so often, and with John, my soul mate alarm bells were ringing in full force.

We adventured, and we played like children. It was sweet, beautiful, and, of course, all sorts of magical. He told me he was not looking for a relationship. I didn't care.

It felt so good and I didn't want it to stop. I knew he was going through a challenging time in his life: he was stressed at work and was grieving a loss in his family. When he told me he wasn't looking for a relationship, I figured he wasn't looking for one right *now*. In my head, he'd eventually change his mind. After all, we had a soul mate connection. And thus began the start of a journey—one that would be full of starts and stops, hope and hurt, and the eventual painful bursting of the bubble that inevitably happens when you refuse to face the facts.

John was easy to fall for. He was handsome, wildly successful, and kind. His gentle nature and southern charm were magnetic. I felt taken care of when I was with him. We lived in different cities and he traveled constantly for his job, so any time we saw each other it was last-minute, spontaneous, and exciting. From fancy dinners to passionate make-out sessions to deep conversations—I experienced only peak moments with John, but never for more than twenty-four hours. There were monthlong lags between our visits, during which I would replay those moments over and over again in my head. Not only would I swoon over the past; I would daydream of our possible future.

"I love you," he told me over lunch. "I think of you often, usually when I meditate."

There are two sides to this story. The whimsical, romantic one, in which you meet and feel all the nonsensical tingles of finding "the one." There can be only one explanation for the intensity of these feelings: destiny has finally delivered your soul mate to you.

The other side is reality, where all of those soul mate feelings are rooted in a wash of chemical reactions, particularly dopamine, heightened by intermittent rewards that can perpetuate an addictive cycle. The growing ache and longing for someone, even when that person is not reciprocating, is your fantasy reflected back at you.

Fantasies can mess with you, because as you continually revisit the emotionally charged memories of the past starring the object of your affection, and daydream about the possibilities of the future, a cascade of feel-good chemicals are produced in the body. Your body can't tell the difference between falling in love with a real person or the person in your head. The dopamine release ensures that both feel totally amazing, leaving you craving more, more, more!

Then the day came when John told me he was now in a committed relationship. I was shocked. I asked him why, after dancing back and forth between gray lines for the last two years, he hadn't chosen to explore a relationship with me. John told me he didn't "see me in the relationship bucket."

Ouch.

Hearing that hurt, like a dart piercing my heart. It took that clear, painful message to burst my fantasy bubble and face reality. Though I had desperately wanted to believe in the mystical soul mate narrative, the reality was that I'd been chasing a unicorn.

I took a handful of loving, beautiful moments, mixed those with a dash of projection and a sprinkle of stardust, and created a romantic story and ideal of a man that wasn't rooted in reality.

The unicorn fantasy was everything I hoped for, and with that taking up a significant portion of my heart and headspace, I hadn't really had to let anyone else in. You see, when you chase someone with an impossible future, you delude yourself into thinking you want a relationship when, really, the unicorn is a reflection of your own unavailability. Unicorns don't require you to go past a certain point of vulnerability, so your heart is always shielded. You don't get to the part where you have to move through issues together, figure out how to fight well, and learn how to coexist with another person in the day-to-day. You don't have to get emotionally intimate, where your deepest vulnerabilities come to the surface and you expose who you really are.

The words of Renew's life coach, Trish Barillas, hit home when it comes to this topic: "Hope will fuck you. Have hope for humanity, have hope for world peace, but do not have hope for a person to change. You cannot hope your relationship into existence."

Time and again, Coach Trish sees how her clients hang on to hope, wishing that their partner would change who they are and what they want or actually start showing up in the relationship. She explains that our personal agendas are often what keep us hanging on, because they distract us from accepting reality. Maybe if I had heeded Trish's advice, I wouldn't have spent so much time hoping that John would eventually choose me.

I held on to hope that maybe John would change his mind about me, maybe the starts and stops would lead to something more, maybe he just needed more time to realize I was his person. He didn't. He hasn't. And he won't.

I share this story because I think my behavior is something all the hopeful romantics out there will recognize: we want the fantasy, the dream, the feeling of finally being whole. This causes us to fill in the spaces with make-believe. The pressure we put on ourselves to find "the one" blinds us to the red flags. It's like using a handful of bread crumbs to make a decadent cake, filling the layers with projections and desires.

FUTURE TRIPPIN'

When you date someone, after a few memorable outings, do you put him on the perfection pedestal? Perhaps you google him and see his career success or his attractive pics on social media. Maybe when he talks about his dream to retire in Bali, your soul mate alarm bells go off: "Omg, that's my dream too!" Instantly, your fantasy brain is off to the races. Suddenly, you're imagining how cute your kids will be, how you'll decorate your three-story house, and, of course, how peaceful it will be to retire together in Bali. You start to idealize him, and the relationship fantasy takes on a life of its own. Instead of staying present and grounded so you can really get to know this person, you've already projected an elaborate future scenario onto him. Unsurprisingly, your feelings start to intensify. But the relationship hasn't caught up, nor have his feelings toward you. Along with these intense feelings, you create expectations of how he should behave and how the relationship should progress, because you like him *sooo* much and the possibilities of your future are *sooo* promising. But it is pretty likely that he doesn't reciprocate your level of feelings. Not yet anyway. Uh-oh. Power imbalance. And when the could-be relationship ends, you're devastated.

Even though you were seeing each other for only a few weeks, you find yourself in deep mourning.

future trippin

WHEN YOU CHASE
SOMEONE WITH AN
IMPOSSIBLE FUTURE,
YOU DELUDE
YOURSELF INTO
THINKING YOU WANT
A RELATIONSHIP
WHEN, REALLY,
THE UNICORN IS A
REFLECTION OF
YOUR OWN
UNAVAILABILITY.

Not just for the times you had. You're mourning all the future plans that haven't been actualized as well.

I don't doubt that in a short period of time, you can connect deeply with someone and feel sparks you haven't felt before. But if your emotional intensity does not realistically match the stage of the relationship, then take this as a sign that your fantasy was in charge. You were future trippin', and that makes the fall a lot harder.

EXERCISE: The Stop Sign (Stop Future Trippin' Before Takeoff)

The building of a relationship takes time. It takes gradual exchanges of vulnerability and sharing—in person. It's a dance. And as two people get to know each other, rapport builds and you become closer and closer. To help you stay present with your current partner, here's an exercise to try the next time your mind starts to wander into the future.

Once the thought creeps up—you imagine a trip you want to take, your destination wedding, living together in a two-story house—catch yourself. Create awareness that your mind is not being present.

Next, imagine a big red stop sign, or say the word "stop" out loud.

If you can, change your body position (if you're sitting down, stand up, and vice versa). Or if possible, go for a walk. It's much easier to get your mind to change when you change your physiology first.

Now, start looking around and observing the things you're grateful for. Be keenly observant. Notice the sky, the trees, the beautiful environment around you, the weather—notice everything and anything and find the gratitude within.

Once you focus your attention on listing off all you're grateful for, your mind will automatically lose track of its grip on the previous thought. Soon you'll forget what you were originally thinking about.

This might be tough the first few times, but with practice, you'll master this! While a daily gratitude ritual helps you rewire your brain for happiness, the stop sign exercise is an in-the-moment hack to help you redirect your thoughts in order to stay present.

IS IT LOVE OR LIMERENCE?

"I'm a hopeless romantic. I fall hard and fast and always for the bad boy. I just don't feel any chemistry with the nice guys." Natalie desired the intensity of fresh romance. She thrived off the thrill that came with longing, with desiring what she couldn't have, and felt high when her latest conquest would give her a little attention. She rationalized that this rush, and the crash that'd inevitably come afterward, was just her being "passionate." If fantasizing were a sport, she'd win a gold medal. But Natalie's longing wasn't about love; it was about getting high. In fact, it's textbook limerence.

First coined by psychologist Dorothy Tennov, "limerence" can be defined as "an involuntary interpersonal state that involves an acute longing for emotional reciprocation, obsessive-compulsive thoughts, feelings, and behaviors, and emotional dependence on another person."[6] Other terms that are often used interchangeably are "lovesick," "infatuated," or "love addicted." Research indicates that the biochemical processes that contribute to limerence last between six months and two years on average. It's not surprising that one study found that 70 percent of straight unmarried couples break up within the first year of dating.[7] The chemical cocktail can often be so strong that it causes people to overlook fundamental differences in compatibility and values, and once the chemistry fades, the relationship has no glue to stay together. We will dive deeper into the chemistry of love later in this chapter, and I'd argue that at least some degree of limerence is necessary to get a relationship going. However, it's helpful to see where on the spectrum you generally stand.

Signs of Limerence

Tennov identified the following core characteristics of limerence:

- Idealization of the other person's characteristics (positive and negative)

- Uncontrollable and intrusive thoughts about the other person

- Extreme shyness, stuttering, nervousness, and confusion around the other person

- Fear of rejection and despair or thoughts of suicide if rejection occurs

- A sense of euphoria in response to real or perceived signs of reciprocation

- Fantasizing about or searching obsessively for signs of reciprocation ("reading into things")

- Being reminded of the person in everything around you

- Replaying in your mind every encounter with the other person in great detail

- Maintaining romantic intensity through adversity

- Endlessly analyzing every word and gesture to determine its possible meaning

- Rearranging your schedule to maximize the chances of seeing the other person[8]

Just because you have strong feelings for someone does not mean there is an actual connection. When you are in a high state of limerence, you are more susceptible to creating a fantasy about a person, becoming addicted to a person, or intensifying your feelings toward a person before the relationship has realistically progressed.

Remember, for a relationship to develop, both parties need to be actively involved. If it's one-sided, if it feels frenetic and angst-ridden, it's not healthy. It's important to do a check-in with yourself, not only about how you feel, but about the reality of the situation.

Does the apple of your eye reciprocate your feelings? Is he communicating his interest and desire to get to know you in both his words and actions? If you can't tell, ask yourself whether the following statements apply:

- He initiates making plans to see me (and not just in the late hours of the evening).

- He initiates communication and is consistent in his contact.

- He makes an effort to see me and is accommodating to my schedule and location (that is, he's not meeting me only when it's convenient for him).

- He sets future plans and schedules time to see each other.

- He's comfortable taking things slowly and not rushing into sex.

- He introduces me to his friends.

- He prioritizes seeing me.

If you answered yes to these statements, great! You can continue moving on to the next section. If you answered no to these statements, seek out expert advice from a coach, a therapist, or a friend who you trust will give you honest feedback.

Do his level of interest and intensity of feelings match yours, give or take a few degrees? Or is it possible that your personal agenda—your hope for the relationship—is blinding you to the fact that you're investing more than the other person? Don't mistake your obsession or hope for his love. The intensity of your obsessive feelings does not signify how deeply in love you are; rather, it reflects the intensity of your limerence. And remember, the right person for you is not going to keep you guessing all the time.

Even when it seems like you're feeling *soo much*—oh, the exquisite agony—this is actually you just dodging feelings. Crush after crush, your target is merely a source of dopamine. This behavior isn't about getting to know the other person; it's about projecting all your desired attributes onto him.

The next time you're craving a big heaping serving of fantasy indulgence, know that afterward you're going to get sick—unless you're into that sort of thing . . . emotional sadism, that is. Recognize when you are in a state of limerence and remember this:

Don't. Feed. The. Fantasy.

"I'M NOT A LOVE ADDICT," SAID THE LOVE ADDICT

At one point in my life, Beyoncé's hit song "Crazy in Love" could have been my personal anthem. I'd been obsessing over boys since the age of four, when my yearning for attention started. Growing up, my friends joked I was "boy crazy." Everything I did was centered around getting the opposite sex to notice me, from joining sports teams at school to taking waitressing jobs to becoming a club promoter—the key objective was to meet guys. Thinking, talking, and fantasizing about relationships was my hobby—I didn't know a different way to be, and I thought everyone else was just like me.

Finally, I learned about love addiction. I had exhibited the signs of being a love addict for years, constantly preoccupied with romance, chasing the roller-coaster highs and lows of unavailable partners, feeling angst about whether my affections were returned by the crush du jour. But no, I wasn't a full-blown addict! An anxiously attached person, sure. But addict? No, not me.

When I thought of the word "addict," I imagined a junkie in a dark alley getting high. The word was not a label I wished to be identified with.

It wasn't until I sobered up that I realized I had a full-blown addiction and had for the majority of my life. Love addiction was really a symptom of my lack of self-worth and an inability to self-soothe. As I started to tackle the limiting beliefs that ruled my emotions and actions, healing my wounds, becoming more secure in my attachment style, making healthier decisions in relationships, and practicing self-care, I became less reliant on validation from men as a way to feel okay. Coming out of this was like coming out of a daze. I could experience a reality where my waking hours weren't consumed with thoughts of my latest romantic obsession. I didn't have a constant, chronic angst about whom I liked or who liked me back. I stopped chasing highs. It wasn't until I was out of it that I realized I had been a textbook love addict.

The truth is love addiction is more common than we think. It's a spectrum, and it's likely we've all experienced it at some point. People who are unable to self-soothe and have a highly dysregulated nervous system are more prone to all types of addiction, including love addiction.[9] Dr. Alexandra Katehakis, the founder of the Center for Healthy Sex and a thought leader in the field of integrative sex therapy, suggests that a lack of healthy modeling on how to self-soothe as a child can result in addiction issues as adults:

> Addicts, whether they're using drugs, alcohol, food, love, or sex to soothe themselves, are typically chronically dysregulated. They're seeking relief from underlying issues like depression or anxiety and can't get it. Because they didn't get the appropriate input and modeling for how to seek and receive comfort from the adults in their lives, they turn to substances or behaviors that will give them temporary relief from their own internal dysregulation.[10]

Having an addiction can be best described as reaching for something external to soothe an uncomfortable feeling, whether it be boredom, anxiety, loneliness, sadness, or all of the above. Whatever the vice, an addict cannot self-soothe and thus repeatedly reaches out for something (or someone) in order to seek temporary relief, despite unhealthy consequences that follow. Over time, this behavior becomes habitualized and reinforced, turning into a pattern that becomes difficult to stop.

While limerence is characterized by obsession for a particular person, love addiction is characterized by chasing the "high" and often transfers from person to person. The love addict cannot move beyond the rush. She confuses the fantasy she's created about the person of the moment, believing that they are in love, when really she is objectifying the person through said fantasy. The paramour of the moment becomes her "drug dealer," giving that hit of intensity and emotionally elevated state she desperately craves.[11]

This intensity usually works in the beginning, but then the anxiety starts to creep in. The addiction is characterized by a tendency to equate love with anxiety in the nervous system. Suddenly, the love addict's fears of being abandoned and of losing that intense feeling start to grow. This leaves her grasping, begging for attention and even tolerating disrespect or poor behavior, because she is desperate to get the relief from her "drug dealer." Not until she gets that chemical fix can she function again. The cycle repeats. The heart palpitations, the sweaty palms, the tightening of the chest—the love addict confuses this for love, when really, it's the body going into withdrawal before the next fix.

A degree of obsession, fantasy, and chemistry is healthy and is often pivotal in the beginning stages of a relationship. The neurobiological rush is the fuel that can help a couple grow into the more mature intimacy that is characteristic of long-term relationships.[12] Dr. Robert Weiss, author and expert in the treatment of adult intimacy disorders and addictions, explains that love addicts live in limerence, hooked on the neurochemical high as a way to escape and disassociate from reality. He notes that "the difference between love addicts and healthy people is that love addicts never make it past limerence; they never 'assign value' to anything beyond the initial intensity they experience. Instead, they seek to continually stimulate their brain's pleasure center with one new relationship after another, just as alcoholics stimulate their brains with one drink after another."[13]

QUIZ: Do You Have Love Addiction?

ANSWER YES OR NO TO THE FOLLOWING STATEMENTS:

1. I tend to feel needy in my romantic relationships.

2. I fall in love very quickly.

3. I have a tendency to stay in a relationship even though I know it's unhealthy or toxic for me.

4. When I have romantic feelings toward someone, I can't stop fantasizing and thinking about him, which sometimes causes a disruption in my daily life.

5. I've been told that I've been smothering in relationships.

6. In the past, when I had romantic feelings toward someone, I have ignored red flags.

7. I find myself investing more into a relationship than my partner.

8. In the past, I've gotten romantically involved with someone to avoid being lonely.

9. I have worked hard to mold myself to the person my partner wants me to be. I will edit myself and sacrifice my needs and values in order to please him.

10. I am petrified of being abandoned. Even the slightest sign of rejection causes me to feel unsafe or worthless.

11. I have more than once chased after people who have rejected me and tried desperately to change their minds.

12. Even if I am not in a relationship, I find myself fantasizing about love all the time—either about someone from my past or about the perfect person who I hope I to meet.

13. I feel powerless when I fall in love, and have a tendency to make unhealthy choices because my feelings are so strong.

14. I need a romantic partner in order to feel okay.

15. I consistently choose partners who are emotionally unavailable or avoid intimacy.

16. When I'm in a relationship, I have a tendency to make the relationship the center of my universe.

If you answered yes to more than 50 percent of these statements, this may be an indicator that you are experiencing love addiction.

These statements are adapted from a questionnaire created by Love Addicts Anonymous. To get a full diagnosis, seek a therapist who specializes in relationship issues or check out resources and programs offered at the Meadows treatment center.

WHAT'S YOUR RELATIONSHIP TO RELATIONSHIP?

When Nicole Boyar, a love coach who helps women shift from love addicted to love connected, passes this quiz around during her workshop at Renew, you can hear the gasps in the room. The women go through each statement, murmuring, "Yep," and "Omg, that's so me."

Karen, the divorcée who uncovered her belief that "there are no good men left" (see chapter three), raises her hand and objects: "Both of my exes were addicts. They were out of control. I was the one keeping everything together. Imagining myself as an addict seems very harsh, when I know what an addict looks like."

Nicole encourages Karen to suspend judgment of the label and instead to explore her "relationship to relationship." "The definition of 'addiction' is continually repeating a behavior, any behavior at all, despite the negative consequence. Did you stay in the relationship despite the negative consequences to your emotional and physical health?" Nicole asks.

"Yes, I stayed way longer than I should have. It's confusing because I didn't start out thinking I was going to get into a toxic or abusive relationship. It kinda just happened. But I know something is wrong because it kinda just happened twice now," Karen admits.

Many of the participants at Renew have dated people with drug and alcohol addictions. Nicole explains that this is a common pairing. People with love addiction have a process addiction as opposed to a substance addiction, but the intense cycle of push and pull is all the same.

"With love addiction, we are willing to be in a cycle of push and pull with drama and intensity. Being drawn to someone who has a substance addiction makes sense, because we are willing to tolerate that back and forth and the roller coaster that they are on. We get so consumed by their journey and trying to heal them that we are not healing our own issues. We believe we are in love when in fact it is intensity, not intimacy. It's that intensity that we get addicted to."

She adds that love addiction is much like a substance addiction in the way that the tolerance to the drama gradually keeps increasing. In the case of Karen, she didn't see any signs of addiction or abuse in the beginning. But gradually there was the drunken night that turned into a terrible fight. Then the insults he'd make after a few drinks. He'd apologize profusely the next day, making up for his drunken stupor with grand romantic gestures. Karen let it slide. Until another incident, and she let it slide again. Her tolerance for the drama and the intensity of the lows followed by the highs continually increased over time.

But Those Cravings . . .

The women listen intently to Karen's story, because deep down, there's a part of Karen's story that echoes their own experiences—feeling addicted to someone who is toxic, chasing intensity, and coping with unbearable withdrawal. Nicole explains that withdrawal symptoms are a natural part of the healing process:

"As you remove this person from your life you can feel intense cravings for them the same way someone with a substance addiction may crave that substance. This could be in the form of obsessive thoughts or an intense desire to call or see them. The good news is cravings usually last only ten to twenty minutes. If you can make it through that time without giving in, the craving will stop!"

The next time you experience symptoms of withdrawal from your ex, give yourself ten to twenty minutes for the craving to pass. Remind yourself that your brain is craving dopamine and it has associated your ex with getting that reward. Find a healthier way to get your hit of dopamine.[14]

Nicole concludes that we lose ourselves in our relationships because the idea of the new relationship feels better than our current life: "When our lives are not that exciting and this new thing comes along, we quickly and blindly dive in as a way to fill the emptiness of our own lives."

This brings us to our next point: when we aren't feeling whole, we are much more susceptible to a good ol' fantasy hijacking.

THE FANTASY DEALER

Whether you're high on nostalgia for the past or drunk on hope for the future, the fantasy of someone can make you feel like you've found Mr. Perfect. Sometimes this is actually the case, and you're fortunate enough to have met a partner who is consistent with the idea projected in the beginning throes of love. But not everyone is so fortunate. In fact, most women aren't. Those who are most susceptible to fantasy bias are those who fall prey to the ultimate fantasy dealer, the narcissist.

"He swept me off my feet." Tracy sighed.

Tracy, a participant at Renew, shared the story of how she and her now ex-fiancé, Tom, met. They had known each other as kids and through chance reunited thirty years later. It was fast and furious, filled with romantic getaways, talks about the future, lavish gifts, and hot, passionate sex. Tracy had, just a few years prior to reconnecting with Tom, left a boring and unfulfilling marriage. Her bond with Tom was utterly intoxicating. He filled all the voids left from her first marriage.

"It was like he knew me more than I knew myself. He was so fun and exciting, and he made me feel so alive."

But a month before the big wedding, Tracy received a call.

The call.

From the other woman.

Apparently, perfect Tom had been living a double life with someone else for their entire relationship. In fact, Tom had been involved with the other woman for so long that by the end of the call, neither one could tell if she was the "other woman."

After coming to Renew and dissecting the relationship a bit more, it became clear to Tracy there had been red flags all along. But the lifestyle, the house in the Hamptons, the dreamboat guy—they had been enough to make her overlook them. For example, life had to revolve around Tom's needs—his career, his social functions, and his preferences in where they should live. If she ever felt upset or questioned him, her feelings or concerns were invalidated; she'd be accused of being "too sensitive" and "acting crazy" (hello, gaslighting). Tracy felt lucky that a charming guy like Tom chose her, and bit by bit, she bought into the story he was telling her and stopped doubting him.

Tracy was a prime target for a narcissist. She was beautiful and smart (required traits for a narcissist, who needs his partner to boost his status and validation), she was overaccommodating and habitually put the needs of others before her own, and since she had exited a loveless marriage, she was starved for passion and excitement. When Tom came along, it was as if he were the remedy to everything that ailed her. He had the finances, the lifestyle, the good looks, and the promise of an exciting life. Tracy wanted so badly for Tom to be "the one" that she filled in the gaps with projection and fantasy. She had a virtual PICK ME sign above her head.

Tracy's story is unfortunately not unique. At Renew, approximately 30 percent of the participants are getting over a breakup with a narcissist or come to bootcamp because they are still in a relationship with one they can't seem to leave.

You would think that spotting a narcissist is easy; however, they can be incredibly charming, attractive, and seductive. In fact, an experiment with speed dating showed that those with the highest scores on the narcissism scale were perceived as the most desirable and datable by the opposite sex.[15] These people are often in powerful positions and overrepresented in fields where being the center of attention is an asset, such as entertainment, entrepreneurship, or politics.[16] They're the life of the party, tend to surround themselves with

people, and invest in their appearance (i.e., they're hot). People are usually pining for their attention, and this can feel extremely validating when that prized attention is directed at you.

When the popular, powerful hot guy suddenly directs his laser-focused attention on you, it naturally feels great! You feel lucky that out of everyone he could have chosen, he chose *you*. Because he's skilled at being likable, he says all the things you want to hear. He may even engage in big romantic gestures: flowers, trips, gifts, and promises of the future. Suddenly, intoxicated by the whirlwind of romance, you think you've found your Prince Charming, Mr. Big, and Harry Styles all in one. You're hooked. And once you're hooked, the switch happens. Suddenly, Mr. Perfect withdraws, and you don't feel so special anymore. You start clamoring for his attention, his time, that rush of feel-good chemicals that you were flooded with in the beginning. You might even start sacrificing your needs to please him, to reclaim his validation and attention. And as soon as you're on the brink of cutting him off, he comes back strong and love bombs you, overwhelming you with tokens of affection to regain your interest. A tornado of excessive flattery, gifts, and romantic gestures sweeps you back up into his vortex, and suddenly you're hooked again.

Narcissists also present a false self, where they appear to be the loving and attentive person of your dreams until you don't do what they want. They will then become punishing, distant, and cold. They gaslight, a term used by psychologists that describes when someone uses manipulation so that his target doubts her own sanity, judgment, and memory. Psychotherapist Jeremy Bergen explains: "It's a tactic one partner uses in an effort to exert power over, gain control over, and inflict emotional damage on the other." He adds, "One of the big warning signs is this persistent sense that what you saw, you didn't really see. And what you experienced, you didn't really experience. What you felt, you didn't really feel."[17]

Without the awareness that this is all typical narcissistic behavior, you feel confused and start blaming yourself, convinced that if only you behave in the right way, do more of this or less of that, the Prince Charming you once knew will reappear.

NARCISSISM AS THE NEW SCAPEGOAT

Narcissism is a spectrum disorder and exists on a continuum ranging from a few narcissistic traits to a full-blown personality disorder, which is a mental illness. There's no doubt that understanding the clinical terminology can help us make sense of things, but we need to be careful of falsely pathologizing others as a catchall for bad relationships. Today, with our vocabularies woke AF, we've armed ourselves with a new lexicon where the people who piss us off are now diagnosed as having a personality disorder.

He might have been noncommittal. He might have been an asshole. But this doesn't automatically make him a narcissist.

When we point the finger of blame by falsely accusing someone of having a personality disorder, we don't see or accept the reality of the situation. When we can't accept reality, we cannot grow. We stay stuck repeating the same emotional experiences, just with different people: "It's the treadmill's fault! Not the fact that I keep running on it."

Whatever you want to call your ex—asshole, narcissist, avoidant, or crazy—if you're consistently choosing toxic people, this says a lot more about your patterns than anything else.

NARCISSIST PROOFING

You know what the best narcissist repellant is? A strong sense of self-worth. People who don't outsource their validation and need to feel "special" to someone else are hard targets for the narcissist to manipulate. If you've fallen for one, you have to take accountability for how you fell for the narcissist in the first place.

What made you want the connection so badly that you ignored the signs? Because, let's be honest, there are always signs.

Did you play into the fantasy he presented? Were you yearning for external validation to feel special? Did you get intoxicated by the lure of the image he projected because you thought it could be a ticket out of your current status? Were you, perhaps, trying to up-level your lifestyle?

It's easy to point the finger at someone for being a narcissist. But how many of us can admit to having some narcissistic characteristics too? Have you dated someone because it was easier to latch on to his life, his success, and his power rather than create that on your own? Have you ever dated someone to boost your self-esteem or status?

Mic drop.

THE LOVE SPELL:
A PROVOCATIVE CONCOCTION OF CHEMICALS

Speaking of narcissists . . .

Meet Justin.

Justin was the quintessential bad boy: a well-known, perpetu-ally single New York player, a successful lawyer with an impres-sive Tribeca loft. We met at a festival, where I was drinking tequila straight from the bottle, and he was partying in the VIP section. We danced. He kissed me. So began our romance.

Justin whisked me off to St. Kitts on our second date. By month two, we were jetting off to Tulum. Every experience we had together was intense, exciting, and passionate. Of course, we were principally opposite in the most important ways: I believed in monogamy, and he didn't. He told me he wanted to be emotionally but not sexually monogamous:

> JUSTIN: All I'm saying is, if I casually hooked up with someone, that shouldn't mean the end of the relationship. All guys cheat; they just lie about it. I want to be honest.

> AMY: Actually, I don't think *all* guys cheat. I want a monogamous relationship and know I can find someone who wants the same thing. What's the value of me getting into a relationship with you? Because I don't like what you're offering!

> JUSTIN: You'd get street cred for taming me.

Can you say "heart melt"?

So, what did I do? I stayed with him, *duh*. I convinced myself that I could manage my emotions with him and keep things casual.

Unsurprisingly, Justin dominated my headspace. I was physically addicted to him even though we had nothing in common except for sex and tequila. I was thrown off by my chemical response to this man: the tingle in the pit of my stomach, the warm flush lighting up my cheeks. My. Heart. Wouldn't. Stop. Racing.

That was Mother Nature screwing with me. And you know the feeling.

Love is not an emotion; rather, it's a motivation system designed for humans to mate and procreate.

When we fall for someone, there's a flurry of chemicals and hormones reacting in our brain. If you're so lucky, the chemical cocktail brings you closer to a suitable mate, but our primal mating drives can often trick us into getting attached to someone who's not a compatible partner.

Human behavior researcher Helen Fisher discovered there are three mating drives that intertwine to convince us we're in love: the first is *lust,* driven by testosterone; the second is *romantic attraction,* driven by high dopamine and norepinephrine levels and low serotonin; and the third is *attachment,* driven by oxytocin and vasopressin.[18]

The Spark

Lust is driven by the hormone testosterone, which promotes aggression, risk-taking, assertiveness, and self-confidence and enhances the visual (spatial ability)—it's our sex drive working at full force.

We know "the gaze" all too well. The gravitational pull that draws us together, which neuroscience terms our "adaptive oscillators." Should the gaze become mutual—perhaps made more uninhibited by a nightclub setting, sexy clothes, and booze—and you fall into another person's eyes, that's your adaptive oscillators locking and forming. The stronger this gaze becomes, the more overwhelming your lust. It takes less than a second for a person to find someone physically attractive and initiate a gaze.

For men, who tend to produce ten times more testosterone than women, the spark of the gaze is a lot more visual. Within microseconds, a man's brain judges a woman's physicality and her receptivity to him (animal brains assessing potential for sex/mating). This is why men report love at first sight much more often than women. Some research suggests that men with higher baseline levels of testosterone, while impetuous and aggressively romantic and sexual during the lust phase, tend to marry less frequently, have more adulterous affairs, and divorce more often.[19]

For women, visual stimulants infer character, status, dominance, and wealth. Rather than sex/mating dictating her gaze, she is subconsciously assessing if a relationship might be in the future, as well as signs of the man's ability to provide and protect. Once he checks out physically, the next assessment is his voice. Women generally perceive men with deep voices who speak rapidly as more educated and better looking. The female brain is driven to seek security and reliability in a potential mate before she has sex. In a study using the brain scans of women who had recently fallen in love, the women showed more brain activity in regions associated with reward, attention, and emotion. The scans of men's brains showed that most activity was in the visual processing areas and sexual arousal.[20]

The Flame

Although lust motivates people to have sex with as many partners as possible, romantic attraction takes the process a step further, helping to focus one's mating energy on just one person at a time. This mating drive is often referred to as "passionate love" or "infatuation" and is characterized by obsessive thinking about a person and a strong desire for emotional union.[21]

Playboy Justin soon told me he was at a stage in his life where he was ready to settle down. He told me he was convinced I was the person he'd do that with. He said, "I knew within the first twenty minutes of meeting you that we're going to be together."

I became addicted to how special he made me feel. The rewards

I received from his promises fed my addiction and perpetuated the romantic attraction. Justin would shower me with attention, desire, and passion, and right when it felt like we were getting closer, he'd pull back. He'd become unresponsive, sometimes disappearing completely. He'd push me away and sleep with other women. Despite his behavior toward me, I craved him more. This was because of a hormone related to dopamine called norepinephrine, which is released during attraction. It is responsible for the surge of energy, the giddy feelings, and the loss of appetite and need for sleep when you're in the throes of romantic attraction. Although more scientific research needs to be done, many scientists believe that during the attraction phase, there is also a reduction of serotonin, which is characterized by the feelings of intense infatuation and obsession. People who suffer from obsessive-compulsive disorder also show similarly low levels of serotonin.

The Burn

Before Justin, I couldn't even have a crush on two people at once without feeling like I was cheating. Now, three months in, I was surrendering my values to see if I could make this relationship work. My feelings were building. Wild date nights were morphing into me staying over, packing lunches for him for work, and making future plans. Justin went from being the hot extra to the protagonist of my movie reel. I was getting attached. I should have known better. This was just Mother Nature running her course.

According to Helen Fisher, this drive of attachment enabled our ancient ancestors to live with a mate long enough to rear a single child through infancy.[22] When there was a couple, a child's chance of survival was more likely. The hormone at play here is oxytocin, which has a significant role in pair bonding. It promotes trust, empathy, generosity, and affection. Oxytocin levels increase when we hug or kiss a loved one, when we orgasm, and when a woman gives birth and when she breastfeeds. Because the level of oxytocin is enhanced by estrogen, women tend to have stronger reactions to oxytocin. So, women are more likely to fall first . . . and hard.

Attachment is characterized by feelings of calm, security, social comfort, and emotional union. Because its primary drive is to ensure successful mating, it's helpful to look at the chemicals in a man's brain when his female partner is pregnant. During pregnancy, a man picks up on his partner's pheromones, secreted chemicals that can trigger physiological responses. This stimulates his brain to produce the hormone prolactin. Men with higher levels of prolactin appear to be more alert and responsive to their infants' cries once the baby is born and are more likely to encourage their child to explore and interact with toys. Also, the woman's pheromones cause the man's testosterone levels to drop by about 30 percent. It's arguable that this is biology's way of dissuading men from seeking sex with other partners, instead encouraging them to focus on their families just after the birth of a child. Men with higher testosterone levels, however, appear less likely to be attentive to their children's needs.[23]

In the end, we need to understand that what we know as love is more a convergence of biological factors that once ensured our survival as a species than a swell of true emotion. We can't always trust what our bodies are naturally wired to do. Love does not necessarily evolve in a linear fashion from lust to attraction to attachment either. That's why you can have sex with someone and never get to a stage of bonding. Or, after years of platonic friendship, you suddenly develop lust for your best friend.

Our mating drives developed in the most primal part of our brains. As "evolved" as we may think we are as a species, our brains are still operating with the same basic programming. It is up to us to be cognizant of this biological reality and be aware of the true nature of potential partnership. Even if biology leads us down the path to couplehood, it may not be right for you. So it was with Justin.

We all subconsciously build defense mechanisms to protect us from pain; we develop habits and coping mechanisms to help us survive; we create story lines to make sense of the past. Without knowing, dysfunction builds, one layer on top of another, creating our baseline. Soon, we become comfortable with that new normal.

Add chemistry, societal pressure, false ideals, fantasies, and the absence of models of what a healthy relationship looks and feels like to this mix, and we are left with a complicated cycle. We say we want one thing, but we are ruled by our patterns, subconscious conditioning, and biological imperatives, so we behave and attract another thing. This cycle continues with the same end playing out each time.

Armed with self-awareness and acknowledgment of chemical impetuses, you have the tools to break the cycle, choose differently, and create a new beginning.

A NEW STANDARD FOR LOVE

You don't get to choose if you get hurt in this world . . .
but you do have some say in who hurts you.

John Green, The Fault in Our Stars

In previous chapters, we've discussed how our wounds from early life impact whom we are drawn to. Our chemistry compass steers our partner choices, and when we find ourselves consistently drawn to the "wrong" types of partners, this is likely an indication that our chemistry compass needs some fine-tuning.

In the past, my romantic life was defined by a pattern of short-lived romances that ended in disaster. I habitually fell head over heels for guys who were emotionally unavailable and never gave the "nice guy" a chance. My breakup with Adam was the catalyst for me to start reflecting on my patterns in relationships. If I wanted to be in a healthy, committed relationship one day, I would need to take a look deep within and make a serious change.

As a highly analytical person, I set out to discover the patterns I was enacting and the defense mechanisms I had built around my heart. Quickly, I saw that I had a type. The men I was drawn to were all busy entrepreneurs, all married to their work. I had developed a warped sense of attraction, equating unavailability and inconsistency with excitement, and excitement with love. My model of what love felt like was not a healthy one.

I realized that my chemistry compass was pointing me in the wrong direction. Hell, let's be real, the entire damn thing was broken. I became determined to fix my chemistry compass so that I could develop attraction toward more emotionally available men. So, I did what any relationship expert would do—I conducted an experiment on myself.

Could I reprogram myself to feel chemistry toward men who were good for me? Could I be open to men outside my usual type? I was going to find out.

THE EXPERIMENT BEGINS . . .

The first order of business was to open my mind. I made the decision to be receptive to dating people outside my classic type. That type usually meant a certain height and status, with a chiseled jawline with a five o'clock shadow and a bunch of other superficial qualities. I tossed the list aside. If someone wanted to go on a date with me and seemed to be kind, emotionally healthy, and available, then I'd give it a shot. And guess what? The moment I did this, I suddenly started to notice men whom I had completely overlooked before! I swiped right on guys I typically wouldn't have chosen in the past and struck up online conversations. Newly open-minded, I decided to give the "nice guys" a chance. And so, I went on dates. And I went in with no expectations; my only intention was to be curious and have fun.

I STARTED TO "CATCH FEELINGS"

Six months into my experiment, I had gone on many dates. While the men were lovely, thoughtful, and attentive, I just wasn't developing any feelings. This was really frustrating at first. Date after date, despite my attempts to be curious and have fun, I was, well . . . bored. But then something unexpected happened.

I was having dinner with a guy named Carter, whom I had seen several times over the previous six months but with whom I, frankly, felt *zero* sexual chemistry. Early on, I was up front that I didn't have a romantic interest in him but was open to still meeting as friends. He expressed that he had no expectations but still wanted to have me in his life. Without any pressure, I felt free to spend time with him casually.

We met up for dinner one evening, maybe for the sixth or seventh time. And something changed. I remember the distinct moment when I looked at him across the dinner table and for the first time noticed how handsome he was.

Oh. Hello.

And just like that, the elusive spark was lit. I became attracted to him—not only physically but to his character and soul. This was a type of intimacy I hadn't experienced before. It was different: slow and steady, calm and peaceful. It didn't have the extreme highs and lows that I knew so well, but it was something far healthier.

IT TAKES TIME TO BUILD A HEALTHY CONNECTION

Perhaps the chemistry had always been there and I just hadn't recognized it. Perhaps my platonic admiration simply turned romantic. Whatever the explanation, my experiment worked! I learned that it takes time to build a healthy connection, because it is based on getting to really know someone for who they are, not just what he superficially represents.

What made me feel happy about the outcome with Carter was that I felt my true power in choosing a mate. I was not acting as a slave to chemistry. I realized that I could take my time and let things develop, be open to different types of men, and even have a lasting connection with someone who wasn't my typical type.

But here's the thing with the guys before Carter: even though I thought the chemistry exercise wasn't working, it actually was—just how I thought it would. You see, each guy before Carter was showing up beautifully for me. They were available, present, and interested in dating me. While I didn't feel chemistry with them, I *was* getting more and more familiar with what a healthy, available man *felt* like. Without even knowing, I was embracing a new normal. And that is what opened my eyes to Carter.

Turns out, there was actual science behind my experiment! If researchers had scanned my brain during my dates, they would have been able to provide a scientific explanation of what unfolded with Carter. You see, in that scenario, the part of my brain responsible for attachment and bonding was activated *before* the part of my brain responsible for sexual attraction was. Which, of course, made all the difference. As we discussed in the last chapter, there are three different mating drives in the brain, any one of which can spark love. In the case of Carter, lust was the last to get sparked, as we first developed an attachment as friends.

You can feel lust or attraction for someone, but that does not necessarily lead to attachment and bonding. If, like me, the first or second mating drive is what keeps landing you in trouble, consider starting from the third drive, by building connection and emotional intimacy first.

Understanding the science behind your feelings can help shift your perspective when it comes to falling in love. Don't write off a person you are compatible with because you don't feel the intense flame of lust—those sparks can grow over time. Research (and, for what it's worth, my experiment) confirms this.

FAMILIARITY BREEDS LIKABILITY

Who knew? This is called the "mere exposure effect." Psychologists argue that the more you interact with a person you like (even if it's only mild interest), the more attractive he becomes.[1]

That was clearly true with Carter.

But keep in mind that repeated exposure only amplifies something that's already there. This is why, regardless of how many meetings you have with the annoying guy at work, you don't fall in love with him. Repeated exposure merely intensifies the dominant emotion in the relationship. Thus, when the dominant emotion is disgust, repeated exposure enhances the disgust. However, when the dominant emotion is attraction, repeated exposure enhances the attraction.

If you are looking for a long-lasting partnership, it's crucial to look at the values that make up someone's character. That spark, no matter how powerful, fades—but character, values, and a shared commitment to teamwork will be the glue that will hold two people together in a relationship for the long term. Now, I'm not saying you force yourself to like someone you have no physical attraction for. I'm suggesting that you shouldn't be so quick to write someone off because you don't feel fireworks . . . at first.

With Carter, I enjoyed spending time with him and looked forward to it, even if I didn't cognitively process that as "romantic chemistry." Sometimes chemistry is there, but your conscious mind hasn't processed it yet. Check in with yourself and see if you enjoy spending time with the person. That's it. If you do, then that's enough to warrant seeing him again.

And as for your type? Know that if you meet someone who fits your "type," you might feel a bigger spark, because that's what's familiar to you. If your chemistry compass is working and that happens, great! But remember, love can be triggered in a variety of ways—a fiery spark, a flicker of interest, a slow-burning flame. There is no right or wrong way.

If you have a history of being attracted to men who are terrible for you (explosive beginnings, quick to smolder), consider being open to dating guys outside your normal type. You might need to give someone more time to warm up and catch fire, but you might be pleasantly surprised. After all, science is in your favor!

SPECTRUM OF ATTRACTION

Attraction is a spectrum. On one end of the spectrum are the potential partners for whom we have no attraction at all. Then on the other end is our "dream type"—the ones we're magnetically attracted to and make us weak in the knees. These are the ones who ring soul mate alarm bells, who you might even perceive as superior to you in some ways. The ones on this extreme end of the spectrum of attraction trigger both our longing and our insecurity.

As stated, the immediate, intense feelings of attraction can easily be confused with love. They evoke all the anxiety, yearning, and excitement that make us feel high. The allure, fantasy, and heightened sense of arousal feel soooo good.

These are the ones you *do not* go for. But you know that by now . . . right?!

If I haven't made this loud and clear, there's a reason there is this intense charge, and as we now know, it's not because he's your soul mate. The ones who fall into the stage ten attraction level are of-

SPECTRUM OF ATTRACTION

ten rife with wounding patterns—your subconscious can detect the qualities that remind you of your own trauma. You also don't want to go for the person on the opposite end of the spectrum either, which some people resort to after heartbreak. Traumatized, they become so frightened by the risk of pain that they choose people whom they feel zero chemistry with but who seem kind and caring—because that feels safer. While it's true that some chemistry can lead to more chemistry, unfortunately, absolute zero chemistry usually results in a bland, asexual dynamic. The challenge with this scenario is that devoid of any spark, the relationship can quickly become stagnant owing to boredom and lack of passion.

Teresa AND THE PERFECT GUY ON PAPER

TERESA IS A SUCCESSFUL EXECUTIVE at a hedge fund in New York. Her therapist recommended she come to Renew after her breakup with Arnold.

"Arnold was super nice. Successful. He had an apartment, drove a Range Rover. We shared fancy dinners and nice trips. But I wasn't attracted to him. The first time we had sex, I had to drink a full bottle of wine beforehand just to make it bearable. I thought I could force myself to like him in a romantic context and that with enough willpower I could become attracted to him. We dated for over a year, but the attraction never came."

Teresa had a history of doubting her gut feelings, so even when she questioned herself about why she was in the relationship, she'd rationalize reasons to stay.

"I knew he was stable. I thought I could stay in control and create a good life for myself. I stayed partly because I was afraid of being hurt, and with Arnold, I'd never have to fully be vulnerable. I stayed partly because I wasn't being true to what I wanted and partly because I was trying to obtain this perfect life through making a decision that wasn't right for me."

Teresa told me during our call a few months after she attended Renew that she is now learning to listen to her intuition more. She has also started taking dance classes to get more connected to her body.

"I'm a lot more aware now. Recently I went on a few dates with another Mr. Perfect on Paper. But I realized my favorite part of the date would be when I was leaving his house. I would feel excited—'I'm freeeee!'"

While in the past, this could very likely have turned into a multiyear relationship, Teresa realized right away she was repeating a pattern and broke it off.

"Renew forced me to look at stuff about myself that I don't like. I started to recognize these behaviors and not hide from them. You have to face your shit—it doesn't just go away."

Amen.

If you've dated people on one extreme or the other and it hasn't given you the results you want, I challenge you: Stop going for the extremes. Aim for the middle. You might not get that high you've witnessed in movies or feel that familiar chaos of the passionate ex who "got away," but the option from the middle is more likely to result in a connection that is healthier and sustainable.

In my experience, people who only date those on the high end of their attraction spectrum are much more likely to remain single. By contrast, however, attraction to people in the middle of our spectrum is rarely immediate; it usually takes more time to get a sense of how interested we really are in such people.

Dr. Ken Page

By changing where you aim, you change your expectations. And this alone can be a game changer. You stop basing mate potentiality on an immediate I-want-to-rip-your-clothes-off chemistry and become open to exploring the you-seem-interesting-let's-get-to-know-each-other-more chemistry. You stop writing people off because they don't intoxicate you, because you've stopped confusing intensity and angst as a foundation for lasting love.

WHO'S RUNNING YOUR COMPANY?

We have standards and guidelines when it comes to our professional lives, but often when it comes to our romantic relationships, our method for screening goes out the window. To drive home this point, Coach Trish asks the women at Renew if any of them have ever had to hire someone. Karen's hand is the first to go up.

Trish asks Karen, "When you're looking to hire someone, what does the candidate bring?"

"A résumé," Karen answers.

"Exactly. And what are you looking for on that résumé?"

"Their experience and work history. Basically I want to know if they're qualified for the job."

"So what happens if someone comes to the interview and you notice they haven't had a job for over a few months? Or they don't have any qualifications or the skill set you're looking for? What do you do?"

Karen chuckles. "Uh, I'd say bye!"

"Yes! If someone comes for a job interview and doesn't meet the criteria for the role, you'd say, 'Thanks, but this isn't the right fit.' Now, do you use the same diligence you do when hiring as you do when you're dating? If someone doesn't meet the qualities that are important to you, do you still pursue them?"

"Ugh. You're right. I have such high standards when I'm hiring, and I don't even own the company! But with my love life, it's like I'm willing to accept anyone who walks in the door," Karen says, and sighs.

The rest of the women can relate. There are murmurs of "I do this all the time" and "This is so true."

"Why are we so clear and strict on hiring the right person for a company that we work for, but when it comes to our personal lives, we have no guidelines for who we let into the most intimate parts of our lives?"

We need to be clear on what we want in a partner, and it starts by getting honest and realistic about our needs.

WHAT DO YOU ~~WANT~~ *NEED*?

Hand it over.

I'm talking about your list.

Either on paper or in your head, it exists somewhere. The list that specifies your dream partner's height, job, status, and preferred brand of jeans. With the visualization of how this perfect person looks, you may think that you're closer to manifesting him into reality. Perhaps you'll lock eyes with him across a crowded room and just "know." Unfortunately, while this rom-com scene seems super dreamy, this well-crafted notion may be the very thing that's blocking you from meeting your match. A few scenarios will play out if you're stubbornly holding out for the perfect-on-paper person:

- You meet someone who resembles the idea of your perfect type and become so attached to making him "the one" that you ignore the reality of who he really is.

- You narrow your focus so much that you do not notice men whom you might actually be compatible with.

- You get into a relationship with someone even though your intuition tells you not to, simply because he checks all the boxes.

The quicker you throw out your list of superficial qualities, the quicker you will have a real chance at meeting the right match—for you. And how this person comes packaged may look completely different from what you thought you wanted.

Our friend Priya from chapter two shared the list she wrote in her journal when she was twenty-five and also the one she wrote at thirty-five:

Priya's List
(written at age twenty-five)

- Tall
- Muscular and athletic
- Handsome
- Rich
- Great career
- Well educated
- Well traveled
- Dresses well
- Romantic
- Owns property

Priya's List
(written at age thirty-five)

- Kind
- Compassionate
- Generous
- Intelligent
- Curious
- A great listener
- High integrity
- Spiritual (or committed to doing self-work)
- Takes care of his health

"Looks for me are last on my list now, as I'm more attracted to someone's energy, smell, and hygiene," Priya says with a laugh. "If I'm totally honest, I still struggle with the money part. I know that a rich guy won't make me happy, but I still want a guy who is at least equal to me in finances."

Priya is currently dating someone who is much older than her maximum age preference specified on dating apps. She met Nick, a man eighteen years older, through work. While he's not her typical type, he's fun, and they have a good time together.

"I would have never imagined dating a guy that's so much older than me. I don't know what will happen, but right now I'm having fun, and he's super sweet, so I'm just going to keep going."

Nick would have never made the cut if Priya hadn't listened to what she needed instead of what she thought she wanted.

HOW TO CHOOSE BETTER

We all have needs that are unique to us. Throughout your dating adventure you will meet many people; some of them might be amazing, but they may not be capable of or willing to meet your core needs in a relationship. For example, I need healthy, consistent communication (which comes from high emotional intelligence). This is a nonnegotiable for me. There are other things that are preferences, but those are not the same as core needs. I have a preference for adventure in my relationships, but if my partner isn't so into exploring or doing wild, crazy things—that's okay. I can fill that preference with friends and community. A compatible partner doesn't mean you find someone who is just like you; rather you find someone who shares the same core values, where both of you can meet each other's deepest needs. Any connection beyond that is considered a wonderful bonus.

It's key to know what you need (and that this may look different from what you think you want).

As we now know, when our chemistry compass is broken, we tend to feel drawn toward people who are not healthy partner choices for us. And the chemical rush from that attraction may lead us into relationships (and to stay in them) even if they're bound to fail. To help us with our decision-making, let's take a look at our values.

EXERCISE 1: Choose Your Values

Do you have a tendency to stay too long with someone who is not right for you? Or do you tend to discard someone quickly before really giving him a chance? Are you blinded by chemistry and not paying attention to compatibility of values?

Try this exercise to find out.

What are the values that matter to you? Review the list below and on the next page and circle your top ten. Once you're clear on your values, you have a good starting point for the values you want in a partner.

Which are the ten values that are most important to you?

**Achievement/
Accomplishment:**

advancement

building something

challenge

competence

competition

creating beauty

creating change

creating information

efficiency

entrepreneurship

excellence

expertise

innovation

Justice:

autonomy

democracy

diversity

equality

fairness

leadership

teamwork

Courage:

adventure

authenticity

excitement/risk

honesty

independence

perseverance

self-expression

self-respect

tenacity

zest

Positive Emotion:

fun

gratitude

joy

leisure

play

Safety:

financial security

physical security

stability

Humanity:

altruism

belonging to a group

care

collaboration

compassion

connection

cooperation

country

family

freedom

friendships

helping others

kindness

listening

love

social intelligence

Status:

fame

getting recognition

influencing people

sophistication

wealth

Temperance:	Transcendence:	Wisdom:
balance	awe	arts
conscientiousness	faith	creativity
eco-consciousness	hope	curiosity
forgiveness	humor	decision-making
harmony	inspiration	decisiveness
health	serenity	discernment
humility	spirituality	exploring/research
integrity	time in nature	love of learning
order	wonder	meaning in life
physical activity		meaningful work
prudence		perspective
respect		self-awareness
responsibility		self-development
self-regulation		self-realization
tradition		

Write down those top ten values that are important to you in column one of the worksheet opposite. In the next column, rate yourself from 0 (not at all) to 10 (fully expressed in this value) according to where you think you score in terms of these values. Now, in chronological order, assess the last three relationships or love interests you've had and rate how they score according to these values.

How do your past partners score in comparison to you? Are you scoring above 70 yourself? If not, is it realistic for you to want a partner who scores 100 when you yourself are not there? For example, if you value generosity but you yourself are calculative, have a tit-for-tat approach, and live in a scarcity mindset, is it realistic or fair that you expect your partner to be generous when you are not?

Is each partner getting closer to your values or further from them? If you've typically been a slave to chemistry, the next time you evaluate if you want to invest in a romantic partner, cross-check with this list. If you find that he is scoring low on compatibility, save yourself the months (if not years) of a relationship that will eventually combust.

	VALUE	ME	NAME	NAME	NAME
1					
2					
3					
4					
5					
6					
7					
8					
9					
10					
SCORE					

EXERCISE 2: Identifying Healthy Love

Now, take stock of what unhealthy ~~love~~ relating is. (It's not love because it was never love in the first place.) If you're reading this book, it's likely because you've had a history of unhealthy connections;

hence, you now know that what you thought was love wasn't. Next, write down a list of what healthy love and support feels like. If you don't have romantic examples from your life, see if you can find examples of feeling love from friends or family members. Let's take a look at Sheena's list. Sheena came to Renew Breakup Bootcamp months after her divorce from an emotionally abusive man was finalized.

Sheena's List

UNHEALTHY RELATING IS:

- *Emotional unavailability*
- *Verbal abuse*
- *Criticism of every aspect of my life*
- *Calculative—taking note of every transaction (including $2.75 for the subway)*
- *Controlling (for example, I was not allowed to use "his knife" and had to buy my own for cooking)*
- *Not being prioritized*

When asked to write her list for healthy love, she wasn't able to come up with anything based on actual experience. She had no idea what healthy love was because she had not experienced it from her parents or romantic partners.

As a starting point, Sheena reflected on how love and support felt like when she was with her most trusted friends. She was then able to craft a list of her ideas of what healthy love could look like.

HEALTHY LOVE IS:

- *Patience*
- *Boundaries are respected*

- *Honesty*
- *Kindness*
- *Open and direct communication*
- *Compromise*
- *Stability*
- *Showing up and being supportive*

Sheena had to start from ground zero, piecing together what healthy love looks like, since most of what she's experienced romantically has been the opposite.

Now it's your turn.

Unhealthy Relating Is:

_____

_____

_____

Healthy Love Is:

_____

_____

_____

Start here. Embrace the difference on a cerebral level so that you can start recognizing healthy love on an experiential level. With awareness as the first step, the second step is to stop choosing people who show signs of emotional dysfunction.

As you continue adjusting your chemistry compass and choose partners who are healthier, you may run into another hurdle. You might meet someone whom you have both chemistry and compatibility with, but then face a blockage that renders you unable to receive his love. And it happens to the most giving of us.

NOT ALL GIVING IS CREATED EQUAL

Do you identify as being a giver? Have you had a tendency to over-give? When I ask this question at Renew, the entire room raises their hand. I get it—many of us have been socialized to nurture, to give, and to give some more. We take pride in being a giver. But what if I told you that your overgiving is actually a disguised form of taking?

There are different motivations for giving. Sure, the gift may appear the same on the outside, but it is the *root* of the gift that creates the energy. What motivates your desire to give?

- Do you give from a *place of insecurity,* where you're overcompensating to earn validation?

- Do you give from a *place of scarcity,* constantly running through the mental calculation of what the recipient owes you?

- Do you give from a *place of manipulation,* where the reason for your giving is personal gain? The gift indebts someone to you or gives you power or control over someone. You may even withhold love as a way to punish.

- Do you give from a *place of abundance*? You give out of love. Regardless of how the other person receives it—and even if you don't get credit—you give without expectations and without keeping tabs.

If the root of your giving is insecurity, scarcity, or personal gain, you are not truly giving—you are withdrawing energy from the recipient of your "gift." This is a selfish act, not a giving act. We've all been guilty of giving from an impure place at some point, and often this is done unconsciously due to lack of awareness. It's important that you start recognizing the real intention behind your giving. If it's not coming from a pure place, take a pause and reassess if you should move forward with your "gift."

You may have been on the flip side of impure intentions. Have you ever received a compliment, a favor, or a gift and felt uneasy, sensing that something was off? Instead of experiencing joy, you felt a sinking feeling in your gut? Or anxiety? This might have been a case where the person who was giving to you was not well-intentioned, and you subconsciously sensed it. That person appeared to be giving to you but was actually taking your energy because their intentions were impure.

HI, MY NAME IS AMY, AND I'M AN OVERGIVER

For the majority of my life, I prided myself on being a giver. Whether it was at work, with friends, or with romantic partners, I was generous to a fault and then ended up resenting those to whom I gave. I would conclude that people were "taking" too much from me and be left feeling exhausted and disappointed. But in most cases I was not actually giving—I was overcompensating.

Whenever I started to develop feelings for someone, I'd put my foot to the gas pedal on giving. I'd cook him multicourse dinners, pack him snack bags, and buy him thoughtful gifts. It didn't matter to me that the person never asked me to do these things, nor wanted them for that matter. I had so much love to give and I just wanted to give it! But all this giving had the opposite effect on my desired outcome of creating more connection. Either he'd start to pull away, or I'd start to feel resentful that my efforts weren't being reciprocated and anxious at the growing imbalance. One guy with whom I dived into nurturing girlfriend mode by week two of dating told me, "I appreciate how loving you are, but I didn't earn any of this." I didn't stop to reflect on his words and instead got defensive.

At the time I didn't realize that I wasn't giving because I had "so much love to give." It was because, at my core, I believed that I was lovable only if I was useful. I didn't feel that I was enough, so love was something that needed to be *earned*.

Today, as a recovering overgiver, I still need to pause before I fall into my old habits. There are times when someone does something nice for me and I immediately want to balance it out or even one-up what they just did for me. In those moments, I make sure I check in with my intentions to see what the root of my giving is, and many times I've had to stop myself from giving.

I'M A GIVER AND I'LL CRY IF I WANT TO

It's a lot easier to play the victim and blame someone else for your emotional experience. In the case of overgiving, you might resent others for not being appreciative or reciprocating. But remember, *you* appointed yourself to this role.

To illustrate this idea visually during a session at Renew, I ask for a volunteer. Miki, a forty-five-year-old single mother from Miami, willingly accepts and comes to the front of the room. I ask Miki to hold an empty glass. Holding a pitcher of water, I ask her if she is thirsty. Miki says no. I ask again, offering her water. Confused, she answers no a second time. I then pour water into her glass and keep pouring until the water overflows, spilling all over the floor.

"What are you doing?! Stop!" she shrieks.

"Well, I have all this water, and I want to give it to you. Even though you didn't want it, and your cup could only hold so much water, I had all this water that I wanted to give, so I kept pouring."

The room erupts in laughter.

"How often do we do this in our daily lives?" I ask the room. "We give to someone who may not even want what we are offering. But we have so much to give! We give even if the person doesn't want what we have, isn't ready to receive it, or doesn't have the capacity to handle it."

The room is quiet. The women sit with stunned looks on their faces. I hear murmurs of "Oh my god, that's exactly what I do."

Miki confides that at first she didn't understand what I was doing. But as a prideful overgiver, the visual demonstration made her think about how often in her life she overextended herself, often without stopping to reflect if the person she was giving to even wanted what she was offering.

THE RECEIVING EQUATION

Now that we've covered giving, let's look at the other side of the equation: receiving. Check any that apply:

- I am uncomfortable counting on others to meet my needs.

- I do not ask for anything from anyone.

- I feel shame around having needs or being needy.

- When I'm presented with a gift (psychological, spiritual, or physical), I don't feel comfortable accepting, because I am afraid I will be indebted to the person or I doubt their intentions for giving to me.

- I feel resentful of others for taking too much from me.

- I feel that my tank is often empty from tending to the needs of everyone else.

- I find myself overinvesting in relationships.

- If someone gives to me, I feel the need to balance it out immediately or give even more back.

- I'm uncomfortable when someone compliments me.

If you answered yes to any of these scenarios, it's possible you have a blockage in receiving and subconscious defense mechanisms that prevent you from receiving openly.

Giving and receiving are part of the same circuit—polarities of the same continuum. You can't have one without the other. You may have the belief that it's generous to give, and it is, but you also need to add the belief that it's generous to receive. If you do not receive, you rob someone else's ability to complete the circuit and the flow between you two stops.

One of the reasons you may have difficulty receiving is because you may be confusing receiving with taking. There's a negative connotation to being a taker, one you don't want to be associated with. It's important you understand the difference between the two.

Takers "take" without any intention of giving in return—well, unless there's something in it for them.

Receivers, on the other hand, don't have agendas or think in a transactional way. Instead, they understand the energy flow that happens between two people when giving and receiving occurs, with a consciousness established in abundance and love, not lack. A person receiving accepts what's being given because she believes she is worthy of receiving.

Some additional explanations as to why you may be resistant to receiving:

- **You want to control.** As we discussed, to receive means to become vulnerable, and vulnerability can trigger fear. Being in the giving position offers a feeling of control (*you're* the one doing

GIVING AND RECEIVING ARE PART OF THE SAME CIRCUIT—POLARITIES OF THE SAME CONTINUUM. YOU CAN'T HAVE ONE WITHOUT THE OTHER.

the favors, *you're* the one taking care, *you're* the one proving how indispensable you are). By refusing to receive, you think you're maintaining a power position, which might feed your ego, but not your soul.

- **Deep down, you don't feel worthy of love.** Your logical mind knows that you want and deserve love, but you have a subconscious belief that you are unworthy. This may materialize in the form of sabotaging healthy relationships and clinging to people who reinforce your feelings of unworthiness. Whether someone is giving you a compliment, a gift, or a loving act of kindness, you can't absorb it. You may develop the ability to fake gratitude, but deep down, you don't feel deserving of the love and support or the gift. You may gloss over it, deflect it, or reject it.

- **It's a defense mechanism to keep yourself from getting too intimate with someone.** For a relationship to deepen, there needs to be a connection, and for there to be a connection, there needs to be a flow of both giving and receiving. Think of it like a circuit: if you're only giving or only receiving, you're short-circuiting the connection. When you block receiving, you block connection, which keeps you from getting close and intimate with someone. If you find yourself having a hard time receiving, ask yourself if the root of it is because you're actually afraid of letting someone get too close to you.

HOW TO START RECEIVING LOVE IN ITS MANY FORMS

You're not going to swing from being an overgiver to an openhearted receiver in an instant. If you haven't been able to receive for most of your life, you're going to need to build your muscles for receiving. The good news is you can practice . . . and it's fun!

EXERCISE: Start by Accepting Compliments

When someone compliments you, do you deflect, downplay, disagree, or minimize? For example, if someone says, "I love your outfit!" do you respond with "Oh, this old thing? Got it on sale." Or if someone provides positive feedback: "You were great in that presentation today!" do you reply, "Ugh, really? I was so nervous and rushed through the opening."

The next time someone compliments you, resist your urge to downplay and deflect. Instead, follow these steps:

- Pause to take the words in

- Listen to what's being said

- Feel the love and positivity behind them

- Articulate your thanks and accept the compliment

Even if you don't want to receive the compliment, the first step is saying "thank you." Give yourself permission to feel the discomfort. The more you practice, the easier it becomes. Soon, compliments will even feel good!

EXERCISE: Notice Your Tendency to Give Back Right Away to "Balance Things Out"

How do you respond when someone gives you something? Is your inclination to immediately return the favor in order to keep balance? Your practice for the next week is to simply accept whatever gift, favor, or compliment comes your way. Sure, you'll probably feel the urge to give back, but resist and relish in the feelings of just receiving.

Remind yourself that you are worthy of receiving. In the words of Renew's tantra coach, Lauren Harkness, "It's generous to receive." Give someone the opportunity to give to you. That is a gift in itself.

EXERCISE: Make a List

You are now familiar with the power of cultivating gratitude and journaling. Using these tools, keep track of all the receiving you experience on a daily basis. This will help you notice how much you're actually getting from others and thus grow your capacity for doing so. So, for the next week, keep a journal of every time you receive something. This could be as simple as a stranger opening a door for you, a compliment from a coworker, or a favor from a friend. The purpose of this exercise is to create awareness around receiving.

EXERCISE: One Week of Asks

For the next seven days, your practice is to ask someone to help you. Depending on how comfortable you already are asking/receiving, you can ease into this by starting with small asks and gradually increase the size of ask. Here are some examples:

Low

(low commitment from the person who is helping, instant/completed quickly):

- At the grocery store, ask a staff member to help you with picking out the perfect squash.

- On the subway, ask a stranger for their seat if your feet are aching.

Medium

(medium commitment, requires some time/effort):

• Ask someone if you can borrow a book (or another practical item).

• Ask someone to bring a dish to the dinner party you're hosting.

High

(higher commitment, requires someone to make effort—what you might consider "going out of their way"—in order to help you):

• Ask a friend if she would be willing to hop on a phone call with you to work through a job-related problem.

• Ask a love interest to help you fix something in your home that is broken.

Balancing giving and receiving is an art form. As we've discussed, it takes practice and time: the discomfort of asking for what you want starts to fade, and being able to receive without guilt or doubt eventually becomes more natural.

INTIMACY REQUIRES BALANCE

If you can't give, you can't get intimate. If you can't receive, you can't get intimate. Intimacy requires balance to grow and sustain in a healthy way. This doesn't mean you keep score or play tit for tat. There will be natural fluctuations in all relationships, where you may be more on the receiving or giving end at certain times, but overall, there's a balance. And if that balance doesn't naturally ebb and flow, dysfunction will form, showing up in resentment, disconnection, and power struggles.

To dive deeper into how intimacy and power are connected, let's heed the confessions of a Dominatrix.

TAPPING INTO YOUR INNER DOMINATRIX

I'm tough, I'm ambitious, and I know exactly what I want.
If that makes me a bitch, okay.

Madonna

That tightness in your chest when he doesn't call. That proverbial punch to the stomach when he breaks up with you. That angst when you want more and he wants to keep it casual. That sinking feeling... when you know you've lost your power.

You know this feeling. I know it too. We've all been there.

The women who come to Renew certainly know this feeling. There was Kathleen, the feisty, funny, fifty-eight-year-old chief financial officer for a billionaire media mogul who kept dating narcissistic men. There was thirty-one-year-old Loretta, who sold her first company at twenty-eight and, a few years into her relationship, found out her boyfriend had a second girlfriend but still couldn't let him go. There's Tammy, who was raising five children while performing at a top level as partner at her law firm and, years later, was still obsessing about the ex-boyfriend who had left her. These are some badass women. They are all powerful and accomplished, but when it came to their romantic relationships, they'd surrendered themselves and turned that power over to someone else.

Culturally, many people believe that power is gained through aggression, taken by force or through exerting control over someone else. This idea leads us further and further astray from what power really is. True power comes from within. It's a mindset. It's an energy. You don't exert power; you live empowered. The former is fake—it's overcompensating behavior to make up for what's lacking on the inside. The latter is earned. Empowerment doesn't come from hardening; rather quite the opposite. It comes from being so strong, resilient, compassionate, and full of love on the inside that you are comfortable in your own skin, able to withstand difficulty without having to create defensive walls that block you from feeling.

We all have power. The key is tapping into the power within. So how do we learn how to do this?

Let's start with some confessions from a Dominatrix.

A DOMINATRIX BARES ALL

At Renew, one of the highlights of the weekend is when professional Dominatrix Colette Pervette leads a workshop about power dynamics. At first glance, you wouldn't guess that Colette's job is to help her clients play out their wildest sexual fantasies using BDSM (the acronym for bondage/discipline, dominance/submission, sadism/masochism).

Colette stands at five foot three inches tall, with long black hair and side-swept bangs that frame her delicate face. She wears no makeup and speaks softly with a calm demeanor. Throughout the weekend, she inconspicuously blends in with the other women and is best described as "cute" and "sweet." Little do the women know that Colette has a Ph.D. from Berkeley, is the recipient of a Bill and Melinda Gates Foundation scholarship, and has been a professional Dominatrix for fourteen years. You can imagine their surprise when during her session, Colette completely transforms from an unassuming, innocent-looking girl into the ultimate symbol of power.

THE SESSION BEGINS

Colette stands before the group of women in her typical attire of black sweatpants and T-shirt with the added flair of a lace mask.

"I have some things to tell you," she confides. "I was that girl who would starve herself and, when she did eat, would throw up.

"I was that girl who had every type of eating disorder. I would vomit in the stairwells of my dorms because it gave me more privacy than the public bathroom. I took diet pills until the age of twenty-nine, when my whole body shut down and I was pooing out blood for months.

"I was the Asian girl who wanted to be white. My mom gave me a Vietnamese name, which I was so ashamed of, I would beg her to change it to Sarah, something super normal, so that no one would know I was the daughter of immigrant parents.

"I had ideas of what perfect was. Perfect to me was being white. Perfect to me was being super skinny. Perfect to me was being rich. And that was everything I wasn't. I didn't realize that the thing that was holding me back from being perfect was simply the idea that I wasn't."

Colette shakes when she tells the group her story. You can feel her struggle radiating from her body. It's palpable. Some of the women have tears streaming down their faces as she recounts her past. They too can identify with her pain—of hiding, of not being enough.

She then takes off pieces of clothing, starting with her socks.

"Now, I'm ready. I'm ready to let go of the shame of my body and be comfortable with my shape. I'm ready to let go of the shame of my race."

She then proceeds to take off her black T-shirt.

"I'm proud to be the daughter of Vietnamese immigrant parents who risked their lives to come here in a boat. My mom smeared my sister's feces all over her thighs so that she wouldn't be raped by pirates. I am so proud to be the daughter of such a courageous mother."

Colette then removes her last piece of clothing, her baggy sweatpants, to reveal her full outfit: a black corset, a strappy leather bodysuit, and fishnet stockings. She then puts on five-inch stilettos and walks to the center of the room.

"I'm ready to step into my truth. I'm ready to step into my power.

"The name my mother gave me, my name, is Hanh."

She removes her lace mask and throws it to the floor.

"I love my name. I love all of myself.

"Why did I tell you this? Because we are all looking for our power. We are all looking for intimacy. And sometimes we don't know where or how to find our power, and so we look outside of ourselves to find it. And we think maybe power is in having that right job, or that right amount of money, or that right man. We have an idea of what power looks like, so we keep looking outside of ourselves.

"But power is in the truth that's inside us, waiting to come out. That truth is that thing we've been hiding. That shame we silence. How we alchemize that shame into power is our expression. And that becomes our power, once we let it out. It's by letting it out. It's by speaking it out. It's by owning it.

"The minute you can own your story, you can own all of yourself... that is your power.

"There is power in vulnerability, because when you can get vulnerable, you can get intimate. And the most important person that you need to get intimate with first is yourself."

Colette explains that for the first half of her career as a Dominatrix, she appeared to be a woman of power on the outside but didn't feel powerful on the inside. She led a double life—hiding her profession from her parents and certain friends who she was afraid would judge or reject her. But the truth was going to come out one way or another, and one day, her sister exposed her to their parents. Her sister told their parents Colette's secret, painting a grim picture of how Colette was putting herself in danger. This created a huge rift in the family, and Colette's parents demanded she quit her job. Colette refused and decided that from that moment on she was going to start telling the truth. She went on a quest to confront her shame and began a five-year journey of self-exploration to learn to first accept and then love herself. She went on dozens of silent retreats, immersed herself in spiritual study, explored various plant medicine ceremonies, and launched a disciplined practice of self-care, along with a daily meditation practice. Each time she felt intense emotion, she would sit with it, explore it, and learn from it.

Who would have thought—a Dominatrix, the ultimate symbol of a woman in power, only became truly powerful when that power came from inside out, not outside in?

Watching Colette morph from a quiet, soft-spoken introvert into a ball-busting (no pun intended) leather-clad Dominatrix delivering an important lesson to the women at Renew is very powerful. She teaches that change can happen in an instant—that inner Domme lives inside each and every one of us, waiting to be unleashed. The decision to embrace her is yours.

POWER IS TRUTH. TRUTH IS POWER.

Colette shows the women that by accepting all parts of herself, including the aspects that she felt shame around, she discovered her truth. Standing in her truth is where she found her power. Power is not something you can outsource, because the minute you do, you lose it. When you base your validation, your love, your sense of happiness, or your self-esteem on anything outside of yourself, you lose your power.

Think about how you feel when you're very hungry. You're more likely to eat junk food or whatever you can get your hands on fastest in these moments, to alleviate the discomfort. But if you're well nourished, you are much more selective in choosing what you want to eat. You're not just trying to alleviate the pain of hunger as fast as you possibly can; you're choosing to honor your body.

Relationships are no different. If you're starving for attention, love, or validation, you become desperate and needy, and other people can sense it. When you are desperate you do not have power.

Colette's profession consists of a transaction where the roles of her as a Dominant and her client as a submissive are clearly defined. A submissive seeks her services so that he can consciously give up his power. He has fantasies of what she will do to him and how he will feel. Typically, these men are highly dominant in their daily lives, and in the hands (or cuffs) of Colette, they get to experience not having to control, not having to decide, not having to give directions. They can, for those few hours, surrender and feel the satisfaction of having their fantasies met.

This dynamic is no different from when you go on a date and immediately start checking off boxes because the guy fits a fantasy you have been conjuring in your mind. When you leave the present and start to fast-forward into the future, attaching him to how he's supposed to make you feel—desirable, loved, special—you've become the submissive. The more you hope for your fantasy to come true, the more you blur reality with projection, the more you create expectations—the more power you relinquish.

What's different is that in the case of Colette, her clients pay her to play the part of fantasy dealer. And once the session is over, both Colette and her client go back to their regular lives. But when we date and begin to attach our fantasies, expectations, and projections to a partner, the relinquishing of power is neither conscious nor consensual.

Colette distinguishes two types of fantasies: ones that disempower you and ones that empower you. Disempowering fantasies are centered around people or situations that are out of your control. These include wishing for the past to be different, getting stuck in what your ex should have done differently, or hoping your ex will change his mind.

Empowering fantasies are ones where you have full control to actualize. These could be in the form of a goal, developing mastery in a skill or hobby, or writing that book you always dreamed of. She suggests that if you're stuck in a loop with a disempowering fantasy, examine it closely, identify the unmet need, and try to meet it yourself.

The fantasies and projections we associate with others can help us discover our unmet needs. Your fantasies live outside of you and reveal insightful information about the feelings, emotions, desires, wants, and needs that have been suppressed or ignored.

Colette encourages the women to practice exploring the reality of the situation when fantasies arise. "There's a fruitful way to engage with our fantasies, by examining them and trying to understand their roots and finding ways to fulfill those needs positively (practicing self-love and care). There's also an unfruitful way to engage with our fantasies, which is to get lost in them and addictively feed off their feel-good chemicals, to chase them or try to re-create them in real life (i.e., thinking we need that 'person' in said fantasy to feel this way) in order to feel good again. And that's what leads us to feeling powerless. That causes us to lose our grip on reality, which diminishes our perception of the choices that we have."

AUTHENTIC SELF

A wound developed in childhood is the rejection of the authentic self, and as long as we reject our authentic self, we are disempowered. John Bradshaw, father of the self-help movement, explains in his book *Homecoming: Reclaiming and Championing Your Inner Child:*

> When a parent cannot affirm his child's feelings, needs, and desires, he rejects that child's authentic self. Then, a false self must be set up. In order to believe he is loved, the wounded child behaves the way he thinks he is supposed to. This false self develops over the years and is reinforced by the family system's needs and by cultural sex roles. Gradually, the false self becomes who the person really thinks he is. He forgets that the false self is an adaptation, an act based on a script someone else wrote. It is impossible to be intimate if you have no sense of self.[1]

The following exercises will help you explore the different sides of yourself so that you can start acknowledging the hidden parts of yourself and bring your authentic self to life. The more we bring the shadows into the light and accept and embrace our many sides, the more we become an integrated, fully expressed, whole self.

EXERCISE: Bring the Shadow into the Light

Take out your journal. This writing exercise is to help you explore your shadows. Your shadows are the parts of you that you hide—your insecurities, your trauma, your wounds, your darkness. The longer we suppress and hide those parts of ourselves, the harder they become to access. Sometimes, in a subconscious effort to restore balance, those parts express themselves in unhealthy ways. Let's bring them into the light.

PART 1: THE WARM-UP

As you ponder the following questions, look for common themes and patterns that you experienced growing up. The prompts are to help you explore how and why you adapted certain ideas around what you "should" and "shouldn't" be.

- What was the first/predominant message you were taught about sex and sexuality growing up? Was the topic discussed with openness, or were you taught that sex was bad or sinful? Reflect on the messages that you may have absorbed from your family, culture, and society around sexuality growing up and how that has affected your relationship with sexuality today.

- Who did you have to be for your mother growing up? Who did you have to be for your father? How did that shape who you are today?

- Are there sides of you that you didn't feel safe to express as a child? In past relationships? Were there parts of you that you felt shame around and had to hide?

Go to a blank page in your journal. Set a timer for ten minutes. Commit to writing without taking your pen off the paper, and let anything that comes to mind flow as words onto the page. Are you ready? The prompt is: "The truth I've been hiding is . . ."

As we've learned previously about shame, the more we hide, the more shame grows. Shame has power over us as long as we continue to bury it. To complete this exercise, think of someone you can trust, who you know will not reject you for telling the truth. Read your journal entry to this person.

PART 2: THE MASK

Did you grow up with an idea of who and how you "should" be? Whether this idea was crafted from the expectations of parents, cultural norms, or societal pressures, chances are there's an image in your head around this, and the parts of you that don't fit into that picture have been suppressed, hidden, or edited.

On the mask below, write down words to describe the person who you've learned that you "should" be. This is the mask you wear for the world—the "you" that is expected.

Next, write down words to describe parts of you that you've hidden, parts that want to be expressed. Maybe they completely contradict the side that you have been showing to the world.

Now it's time to pick a Domme name. This is your fully expressed self. She is all the things you've ever wanted to be, all your sides. Choose a name that encapsulates her. Using the outline below, write adjectives that describe her. Some of the words may contradict—that's perfectly okay! Be bold and unafraid to describe your integrated self, uninhibited, fully expressed—the you that is inside you, wanting to come out. Bring her to life below.

PART 3: VISUALIZE YOUR INNER DOMME IN ACTION

1. Recall a scenario in the past in which you felt you lost your power. What happened, and most important, how did you react? Picture yourself: How were you standing? What was the expression on your face? How did your voice sound? How did you feel?

2. Use your imagination to envision your Domme self. How does she live, express love, and connect to others? How does she handle rejection? How does she walk into a room? How does she get what she wants? How does she handle boundaries?

3. Now, close your eyes and revisit the scenario you described in number 1. How would your Domme self handle that same situation? Replay the scenario in your head, but this time, approach the situation as a fully realized, powerful Domme.

My challenge to you is to channel your inner Domme at least once a day. Maybe you're at a restaurant and you get the wrong order, and your "should-be" self doesn't want to cause inconvenience. That's the moment you channel your inner Domme. What would she do in that situation? Channel her when you need some extra oomph to draw boundaries, ask for what you want, walk taller, flirt with the handsome guy next to you on the train—any situation where you want to draw out your fierce, raw, sensual, confident, playful, powerful self. She's in you. You just need to let her out. She's begging you to release her.

STOP GIVING AWAY YOUR POWER

Power is not something you can fake—at least, not for long. Power isn't about how long you wait to text back or how aloof you appear in those messages; power is an energy that can be felt. Power is not about perfection. When you are operating from a place of fear or neediness—when you're putting out an energy that you need someone else to fill what is missing inside you—you are not in your power.

The previous chapters of this book have educated you on the wounds that create this type of codependence and have shown that as you keep working on yourself, you create a stronger foundation. This means that the more you become your own source of validation, love, peace, and abundance, the sturdier the ground you stand on and the more powerful you become. That is a work in progress; it doesn't happen right away. In the meantime, you need to find ways to practice standing in your power. I've outlined some common situations that may arise when you can practice responding in an empowered way.

Meet the Urge with a Pause

The second you feel that urge to grasp, to chase, to do something drastic, or to create finality out of a situation instead of allowing it the space and time to unfold—this is your signal to pause. Often when we feel emotion—whether that be angst, fear, or hunger for validation—the reaction is to get rid of that discomfort by taking immediate action. So, we distract, medicate with substances, or reach out to the person we feel is the source of that discomfort (or the medication for it) and, like a game of emotional hot potato, assign him the job of giving us relief. Of course, the person on the receiving end feels your neediness on an unconscious level and likely doesn't respond the way you want. Then that original discomfort grows and you become hungrier, more desperate, less powerful. For example, when you get in an argument with your partner, do you send a reactive email or engage in emotional verbal vomit? You might think you're trying to solve the issue, but what you're really doing is reacting to your feelings. You're trying to soothe yourself by seeking a reaction from the other person. As long as you keep reacting to those feelings of discomfort by outsourcing the relief to something external, you will not build your muscle for standing in your power. The simplest, yet the hardest, thing to do is to pause in these moments and do nothing. To get comfortable with discomfort is a practice, but an empowering one.

At Renew, each person receives a blank prescription pad upon arrival. Using all the tools they've learned at the retreat, during one session the

NAME: _____
TO CURE: REACTING IN WAYS THAT DO NOT SERVE YOU

℞

MD: YOUR FUTURE SELF _____
SIGNATURE: _____

women tailor their own prescription with soothing "medication" for use the next time they want to react. Using all the tools you've learned from the book so far—self-care, shaking your body for a state change, deep breathing—what can you prescribe yourself so the next time you want to react you don't give your power away?

Match Your Level of Commitment with Reality

Let's say you were unemployed. Think about how your state of being would be if you had two years' worth of savings in the bank versus two weeks. The former would enable you to be relaxed about your employment situation, and you'd likely take that time to find the best next job for you. The latter situation would make you more desperate and more likely to accept the first position offered.

Let's say you start interviewing, and one of the possible employers tells you they're interested in moving to the next step of the interview process. Would you stop interviewing with all the other companies immediately? If you did, all your eggs would be in that basket. What if you never got another interview, much less a job offer? Where would this leave you?

Obviously, you should keep interviewing with as many companies as possible and, until you get an offer, not cut off other prospects. So why is it that so many of us apply such a faulty strategy when it comes to dating?

Many women (myself included) declare loyalty (albeit in our heads) when we like a guy, even though there's been no talk about commitment or clear indicator that the other person is even as interested as we are.

"I want to keep my energy clear so that I don't mess up my chances with this guy."

"I don't want to hedge—I like to jump in fully and put in a hundred percent."

"I am naturally monogamous. I can't like two people at once."

Have you ever thought or said these things? I sure have. And you know what it got me? Obsessed over one person before he committed to me. I'd cut things off with people, stop dating, and laser focus on the apple of my eye, which would then accelerate my feelings and intensity of attachment to him. While we may have started off balanced in our feelings, the other person would unconsciously pick up my shift, and he would inevitably pull away if he wasn't ready to be where I was. This would leave me yearning for more time, attention, commitment. You know how the story ends.

The lesson here is this: When you start off in scarcity mode (i.e., that two-weeks-of-savings-in-the-bank mentality), you are going to be a lot more desperate and will likely take a bad deal and not negotiate your terms. You need the thing because you're afraid it's all you've got. No options = lack of power.

There Isn't Just One, There's Many

We've already discussed the myth of the soul mate and that there is more than one person out there for you. This may seem absurd—*There's nobody else like him,* you might think, and for good reason! Perhaps you've been in a marriage of twenty years with someone and reached a level of comfort you won't with anyone else; maybe you think you'll never meet someone who will adore your quirks like he did or whose penis was just so perfectly equipped for your yoni.

And maybe that's all true—you won't find someone who's just like him, but you will find someone who is amazing in his own way, and you'll find new, special ways to connect. Remember when you were a kid and only had one BFF? You couldn't imagine life without your BFF. I'm pretty sure you've met many extraordinary friends since then, who bring different values to the table and are unique in different ways.

Train yourself to get out of the "there's only one" mentality. This is helpful in love relationships as well as in work connections, friendships—all relationships, really! Thinking there is only one of anything will catapult you into a scarcity mindset. In that state of fear, you will be desperate for whatever you think you can get—even if that means settling for someone below your standards.

Build Your Abundance Mindset Muscle

Part of having an abundance mindset is knowing your worth and value, and that if you connected with one person, you'll be able to connect with many more. It's also about trust and having faith that sometimes, when you've done your part, the rest can be left up to the universe. Pay attention to flow versus resistance—this is the universe leaving you signs. Flow is a green light. Resistance is a red light telling you to stop, to not press the pedal for more gas.

Resistance does not mean you should exert more energy to get what (you think) you want. Resistance is a sign that a pause and a reassessment are required.

So how does this translate from theory into tactical steps? The next time you're upset and want to send an angry email, write a draft and give it forty-eight hours so you can reread it when you're in a non-activated state and can reassess. If you want to see someone and you keep hearing excuses, step back and let things breathe. When someone isn't showing up for you, remind yourself how awesome you are and that there are plenty of others who will appreciate you and reciprocate.

Stop chasing. The right one won't require you to catch him.

How to Win the Power Struggle When Men Pull Away

Boy likes girl.
Girl likes boy.
Boy pushes girl away.
Girl chases boy.

(You know what happens next.)

The seesaw of power dynamics in a relationship is common, and you may find yourself more often the "distancer" or the "pursuer" of intimacy and connection. The distancer responds to relationship stress by moving away from her partner. She wants physical and emotional distance from the other. The pursuer does the opposite, moving toward her partner with urgency to seek closeness, connection, and repair.

Men are more likely to be distancers, and women, pursuers. One hypothesis is that men are more physiologically sensitive to stressful stimuli and withdraw as a way to self-soothe. Another argument is that men are socialized to be less dependent, whereas women are socialized to be more affiliative and seek closeness.[2] Neither pattern is wrong, but the dynamic can become toxic when both partners become entrenched in their roles of pursuer and distancer.

Part of your practice of staying in your power is to not attach your self-worth to the fluctuations of the seesaw. Staying in the cycle only perpetuates it. Stop the cycle by redirecting your focus from getting him to respond and shift that energy inward. This is your opportunity to practice being more secure in your attachment and getting comfortable with real autonomy. If both partners can have compassion for each other's needs during this time of conflict, it's possible for the relationship to grow stronger.

Understand That Distancing Is a Coping Mechanism Learned from Childhood

Many people are reliving their terrible twos—a developmental stage where the child tests boundaries, bounces between exerting independence and acting clingy, and tries to communicate without having the emotional vocabulary to do so. How the child's caregivers respond can significantly impact how the child learns to deal with getting their needs met. The child may learn that throwing tantrums is the only way to have their needs attended to, or they may withdraw in shame when scolded. These repeated reactions eventually turn into patterns that become their default programming of dealing with conflict, uncomfortable emotions, and confrontation as an adult.

If your partner is distancing, remember that it's not personal and have compassion that he's likely acting out his wounding from childhood. Find a time when you're both feeling connected to have a conversation about your different communication styles. The timing of this conversation is key—you don't want to have it when you're in the midst of a fight. When you are both in a calm state, you can converse without being defensive and guarded, and you can come up with a plan for how to communicate more effectively the next time a moment of disconnection occurs.

Do Not Scold

If you feel provoked by his distance and react by scolding, demanding, or criticizing, the man will stonewall, shut down, or pull away even more, according to leading marital researcher and author Dr. John Gottman.[3]

One theory as to why this occurs is that men are sensitive to being attacked because they have retained the wiring of prehistoric times, when they were constantly on alert for predators. The defense and survival skills were fight or flight. Thousands of years later, men still have this wiring, and when they have an emotionally charged discussion, the same stress hormones flood their systems. Too much emotion creates a physical response—"I have to get out of here"—and he will run from intimacy to create distance.

According to Dr. Shelley Taylor, a psychology professor at the University of California, Los Angeles, women have a different response to stress; they are more likely to "tend and befriend." This response is encouraged by the female reproductive hormone oxytocin and endorphins, which are released in women when feeling stress.[4] Scolding can be received as an attack, and you want to be associated with safety—the opposite of danger.

Step Out of the Game or Change It

During the beginning phase of courtship, you may find that contact, effort, and making time for each other are reciprocal. Or you may experience being pursued, and the overwhelming amount of attention and recognition set your expectations for what you think is going to be the norm. But right when you're comfortable in this newfound cadence of pleasure, he starts to pull away. The inconsistency creates anxiety and you try to pull away. Once you do, guess who comes back? Maybe in the form of an Instagram comment, a sweet text, or a full-blown love bombing. Your partner reengages and you're back to a state of elation. Maybe the previous drop-off was just a blip, you think. Until he does it again. Hot. Cold. Repeat. The cycle keeps going and going, until you decide to stop playing, like for *real* real.

You need to determine if this is in fact a "blip" or if it's a chronic pattern.

A blip is when your partner is emotionally invested and has the intention of growing the connection, but is scared. You can tell the difference if he's willing to communicate and have an open conversation around the fear he's experiencing. With communication and compassion, your connection will continue to move forward. A chronic pattern, on the other hand, reverts to the cold phase as the norm, where he provides bread crumbs of intermittent hope—just enough to keep you from starving, but never full. Whether he's consciously or unconsciously doing this, the root of the hot/cold behavior is control. With him controlling the pressure valve, he can feel the love and connection when he wants and dial it back without getting hurt. When it's a chronic pattern, the only way to stop the cycle is to get out of it. You're worthy of a relationship that doesn't keep you guessing all the time, and the longer you continue feeling like love is just beyond your grasp, the more desperate and disempowered you get.

But—But . . . He's Amaaaazing

If you're dating someone who you think is absolutely amazing but you feel far from amazing because he doesn't prioritize you, pushes you away, or disappears for chunks of time, here's a news flash: he's not amazing *for you*. I have no doubt the guy is awesome—maybe he's handsome, successful, and rescues dogs in his spare time. That's great! But what matters in a partnership is that he is amazing *to you* and *for you*. See the difference? His being amazing in isolation does not matter.

Inconsistency is not amazing. Lack of follow-through is not amazing. Showing up in a loving way only when it's convenient for his schedule is not amazing. He's likely not a bad person, but if someone is not available, ready, and willing, the amount of energy you will need to exert to convince him to want something he does not is going to be exhausting for you. And it isn't going to work.

Get Grounded. Redirect Your Attention.

If you're in the cold phase of this cycle, you might feel powerless. I can empathize with how uncomfortable this is. But this is where you get an opportunity to practice standing in your power. That's right—you get to practice staying grounded and remembering your worth, regardless of how the other person is showing up. Right now, your attention is flowing outward toward what he is and isn't doing. This attention outward is causing your anxiety and helplessness to grow, leading to a state of scarcity. And we now know that scarcity means desperation, and desperation means powerlessness. You need to redirect that attention inward. Focus on what you want and need and what you can do to fill your own love tank. Repeat after me: *I am awesome. I am worthy of love.*

If someone is distancing, do not let this take away your awesome! Do not fall into the trap of analyzing what is wrong with you or blaming yourself. When those insecure thoughts come in, use the hacks from this book to get out of the thinking trap, self-soothe, and return to the present.

Another great way to redirect your attention? Tune in to your sexual energy.

REAL TALK ABOUT SEX

Sexual energy is creative energy. Whether you call it your sexuality, your sensuality, your fire, or your light, this is the wild, free, uninhibited part of you. Whatever your gender, sexual orientation, age, or background, we all have it; it's just that many of us are disconnected from it. And that's okay. But just because that sexual energy may feel a little dull or even nonexistent at times, that doesn't mean it's dead. It just means you have an opportunity to reconnect to it, which requires intention, skill, and practice.

How did you first learn about sex? Did your parents have a conversation about it with you? Did you stumble on porn? Did you get shamed for touching your genitals? Did you have trauma around sex? We all have a story about how we learned about sex, and unfortunately, many of us never received a proper sex education, if any education on the topic at all. This is why at Renew, we have various coaches from tantra masters to sex educators teach about the topic.

We devote an entire morning to learning about sexuality from Amy Jo Goddard, a sexual empowerment coach and the author of *Woman on Fire: 9 Elements to Wake Up Your Erotic Energy, Personal Power, and Sexual Intelligence,* who has been teaching about feminism and sexuality for over two decades.

One by one the women share their challenges around sex. There are overlapping themes of sexual shame—around their bodies, around having (or not having) orgasms, and around feeling the pressure to have sex like a porn star in order to feel desired.

I'VE ALWAYS THOUGHT of sex as for someone else. I never thought of it as for myself.

THERE IS A common misconception that a woman's orgasm is less important than a man's.

I FEEL LIKE I need to want to have sex all the time in order for someone to be attracted to me. This is what we see in the movies. Men want women who always want to have sex. I feel I have to be that way.

I THINK THAT by having sex it will make the guy stay with me. It's not about me and what I want.

I FEEL LIKE a lot of guys in my generation are imitating the porn they've been watching. It takes me out of the moment, and I don't know how to push back on that without feeling boring.

Amy Jo empathizes, noting that it's common for women to think of sexuality as a thing that is for someone else, as if sexuality is something to be performed: "First and foremost, your sexuality is for you. It is not for somebody else. You get to decide if there are people you want to share it with, and it's awesome when you find those people— but it is for you. Even when in a relationship, it's important to be your own sexual self and have your own sexual practices."

Amy Jo discusses the cultural stories around sex and how spontaneous desire is positioned as the norm. She jokes about the typical sex scene in movies, where you don't see any negotiation or talk about birth control or condoms: "Suddenly, we are naked, having mutual, mind-blowing, hanging-from-the-chandelier orgasms, and then we are smoking a cigarette and there is world peace. That is what we are told sex is supposed to be. But sex is impacted by our context."

She calls this our sexual ecosystem, which comprises many different factors, from the dynamic with your partner to your thoughts and environment.

"If you are distracted in life and multitasking all the time and cannot be present with yourself or with your partner, you are going to have trouble in sex too. It is not like we go into the bedroom and magically things will happen differently. We carry exactly who we are being in our lives into our bedroom."

Amy Jo's talk empowers the women to rewrite their scripts around sex, and she shares different ideas on how to do so. She hands the women permission slips, encouraging them to give themselves permission to explore their sexuality, honor their desires that may be outside of typical cultural norms, and embrace their authentic sexual selves. Some ideas she suggests:

Give yourself a masturdate! Masturbating in front of a mirror can be a powerful way to tap into your sexual expression, says Amy Jo. Plan a night of pampering and lovemaking with yourself. Use toys, wear something you feel sexy in, play sensual music, and set the mood. Create a sexy environment to turn yourself on!

Initiate sex. Amy Jo discusses how with couples there's usually one person who initiates sex, which can leave the other person "perpetually passive—responding to what is offered rather than going for what you want." If you usually are more submissive, try being dominant. You now know how to channel your inner Domme. Play with different roles.

Create a sensual practice. Remember, you are responsible for your own turn-ons. Too often we make it someone else's job to make us feel sexy. But what if you got into the practice of lighting your own fire, sparking your own desire, and awakening your own pleasure? Start with creating a sensual practice and explore what makes you feel sensual. Put on a sexy playlist and dance to it. Get some rose oil and slowly rub it over your neck and work into a breast massage. Stand naked in front of a mirror and touch your arms, your legs, your stomach. Adore and appreciate your body.

Talk about sex. Communication, negotiation, and curiosity are sexy! Have a judgment-free conversation about what your desires are, what turns you on, and what turns you off!

Learn about sex. Take initiative in your sex ed. Buy a book on the topic—check out the work from Amy Jo Goddard, Emily Nagoski, Michaela Boehm, Lauren Harkness, Regena Thomashauer (aka Mama Gena), and Esther Perel, to name a few. Try a tantra class, or go to a local sex shop and see what workshops it offers.

Make a yes, no, maybe list. Before you negotiate what you want sexually, it's helpful if you have clarity on what you want and don't want. What's a fuck yes? What's sexy, fun, and hot to you? What's a fantasy you want to explore? Write it down. What's an absolute no? Write it down. What's in your maybe list? This is a possibility, perhaps something novel and exciting, that can be explored in the right context. Amy Jo advises that if it's a maybe, it's a no for right now, because a maybe is not a full-on yes. When it's not a full-on yes, that's when people end up regretting their sexual experiences, letting themselves sway into a yes when it wasn't, and feeling badly after. This list is something you should review regularly. You might try something on your yes list and decide you don't want to try it again, and it goes on your no list. This list is for you. It's a tool to help you create clarity on how you want to play in your sexual playground. Use the template on the next page created by Amy Jo to map it out.

YES	MAYBE SOMEDAY	NO
Things I want to do or like to do sexually/ romantically	*Things I've thought about doing sexually/ romantically but am unsure*	*Things I do not want to do sexually/romantically*

Simone:
A THREESOME GONE AWRY

SIMONE IS A THIRTY-THREE-YEAR-OLD ENGINEER who had been in an on-again, off-again relationship for seven years with Rodney. He wouldn't fully commit; they'd break up, then he'd love bomb his way back into her heart. She changed herself so much during the relationship that by the time she came to Renew, Simone didn't recognize herself anymore. She feared he'd abandon her and would constantly change herself in an effort to keep him.

"Rodney was a very sexually open guy. While I only had two partners before him, he had slept with tons of women. I felt like I had to push myself to be more sexually adventurous even though I wasn't comfortable. He wanted to have a threesome, and even though I wasn't into it, he kept bringing it up, and eventually I gave in."

It did not go well.

"The threesome was with a woman he'd been with from his past, and the entire thing turned into a terrible, dramatic situation."

While the threesome debacle should have been a clue for Simone to stop doing something that she was not comfortable with sexually, it didn't end there. Rodney wanted to go further. He asked her to join a sex club.

"The threesome was just the beginning. Next he wanted to explore having foursomes, fivesomes . . . I filled out an application to join a sex club. I knew I didn't like this—it didn't make me excited or fill my spirit—but I did it anyway."

Now that she's out of the relationship, continuing with a coach and focusing her attention on building her relationship with herself, she feels a lot less stressed.

"It's very stressful walking around being someone you're not. It's like wearing a mask. I now recognize why I did it and how it happened. It doesn't happen right away. I was very much myself in the beginning, but then when I got invested, there was a switch, and then my fear of losing the person made me turn into someone else."

When I asked her what's different now, Simone shared: "The root of my patterns was that I didn't like myself, let alone value myself. That's now changing. It's empowering knowing the things I know now, and my hope is that when I get into a relationship one day, I won't cling on to someone like I did before."

It's been ten months since she's spoken to Rodney. She marks every month on her calendar to keep track.

If you've been outsourcing your power, validation, and sense of self to other people all your life, it's going to take some practice to stop, and it may feel unnatural at first. You can get there, and you've learned how. Now, it's time to integrate. Each time you speak your truth, create healthy boundaries (and maintain them), walk away from the wrong fit, and choose compassion even when you're hurt, you become stronger and more empowered. Soon, your energy begins to shift. People start to react differently to you. Your baseline changes.

In fact, humans have a natural instinct to be drawn to power. When you're feeling grounded, abundant, and strong from the inside, it automatically radiates outward. Your posture shifts, your tone of voice becomes more authoritative, the amount of eye contact you make increases, the energy you emit changes from "I'm easy to take advantage of" to "I have a high bar of self-respect and won't tolerate anything but kindness and honesty."

This entire book has been about working on creating change from the inside out, so that you don't have to fake confidence or put on an act to trick someone into liking you. Your power comes from within, and it doesn't change whether you're single, coupled, or anything in between.

This is power. When you tap into the source that's been inside you all along.

HERE I AM, GIRL UNTAMED

Be more demure. Don't swear. Men like girls who are feminine. Don't show your crazy until you have a ring on your finger. Make sure you look pretty. Make sure he feels needed. Don't cry in front of him. Wear makeup, but not too much. Be smart, but not too smart.

These kinds of messages have been ingrained in my head since I was a little girl—from my family, my peer group, society, culture, magazines, movies, television shows, and self-help books. In response, I worked hard to present the picture-perfect image of the woman I thought I was supposed to be in order to attract and keep a man. This was my priority. I just wanted to be someone's wife, dammit!

Intent on my mission, I would hide the parts of myself that were not perfect. God forbid I exposed to a potential mate that I could get angry or sometimes feel sad, or that I felt destroyed when he liked me just a bit but never enough. So, I would morph into what I thought men wanted: submissive, nurturing, feminine, and helpless but simultaneously independent without needs or demands. Oh and of course, a hot Asian fantasy too. All at the same time.

And when a man treated me badly or rejected me, I would blame myself, analyzing what was wrong with me or what I was doing wrong. *Get better. You're not good enough the way you are. You're too emotional. You're too intense. You showed too much interest!*

How many of you can relate to performing a game of emotional contortionism so that you could fit the mold preferred by the guy you liked? If so, you've probably been disappointed with the results. I know I have.

Lots of mini romances: intense beginnings, and abrupt endings. I tried listening to all the things I was told to do, and it didn't work.

I am now left with . . . just me. Raw, vulnerable, intense, vibrant, emotional, analytical, opinionated, feminine and masculine, me. Not parts of me cherry-picked like a custom-ordered salad. But *all of me.*

I'm done adjusting, accommodating, and placating so I can attract

LOVE WITH ANOTHER
CANNOT EXIST
WHEN YOU DO NOT
HAVE LOVE FOR
YOURSELF.
THE EXTENT OF HOW
MUCH YOU LOVE
YOURSELF IS THE
BAROMETER OF YOUR
CAPACITY TO LOVE
SOMEONE ELSE.

someone who can't handle my awesome. From the guy who didn't like that I initiated sex after our date because "that's a man's job," to the guy who told me that I was too analytical for his liking, to the guy who complained I cared about my career too much, to the guy who tried to convince me that if he were to "accidentally have casual sex with someone," it shouldn't end the relationship because he was emotionally monogamous.

I'm no victim here. I acknowledge I was an active participant in all these scenarios. I take accountability for the sucker I was all those years, taking the discomfort of these men as signals that I needed to change, to tone down, to be more of what they wanted.

Ladies, bait and switch is not a sustainable strategy. If you don't start acknowledging and loving all the parts of yourself—your shadows, your light, your bruises, and your scars—you will constantly be editing. You're the entire package, not just the beautiful bow on top.

You are not "too much" or "too little" of anything. Loving yourself is acknowledging that you're a perfectly flawed human, and that each and every one of us is a work in progress.

Love with another cannot exist when you do not have love for yourself. The extent of how much you love yourself is the barometer of your capacity to love someone else.

It's time to create your new declaration of love—one that doesn't require you to make yourself smaller, or more or less of anything that isn't authentically you. Repeat after me:

Here I am, girl untamed.
If you want to be my partner, know that you better be able to
    match my awesomeness.
Know what you're getting into—because my days of suppressing
    parts of my personality are over.
I love and feel deeply, intensely—and unapologetically.
I'd have it no other way.
I'm powerful, dominant, and wild.

I am both highly analytical and boldly emotional.

I'm not "too much" or "too little" of anything.

Don't think that you can be drawn to my life force—and then punish me for the very emotional range that gives me the capacity to touch your heart.

I don't need your money, your status—or to be your plus-one.

Because I've created all of that on my own.

I'm not looking for you to complete or validate me.

So no, I won't need you—but I may choose you.

I'm not looking to tiptoe around your issues regarding intimacy.

If you're going to dance with me—get ready to unearth those sides of you that have been long suppressed too.

Because I want all of you.

I will not tolerate your bad behavior or chase you if you run from conflict.

But if you're game, I will work through the tough parts with you when your inner child is freaking out.

I can't promise it will be easy, but I do know it will be worth it.

Go through the fire with me.

I'll hold your hand.

We'll dance through the pain and rise through the flames.

This is the type of love worth creating.

»— 9 —→

THE SECRETS

How a person seems to show up for us is intimately
connected to how we choose to show up for them.

Marianne Williamson

We've come a long way together. As you've processed the pain from
your past, healed old wounds, and rewired patterns and unhelpful
beliefs, you are now a different person. With your foundation strong,
your self-worth high, and an arsenal of tools at your disposal to help
you handle the ups and downs of life with resilience and empowerment, you are now ready to rethink your approach to relationships.
To do so, we're going to learn about the science of attraction and the
art of connection.

As explored in this book, lust is the result of a chemical cocktail
that, if mixed and stirred just right, can lead to a committed, bonded
love.

If both men and women experience the same types of chemicals in
the dating process, then why don't more of those hot, steamy hookups
turn into long-term, committed relationships? I'm often asked questions about the right time to have sex, and I hear stories of women
counting the number of dates so they don't "give it up too soon." I also
hear stories of women blaming themselves for having sex too early,
thinking that if only they waited, maybe the guy would have stayed.

There is no firm rule or an ideal amount of time that needs to pass before you have sex. Each person, each situation, and each context is going to be unique. What's more important is for you to be conscious and intentional of whom you're sharing the most intimate parts of yourself with—physically and emotionally. If you have a tendency to get attached quickly after getting intimate, then explore getting to know someone for a longer period of time, letting the bond and trust build before you dive in deeper. There is no one way, but there is research that suggests that men and women experience a different chemical cocktail after sex, which affects how they bond.

To find out more, I interviewed the biologist and expert on the science of love Dawn Maslar. She hypothesizes that women fall in love differently than men do, and it has everything to do with how our brains are wired.

HOW WOMEN FALL IN LOVE

A woman needs a combination of dopamine and oxytocin to fall in love. Maslar explains that this is a gradual buildup until she hits a tipping point, chemically speaking. After she has an orgasm, a woman receives a surge of dopamine and oxytocin that can often push her past a point into *love*-love land. Here's the play-by-play:

Girl meets boy and goes on a date. She has a good time, and dopamine is released. She's very attracted to him, so she gets a lot of dopamine (this makes her feel good, and she wants more). Girl and boy talk on the phone and she starts to think about him. Oxytocin (the bonding chemical) is released. They go on more dates, hold hands, and kiss, and more and more oxytocin floods her brain. Oxytocin is the neurotransmitter of trust, so she starts to feel more comfortable and safer with him. Now when they go on dates, without knowing they're doing it, they're staring into each other's eyes for longer amounts of time, producing more dopamine. There's a positive feedback loop where dopamine triggers more oxytocin, and oxytocin triggers more dopamine. The more oxytocin, the more she wants to be around him. The more the interactions are positive, the more dopamine is produced. All is wonderful, as these chemicals work in tandem. And then they have sex for the first time.

Girl orgasms and a surge of oxytocin is released. It feels amazing, and they keep dating and having sex. Then one day, even though they're technically still in the casual dating phase, girl can't stop thinking of him. She only wants him and his commitment. She's climbed the dopamine-oxytocin mountain up to the summit and has now fallen off the edge—she's in love.

HOW MEN FALL IN LOVE

Men also experience this buildup of dopamine and oxytocin; however, it doesn't affect them the same way as it does women. According to Andrew Trees, author of *Decoding Love,* oxytocin has a greater effect on women, while men also need a buildup of vasopressin. Vasopressin is often referred to as the "commitment hormone"; it's been linked to monogamy for males and also appears to make men more possessive over their mates.[1]

Maslar argues that for a man to fall in love, dopamine and vasopressin must build up over time until levels reach a tipping point, but this takes a longer amount of time for a man than a woman. She explains why: "First, men have much higher levels of testosterone than women, which blunts the bonding effects of oxytocin (technically speaking it blocks oxytocin's ability to bind with the receptor)." Some Science 101: when a neurotransmitter can't bind to a receptor, it blocks the neurotransmitter's ability to affect the brain.[2] Maslar uses this analogy to explain:

"A receptor is like a reactive site. The neurotransmitter is a chemical messenger. They work together like a lock and key. Imagine there's a door with a bunch of locks. Each lock needs a key for it to open. You can think of the neurotransmitters as the keys and the receptors as the locks. The neurotransmitters bind or attach to the receptors. It takes a certain amount of neurotransmitters triggering those receptors until they all are open. Once they all are open, the person falls in love."

So even if the man's getting the same amount of oxytocin, it's not impacting his brain as it would a woman's.

Vasopressin is a hormone linked to long-term attachment. It is needed for a man to bond and commit, but in order for him to feel the effects, the brain needs to have receptors for the neurotransmitter. The formation of these receptors takes time, and the process begins with the presence of the vasopressin, which sends a signal to the body saying, "We need receptors for all this vasopressin!" Same goes for oxytocin.

Here are two play-by-plays of the male brain on love.

Scenario One: Lust Turns into Love

Boy meets girl and goes on a date. Boy wants to have sex and this sexual desire causes vasopressin to increase. But she doesn't have sex with him . . . yet. So, he's thinking about having sex with her (vasopressin is increasing). They Netflix and chill a lot, and their cuddle game is strong (oxytocin is increasing). While he's eagerly waiting until she's ready to go to third base, his receptors for vasopressin and oxytocin are building. After a period of time, he's built up the receptors for vasopressin and oxytocin, which means when the neurotransmitters are present, they actually bind to the receptors, impacting his brain. He feels the bonding effects and wants to commit. His dopamine, oxytocin, and vasopressin have all built up; he's climbed the mountain and has fallen over the tipping point and bam! He wants to go steady. The beginning.

Scenario Two: Lust Stays at Lust

Boy meets girl and goes on a date. Boy wants to have sex and this sexual desire causes vasopressin to increase. Girl has sex with him after their second date. His vasopressin and oxytocin rise after orgasm but so does his testosterone, so it blunts the effects of the bonding neurotransmitters. The day after, his feelings for her remain the same, while hers have skyrocketed. Girl starts to like boy more and more each time they have sex. After a few months, girl is in love and wants to be exclusive, but he doesn't. The end.

BLAME IT ON THE ORGASM

We now know that when two people have sex, a host of chemical changes occur. Men get a jolt of testosterone during orgasm, which suppresses oxytocin. They also get a rush of dopamine, which is the addictive pleasure hormone (translation: they want more sex, but not necessarily with the same person). Women also get a jolt, but because they don't get that same surge of testosterone, they are left with the bonding effects.

For women, during an orgasm, there is a surge of oxytocin in the brain. It is what makes us want to cuddle and bond, breaks down emotional barriers, lowers our defenses, and increases our levels of trust and empathy. Women produce way more of it than men and will often mimic feelings of attachment whether that attachment is reciprocated or not. When he's not around and she's not producing as much oxytocin, her body will crave him.

A woman's body often can't tell the difference between whether she is having casual sex or mating with the love of her life: the same hormones are being released and suppressed regardless. If you're having sex with someone who has marriage potential, this is nature working for you; sex is helping the bonding process with that person.

But if your intention is to keep it hookup-cool, don't be surprised if you get the feels for the person afterward. Women are more likely to regret a hookup and experience shame afterward.[3] Dr. Helen Fisher warns, "Don't copulate with people you don't want to fall in love with because indeed you may do just that. Testosterone can kickstart the two love neurotransmitters while an orgasm can elevate the attachment hormones."[4]

So, although you're wired to fall more in love after orgasm, the guy is wired to have more sex. Oxytocin's a bitch.

FAKE DATING

> If the train doesn't stop at your station, it's not your train.
>
> *Marianne Williamson*

Perhaps the chemicals are to blame for the high amount of women I work with who are fake dating. This is when someone acts like she's in a relationship, but there is no commitment from the other side. It can be tricky to spot, because consciously she might say that she's okay with the casual dynamic and lack of label. But deep down inside, she's only accepting this because she's afraid that's all she can get. Does this sound familiar?

If you want a committed relationship, but have been casually dating someone for a year, hoping for something more, I hate to break it to you, but you're likely "fake dating." It's an all-too-common story of giving the girlfriend experience to someone who refuses to be your boyfriend. You give more, invest more, and sacrifice more, hoping that he'll eventually wake up and have an aha moment that you're the love of his life. I interviewed a few men to get the DL of what really goes on in a guy's head in these scenarios.

CASUALLY DATING MEANS I don't like her enough. If I'm not committing to her in the first few months when it's the most exciting and fun, it's unlikely I'll commit a year later when the honeymoon phase has worn off. I casually dated a girl for five years. She said she was okay with it, but in retrospect, I knew she wanted more. I'd break it off for a few months whenever she'd express it was too much for her, or when I'd meet someone new and have a romance. When that fizzled out, I'd go back to her. The truth is I never liked her enough to want to commit, and no amount of time was going to change that.

Peter, 37, New York

THE LAST PERSON I dated was a great person, a total package. She was kind, funny, smart. She was a model and going to school to become a doctor, and she did everything right. A relationship with her would have been great. I wanted to like her, but at the end, I just didn't feel it. When you love someone, doing stuff feels different. The annoying stuff is part of the package, but when you don't love them, the annoying stuff is just really annoying.

Leslie, 30, Los Angeles

A REASON WHY I wouldn't commit was because I'd sense a shift in her energy around building a fantasy, versus just being. I could feel that she was more concerned with the destination and label. It was more about arriving versus being. Some people want to climb the mountain to get to the summit; others love the climb and the summit is just a nice break. Societal pressures bake conformity into a fear-based monkey mind, and that makes a person fear losing things.

Bob, 53, New York

I'VE STAYED IN casual relationships because the sex was so good and because I like the attention and company. But I'm not that into them, so it doesn't move past casual.

Cameron, 28, Austin

If he tells you he's not looking for a relationship, believe him.

If you're dating someone, whether it's in the early stages of getting to know him or it's been many months, the feedback I've gathered from several men is that it's better to be up front about what you want. Many women are afraid that expressing how they feel and what they want in a relationship will scare the guy away. But in fact, what it does is give both people more data on the situation and the ability to make a conscious choice.

In an interview, Drew, a thirty-five-year-old bachelor in New York, shared that when a woman is up front about how she feels, it provides the clarity he needs to eliminate the gray area: "If someone tells me that they like me and want to explore a relationship and I like them, I'm ecstatic. It gives the reassurance that allows me to lean in and be more vulnerable, which sets up a foundation. But if I don't really like her or see a future with her, and I know fairly early on, it makes it clear that it's not okay to engage with her in a casual way."

The bottom line is this: men often "know" if there's future relationship potential fairly soon in the dating process. Generally, they keep it casual not because they are terrible people, but because they enjoy spending time with the person (and having sex) but don't have strong enough feelings to commit fully. There is nothing you can do to make someone have more feelings for you. Waiting it out, doing more, or trying harder will not change his mind.

If you express your interest and how you feel, but they don't match his, he's not your person. Move on. But if you express that you're into someone and he is equally interested, then this accelerates the connection. Both outcomes are win-win.

Karolina: SETTLING FOR CRUMBS

KAROLINA WAS IN a nonrelationship relationship. In her head, she was dating Ivan exclusively. In Ivan's head, not so much.

This was made clear two years into their "relationship," when he casually told her over Mexican food that he was excited about a date he was going on.

"He broke the news to me in the same casual tone as he'd ask me to pass the salsa," Karolina exclaimed.

Karolina and Ivan were friends for six years, and when he went through his divorce, they crossed the line from friends to lovers. This lasted for about three months. But after that period, while Ivan continued coming to her house daily, sleeping over, eating meals, and running day-to-day errands with her, they were no longer intimate. They didn't have sex or share any physical affection. At first, Karolina would make her needs for touch known and try initiating hugs or kisses. Ivan rebuffed her, telling her, "I just gotta get my life together."

"I opened my heart, my home, my body to him. And even when he didn't reciprocate, I didn't stop giving—I just stopped expecting anything in return."

Karolina knew that Ivan wasn't capable of being in touch with his emotions or deep intimacy. He admitted to never really having opened up his heart to anyone, including his ex-wife of twenty-two years. He confided that communication was an issue with everyone in his life, even his family. But his history didn't matter to Karolina, who thought that what they had was special enough for him to change.

"I knew he wasn't well equipped for a healthy relationship, but I thought he would learn how and change, because he'd think I was worth it."

Karolina thought their lack of intimacy meant a relationship rough spot—just a phase where he was figuring himself out post-divorce. She rationalized that she would keep being supportive and devoted to him, not mentioning things that bothered her to avoid seeming confrontational. This nonrelationship went on for another eighteen months, until that fateful day over nachos when he told her he was going on a date with someone else.

When Karolina told this story upon her arrival at Renew, it was a tale full of projection. She vilified Ivan as the jerk who betrayed her, who took advantage of her heart. But throughout the weekend, as she learned how to separate fact from fiction, she came to the realization that she was never actually in a relationship with Ivan. She had wanted him so badly that she settled for anything she could get, not wanting to discuss the truth of the situation because secretly she was scared she'd lose him.

A few months after Karolina's attendance at Renew, we spoke. While she still goes through ups and downs, she now realizes her part in the situation and embraces lessons she will take with her into the future.

"Having the tools I have now, if I were to go back in time I would have been up front with what I needed before we crossed the line from friends to lovers. And if he wasn't ready, willing, and able, I would have not invested in him the way I did. I also realize that because Ivan 'showed up' by coming by the house daily, and I never got this from other guys I dated, I would rationalize away all the other things I wasn't getting in the relationship."

Her tune about Ivan's character changed from him being a villain to him being a nice guy who ultimately just didn't like her the same way she liked him. Fact. End of story.

The truth may hurt in the moment of realization. But it will ultimately set you free.

REAL DATING

We now know how to *not* date. We know not to invest in people who are not investing in us, that chemistry alone doesn't make a relationship last, and that even if we get hurt in relationships, we have the resilience and tools to get back up, stronger and wiser. Now let's explore what real dating looks like, starting with some dating hacks that will help you increase your personal magnetism.

R.I.P., Resting Bitch Face

When two singles spot each other across the room and feel an immediate attraction, who do you think makes the first move—the man or the woman? Many of you will probably guess that it's the man who makes the first move, but studies show that this isn't necessarily true. A study conducted at Bucknell University revealed that men rarely approach women without significant eye play first. In fact, women had to make an average of thirteen short and direct glances before a man dared to approach.[5]

But before the man approaches, he will subconsciously engage in "space maximization movements," where he will use his body to make himself appear bigger and more dominant. For example, he may stretch his arms across the backs of the chairs, spread his legs while seated, or put his thumbs in his belt loops. These are open body movements that convey social power and persuasive personalities, whereas closed body positions such as folded arms or rounded shoulders convey a lower position in the pecking order. The study showed that men made an average of nineteen space-maximization gestures (all while sneaking glances at the target female to gauge interest) before he approached.

For women who want to enhance their attractiveness and increase their number of interested suitors, it's important to master the eye gaze. Psychologist Monica Moore states that no successful romantic encounter happens without the eyes meeting first, and she identified three main forms of gaze in the courtship dance. First, there is the room-encompassing glance, a five- to ten-second scan of the room (during which a woman raises her chin, arches her back, and sticks out her chest). Second, there is the short darting glance, which is targeted at a specific man and repeated several times. Third, there is the direct gaze that lasts longer than three seconds. Smiling while initiating the gaze is extremely powerful in garnering interest. Once eye contact is made, the dance begins. The woman's head and neck become the focal point, and she subconsciously draws attention to this area by flipping her hair or trailing her fingers along her neck. She might also laugh and nod her head, and adjust her body to face the object of her desire.[6]

Greenlighting

So, is it the prettiest woman who gets the most attention in a room? Nope. It's the most approachable woman. Men are hardwired to avoid rejection, so they are subconsciously looking for cues of how receptive a woman is to him. Approachability is more important than pure looks when it comes to encouraging guys to make a move. A study examining the effects of body language and attraction was conducted on a group of women who all had a similar level of physical attractiveness. The women who displayed more than thirty-five receptive signals an hour were approached by an average of four men, whereas those with less flirtatious body language were not approached whatsoever.

Single ladies, take note. If your body language is closed and intimidating and your vibe is unfriendly, chances are no one will dare approach you.

If you are interested in meeting someone, you want to be greenlighting signals all the time, meaning you have open body language and make eye contact. You appear happy and receptive. You want to be giving off nonverbal signals that you are open to being approached.

Being "attractive" in this way is a learned skill. This is not about how you look. The more you practice, the more it becomes natural and a part of your way of being. One special area of focus should be your eye contact skills.

MY GREENLIGHT BRINGS aLL the BOYS TO THE YARD...

SOME PLAY WORK . . .

When you walk down the street, try to look at people you walk past and hold their gaze. It's an extremely awkward thing to do at first, and you'll notice that most people will look away. But make a point to make eye contact and hold a gaze with all the people you come across, from the barista to the waiter. The more you do this, the better you become at making eye contact and sparking human connection. Eventually this will become a habit and you won't even need to think about it. When you become comfortable with making eye contact (and holding it), eventually when you do meet someone you find intriguing, you'll have the confidence to use your eye contact to signal interest and spark attraction.

Always Be ~~Closing~~ Connecting

The foundation of love is connection. Set your goal not on falling in love but on creating connection. The former is not something you can control; the latter is a choice you make every day.

Connection is an art form. The more you practice, the better you get and this applies to all relationships, not just romantic ones. You get good at relating, a key social skill. The goal is to be a people magnet, where people naturally gravitate toward you.

While some are naturally better at connecting than others, the good news is this is a learned skill. In Neil Strauss's *The Game*, a book chronicling the seduction tactics of pickup artists, he points out the main difference between those who fail at the "game" and those who succeed: "The guy who fails at the game is the one who goes out looking for women to make him feel good about himself. The guy who succeeds at the game is the one who goes out and makes other people feel good about themselves."[7]

Ta-da! It's really that simple. The first type of person is an energy suck, preying on the validation, attention, and reactions of others to fill himself up. The second type of person is easy to be around, exudes charisma and positive energy, and leaves people feeling inspired, comfortable, and joyful. Be *that* person. Not just because you're talking to a hottie—be that person to the waiter, to the Uber driver, to the stranger who strikes up a conversation with you in line. If you make it an intention to treat all people better by being present, curious, and kind, you will become a people magnet.

Here are some tips on how to increase your magnetic factor.

Be curious: Unfortunately, you cannot fake curiosity. If you're rattling off a bunch of obligatory questions to act curious, the other person will be able to sense your insincerity. If you're shy, introverted, or have trouble with small talk, that's okay. To grow your curiosity muscle, whenever you speak to someone—whether it's your local café's barista or a new acquaintance you've just met—play a game of "the one thing I can learn." Have a conversation with the goal of learning one new thing. This turns the interaction from a dreaded obligatory conversation into a fun game. For example, if I notice the taxi driver is particularly cheerful, I'll ask him about his secret to a happy life, or I'll ask him about the most interesting person he's ever had in his car. I've learned some pretty profound wisdom from the most unexpected of people in this way.

Be playful: You might think that you're too busy, too Type A, or too [insert excuse here] to be playful. Or you might think that you just don't have it in you. These are all limiting beliefs that are harming your magnetic factor. We all have little kids inside us waiting to come out to play. The problem is society has told her to hush, to conform, to stop being silly. We've got to learn how to tap back into our playful side—the one that dances, that looks around with awe, that imagines, that giggles, that doesn't take things so seriously. That person is fun to be around and being with her feels good. Other people are drawn to what feels good. So, how do you embrace play again? A good way is to take a class that allows you to express yourself creatively. Take a dance class and get into your body. Take up painting. Do an activity that has no goal or specific outcome other than to simply enjoy yourself.

Build rapport: Building rapport requires a series of steps that are often natural (you probably do many of these already). First, create comfort. That means you match the other person as much as possible in terms of energy level (don't go shrieking with excitement with five exclamation marks after each sentence when the other person is super calm and collected). Match their pace in tone and speed and mirror their body language. Second, make the person feel safe. This means that you actively listen without judgment (and no eye rolling, gasping, or exhibiting disgust). Third, let the conversation build. There's a reason people talk about the weather—it's finding a commonality. Start with an easy, safe topic that the other person can participate in and slowly build from there. Vulnerability is the key to bonding; however, you don't want to flood the person with your deepest, darkest secrets off the bat. Think of the sharing and revealing more like a flicker—you show a bit, he shows a bit, and you gradually go back and forth to build a flame.

VITAMINS VERSUS TOXINS

I have a friend named Devon, and any time I see her, I feel like I'm a better human being. She is curious and compassionate and can find the humor in any situation. Devon has positive energy. This doesn't mean she hasn't been through a lot of hardship in her life, but she has an attitude of gratitude and is refreshingly honest and authentic. Whenever I'm in a situation where I'm feeling judgmental or antisocial, I ask myself, *What would Devon do right now?* Thinking about her inspires me to act with more compassion and grace. Devon is a vitamin. She leaves people feeling lighter, more inspired and connected. On the other hand, I used to have a friend named Pam (I use past tense because I've intentionally stopped spending time with her). Pam loved to gossip and complain and constantly dominated conversations. If it wasn't about her, she'd make it about her. Drama followed her everywhere—there was always some new situation where she was being wronged. Pam is what I call a toxin. She leaves people feeling drained and stressed out.

Do you act like a vitamin or a toxin?

EXERCISE: Be the Vitamin

Think about three people you love being around. These are "vitamins," because they make you feel good *and* are good for you. Write down below what you feel when you're with them and how you feel afterward. Reflect on what they do to make you feel this way. Do they validate your feelings? Do they ask questions and listen carefully? Are they present? Next time you are with these people, pay particular attention to their body language, questions, tone of voice, and any other mannerisms that might contribute to the good feelings you get from your time with them.

Vitamin: _____

Vitamin: _____

Vitamin: _____

Think about three people you dread being around—the "toxins." You know, the folks who leave you feeling drained, negative, and annoyed. What are the three ideas that pop into your head after you're with them? What do these people do to agitate you? What do they not do that you wish they would? Do they interrupt? Brag? Dominate a conversation?

Toxin: _____

Toxin: _____

Toxin: _____

For the next week, when you interact with people, be intentional about how you're making them feel. The goal is to leave them feeling how you feel after you spend time with someone who inspires you. Employ the mannerisms and social savvy of those "vitamins" in your life. If you catch yourself exhibiting behaviors of the "toxins," notice them and stop yourself.

At the end of the day, rate yourself in your interactions. Just the act of being aware of how you want someone to feel when they are around you, and assessing what works and doesn't work can help you to build your social mastery.

Remember, being inspiring, radiating positive energy, and being someone whom people want to be around is a skill, and one you can develop. It is also all-encompassing and shouldn't just be saved for potential romantic partners. Put light out into the world, and your whole world will improve, not just your love life.

TRY A DIFFERENT BRIDGE

Love is not something we need to "find."

Love is always circling around us, waiting for the right conditions to make itself visible to us. We simply need to stop blocking it from our view.

Opening your heart and being vulnerable and comfortable with intimacy take practice. It takes even more practice if you've had a run of bad relationships. There's definitely a lot of work you have to do on yourself first. But there comes a time when you've got to put down this book, put yourself out there, and apply the knowledge you've accumulated.

Don't go repeating your old patterns of dating the same type and crossing the same bridges. I'm suggesting you look for *another* bridge—one that might lead to a new place, one completely out of your comfort zone.

The point of what you've learned is *not* to put pressure on yourself to meet "the one"; it's to get comfortable with expansion and possibility and to open yourself up. You need to be prepared for the next, better relationship in your future. Now, you are.

EXERCISE: Create Your Own Dating Experiment

Being "good" at dating is a skill. This exercise is to help ease you into the dating process so that you can have fun and enjoy the journey even after heartbreak!

Commit to dating three different types of people. The objective is to go outside of where you've always gone before—and to not emit a needy, anxious energy about the future. Your next three dates are not meant for you to find "the one." Your mission, should you choose to accept it:

- If you've never done online dating, create a profile and go out on a date.

- Get set up by a matchmaker.

- Date someone who is not your "type." Maybe he's shorter than your typical height requirement, he works in an industry you'd normally deem boring, or he's of a different cultural background.

LOVE IS NOT
SOMETHING WE NEED
TO "FIND."
LOVE IS ALWAYS
CIRCLING AROUND
US, WAITING FOR THE
RIGHT CONDITIONS
TO MAKE ITSELF
VISIBLE TO US. WE
SIMPLY NEED TO STOP
BLOCKING IT
FROM OUR VIEW.

- Ask your closest friends to suggest someone whom they think you'd be a match with and ask that person out for a coffee.

- If you never initiate, ask someone out on a date.

- If you haven't had sex in months, find a lover.

- If you're dating someone, show up one night as your Dominatrix self. Channel her and make a fun evening out of it.

- Go on a date with someone five to ten years younger.

- Go on a date with someone five to ten years older.

Add to this list as it suits your interests and willingness to be adventurous. Remember, you are *experimenting* and *practicing*. Don't put pressure on yourself to feel sparks or meet your future husband; avoid any of the angst-ridden baggage that led to disaster before. And journal your process—this is important! Reflect on your experiences. What upset you, and what inspired you? What did you learn about your needs, desires, and wants? What is closer to how you want to feel or how you don't want to feel? What can you apply moving forward?

LOVE IS AN ENERGY. TUNE IN TO IT.

Part of manifesting the relationship you want means you need to be vibrating in the frequency of what you want to attract. If you're closed, defensive, guarded, and jaded, it's unlikely you're going to draw light, abundant, loving energy toward you.

Energy doesn't lie. People can sense it, even if they consciously can't process what they are feeling. We are drawn to some people and repelled by others—and it is all about picking up on energy.

"Love promotes love," so that the person
who has let go of a lot of inner negativity is
surrounded by loving thoughts, loving events,
loving people, and loving pets. . . . Because all
living things are connected on vibrational energy
levels, our basic emotional state is picked up and
reacted to by all life forms around us.

David R. Hawkins [8]

You get from the universe what you put into it. The challenge with pop spirituality is that it's often suggested that if you repeat positive mantras until your face is blue, you'll get that million dollars, dream house, and Prince Charming. But if, in your deep subconscious, you don't feel worthy of these things, you're full of doubt, and your default state is one of scarcity, there is no mantra or magic spell that will make decades of negative energy disappear.

This is why so many chapters of this book have focused on getting at those deep-rooted beliefs, which have a ripple effect on your behavior, your environment, and the frequency you emit to the world. This book has been designed to help you create alignment between your conscious—what you say you want—and your subconscious—what you internally believe you're worthy of.

You can't manifest what you don't actually believe is true.

That's right. Manifesting is about believing, without a doubt, that what you want is possible and already on its way. Fully believing and eliminating any doubt is the first step, and the next step is experiencing the emotions of your manifestation as if it's already happened. You're getting into the vibration of already having something, versus the vibration of lack, of seeking something. To demonstrate how we can move beyond doubts and tap into new possibility, try this visualization exercise.

EXERCISE: Move Beyond the Confines of Your Mind

1. Stand up straight with your feet together. With your right hand straight in front of you, use your index finger and point straight ahead.

2. Keeping your feet planted on the floor, turn your body clockwise as far as you can and notice where you naturally stop. Make a mental note of where your index finger is pointing to—this is your stop point.

3. Drop your hand and come back around to the starting position, standing straight, with your hands by your sides this time.

4. Close your eyes, and this time, just visualize yourself doing the exact same exercise. Do not move your body; only visualize your index finger reaching out in front of you, twisting clockwise, and, this time, moving past your stop point and going twice as far.

5. Keep your eyes closed, put a smile on your face, and make a mental note of your new stop point and how much farther you were able to turn. Repeat the visualization one more time, from the beginning, this time with your finger reaching even farther.

6. Open your eyes. You should still be in the starting position. Now, do the exercise like you did in the beginning. Standing up straight with your feet together and your index finger pointing straight ahead, physically move your arm and twist to see how far you can go.

7. How much farther did you go?

When we do this exercise at Renew, every person is shocked at how much farther she is able to reach by using visualization. The potential for going farther was there from the start, but we reach only as far as we believe we can go. How often do we do this in our daily lives? How often are our limiting beliefs and doubts keeping us from reaching our fullest potential? Visualization is a helpful technique to move beyond the confines of the mind and into expansion and possibility.

EXERCISE: Manifest Your Perfect Day

Now that we understand the power of visualization, we are going to take it a step further and use visualization as a tool for manifesting. Remember, the key to manifestation is to create the feelings and energetic state as if what you want is already true—it's tapping into the potential that's already there, just like with the arm exercise we did earlier. You want to imagine that what you want is not something that you're trying to get but something that you're living right here and now, and to generate the warm feelings and gratitude that you'd feel.

There are two parts to this exercise. First, you will visualize your perfect day, and once you've mentally rehearsed it, you will write it down.

PART 1

Close your eyes and do some deep breathing to get yourself in a calm, relaxed state. Fast-forward to a year from now. Imagine you are waking up and you're about to have your perfect day. What do you see? Are you by yourself or with a partner? Is there sunlight pouring through the windows? Can you hear the sounds of the ocean? Visualize what's around you: what you hear, what you see, what you smell, what you feel.

Visualize your partner and feel the warm feelings of love and support you share. How do you feel with your partner? Imagine what the two of you are doing. Play out an experience with your partner that makes you feel everything you dream of feeling, as if it's already true. Embrace this feeling of love. Feel the support, the trust, the peaceful energy.

Now continue visualizing your day. Maybe you go for a walk or head to work. Go through the rest of your perfect day and feel how fulfilled you feel, how loved, how supported; summon all the warm feelings and be excited and thankful for the life you've created.

When you've completed your perfect day, open your eyes.

PART 2

Take out a sheet of paper or use your journal, and on the top of the page, write the date for one year from today. Pretend this is your journal entry a year from now. Recount the visualization you just did, and in first person, write down this perfect day that's just unfolded. Write it in detail, including how you felt. Summon the feelings of warmth, love, and gratitude while you write—just like how you write your gratitude journal.

We do this exercise together on the last day at Renew. The women are encouraged to revisit the letter and use the tool of visualization to bring it to life. On the first anniversary of their retreat, the women open up their journals and share what's come true in their group chat.

Mandy

MANDY CAME TO the Valentine's Breakup Bootcamp in 2018, recovering from a breakup with her first love. She was living in San Francisco at the time and had dreams of moving to Los Angeles. Exactly a year later, she attended her second bootcamp. She was in a new relationship (the one she was reciting her I-hate-you speech for in the car) and wanted to learn how to manage her anxious attachment. She brought her manifestation journal entry she wrote the year before and shared it with the group.

I'm sitting in my beautiful garden in my new house in Los Angeles. The sun is beaming on my face and my dog (a cute French bulldog) is running around, playing in the grass. I'm sipping my cup of tea, writing in my journal, and feel so peaceful and calm. My partner is in the kitchen making breakfast. I feel so grateful for his love and support. He's kind, generous, affectionate, and we have so much fun together. . . .

The journal entry continues to describe how her day unfolds, her fulfilling job in nursing, and the new community of friends she's created. While not every item had manifested, a lot had. She had moved to L.A., was living in a beautiful home with a garden, had gotten a dog, and was accepted to the nursing program she had dreamed of. A year later, on February 4, 2020, I received a text from her:

I wanted to share some wonderful news. I'm finally in a very beautiful, healthy conscious partnership and I owe a lot of reverence to the lessons I have learned from the retreats. We started working on our love contract yesterday and it was a very beautiful, safe, and bonding experience. He loves the values checklist and it helped confirm we're compatible beyond chemistry. So thank you for being a guiding light in my love life. After all the tears, this has been SO worth it.

10

HAPPILY EVER AFTER 2.0

> You can only heal a broken heart through allowing it to
> open again; a closed heart remains a wounded heart.
> Many battles may be lost but you are not broken and
> you are not your wounds.
>
> *Christine Evangelou*[1]

There's a technique in Japan called *kintsugi,* where broken ceramics
are repaired with gold resin. The cracks are not hidden; rather they
are accentuated, making the piece more beautiful than it was before.
Kintsugi can be a great metaphor for life. Our scars, our history—
including the parts of us that once felt broken—are what give us character and beauty.

You are not the same person you were when you started this book.
New seeds have been planted and will continue to grow as you integrate the knowledge into experience. It's important to remember that
the journey doesn't end here; it's actually just beginning. With your
newfound awareness, heightened consciousness, and an arsenal of
tools by your side, the goal is not to sit back and coast, whether you're
single or coupled. Keep doing the work. Keep striving to evolve and
grow. This is a lifetime journey. It's not about chasing the traditional
happily ever after, because that doesn't exist.

This book has taught you how to create a new version of happily ever after, one that has nothing to do with your romantic partners and everything to with *you*. When your emotional core is strong, you can handle ups and downs without falling apart, you stay grounded in reality, you choose compassion . . . you lead with love. Your sense of wholeness is not dictated by your relationship. You feel at peace, regardless of your relationship status. This is the happily ever after I hope you keep fighting for.

HEALED PEOPLE HEAL PEOPLE

I've made it my life's mission to help people heal their hearts. I believe a broken heart is like a deadly weapon, and if the heartbreak goes unattended, people continue to hurt themselves and anyone who crosses their path. The hurt has a domino effect. The same goes for a healed heart. People whose hearts are full of love spread love to others. It's a positive ripple effect.

The final step in your healing process is to help another person. The last exercise we do at Renew is to write a love letter to another woman who is experiencing heartbreak. The women are prompted to channel their inner wise sage and, using the lessons they've learned, write a letter of support to the next class of Renew participants. They all end their letters in the same way:

From one woman to another, you are not alone.

The next group of participants will receive the letters on the first day of the bootcamp. It's a beautiful cycle of sharing love, because after all, we're a connected sisterhood. And we are all in this life together. Your last exercise for this book, if you feel so called, is to write such a letter to another woman.

Channel your own inner wise sage, and write a letter sharing what you now know. Pass on your wisdom and let someone else know that even if she doesn't think so now, she will be okay. When you're done, snap a photo of your letter and send it to us! We'll post a selection of love letters on RenewBreakupBootcamp.com, and this way, women from all over the world will have a chance to feel the strength of other women through times of their deepest hurt.

A LOVE STORY

Adam and I are sitting in my favorite café in SoHo. Seven years after our breakup, here we are, laughing and poking fun at each other. He jokes he should have shares in my business and gives me advice on how to scale. I give him love advice on how to communicate better with his girlfriend. Oh, the irony of it all.

It's taken a traumatic breakup, hurtful words, and a lot of healing of pain to get to a place where we genuinely love each other. Our relationship was not a failure; it was a necessary point in both of our lives that helped us on our paths of healing and self-discovery. Today, I consider Adam one of my closest friends, and we both want nothing but the best for each other.

I believe that all the men who have come in and out of my life were important points along my journey. Each taught me a lesson and in that growth I got closer to a state of being where I truly loved myself. Each forced me to reflect on the childhood wounds and negative story lines I had accumulated through time. Each helped me realize that nobody has the responsibility or power to make me happy or fulfilled but me.

I've learned to base my happiness on the things I can control—my energy, my kindness, my ability to help, inspire, and impact others—my empowerment. With a baseline of joy and peace, life events and hardships may bruise me but will not break me.

Pain is something our society avoids. We stop ourselves from being open and vulnerable, from truly connecting with others out of a fear of trauma. But the emotions that come with pain—the good, the bad, and the ugly—are all a part of the spectrum of feeling that makes life colorful.

And when you happen to experience pain of the romantic kind, you can reach a place of acceptance, with a knowing that a heartbreak will not destroy you. You can choose to bounce back. And you will. That journey is empowering.

This leads me to the love part of this story, and no, there is no prince involved.

You see, this is and always has been my love story—and it has nothing to do with Adam or anyone else for that matter. Rather, this has been a story in the making for a very long time. All the heartaches, the lessons, the highs and lows, the various characters who have made an appearance—they have all been critical to the plot. Because it is through those twists and turns that I have finally realized that love stories begin and end with you. Anyone else who shares a part of that journey is an added bonus.

To know the risks of being vulnerable and openhearted, but to go ahead with reckless abandon in the spirit of creating something spectacular and awe-inspiring—that is courage.

To allow yourself to sit with the negative emotions that come from heartache instead of numbing out—that is strength.

To face your fears of abandonment and rejection without allowing disappointment to harden you, to get back up in the face of it with a blank slate and hope—that is resilience.

To know that nobody has the power to make or break your baseline of joy—that is empowerment.

And in a time when your heart is aching, to hold compassion for yourself as well as for the person who hurt you—that is love.

THE HEARTACHES WERE WORTH IT

When I was twenty-five, my boyfriend came home and told me he wanted to break up because he didn't feel "butterflies" anymore. This was after I bought us an apartment.

When I was twenty-nine, the man I thought I'd eventually marry cheated on me. The pain was so excruciating that I spiraled into depression.

When I was thirty-three, my boyfriend broke up with me, saying he wasn't sexually attracted to me. I'd later find out via Instagram that he had been cheating on me the entire time we were together.

When I was thirty-seven, I finally learned how to love myself enough to truly be able to love someone else.

To say I've struggled in the love department is an understatement. Which is exactly why I made it my life's work to understand this mysterious thing that can bring such joy yet so much pain.

It's taken a lot of heartbreak for me to learn it's not love that hurts; it's what we too often confuse for love. In retrospect, I don't think I ever really knew what love was. I sought love from others to fulfill what I did not have in myself—and that is not love, it's codependence.

It's been quite a ride. I've overturned every rock to understand the origins of my wounds and heal them. I've cultivated practices of self-love, compassion, and mindfulness that through the years have had an enormous cumulative effect on my overall sense of joy and inner peace. I've developed the discipline to pause before reacting to every emotion that pops up. I've learned to be comfortable with discomfort, to self-soothe, and to be perfectly content in my own company. I've also kissed dozens of frogs along the way. I've fallen and gotten back up—on repeat. There've been multiple times when I just wanted to close up my heart for good. Through it all, the one affirmation I've clung to is this:

Our greatest lesson in this lifetime is to practice opening our hearts, even when it hurts. Especially when it hurts.

Opening our hearts is a constant practice of choosing compassion over judgment, love over fear, and softening over hardening. Each time we choose to act with compassion, pause before reacting, or approach a conflict with curiosity versus defensiveness—those are all steps rooted in love. The steps add up. Love is the journey. The good news is each day is a new day, and you are empowered to choose which direction you want.

It took me a few decades to love myself and get to a place where the people I was attracted to (and attracting) were healthy and available. Gone were the days of tolerating bad behavior or chasing men who weren't into me. But even though the quality of men I was meeting was drastically higher, I still wasn't meeting my match. It wasn't until I had an aha moment after a conversation with a friend of mine that I saw that perhaps I wasn't as openhearted as I thought I was.

My friend Hugo is one of the most conscious, self-aware, emotionally intelligent people I know. We were catching up over tea one day, and he was telling me about his new girlfriend. He had committed to her quickly, and I asked him why he had made that choice.

"I decided to jump in with both feet and love her with reckless abandon."

Hugo wasn't doing this out of recklessness, however. His choice to fully open his heart and commit wasn't coming from a place of hurt or insecurity. In fact, it was quite the opposite. Hugo has such a strong foundation, a chemistry compass in good working order, that even if he opened up his heart with full vulnerability and it didn't work out, he'd be okay. His "house" would still be standing. He wouldn't break into a million pieces, because his identity and sense of self-worth would not ever be based on his relationship.

That night I reflected on our conversation. I realized that I still approached love with a gate around my heart. Because I broke into pieces after my past breakups, I had never fully opened my heart for fear of repeating the same trauma. Back then, I wasn't equipped to handle it.

But I was different now. If I opened my heart fully and got hurt, I would be okay. I am resilient. I have a strong foundation, tools for emotional regulation, and healthier relationship skills. I am no longer the codependent, anxiously attached girl who once based my identity and world around a man. The rug would not be pulled out from

OUR GREATEST
LESSON IN THIS
LIFETIME IS TO
PRACTICE OPENING
OUR HEARTS,
EVEN WHEN IT
HURTS.
ESPECIALLY WHEN
IT HURTS.

beneath me ever again, because I would never make someone the ground I was standing on.

I could love unafraid.

I made a decision to open my heart, to follow my chemistry compass that was now in good working order, and to approach love with reckless abandon, like Hugo. My energy shifted. Shortly after, I met Paul.

Apparently, a friend had tried to set me up with Paul before, but I had declined. I don't even remember, but it goes to show how closed I was. I matched with Paul on a dating app, and we had fun banter via text. On my way to our first date, I set an intention. I was going to be completely open, show up with full presence and curiosity, and have a good time.

We met for a drink and the conversation was easy. There was a connection—what kind of connection I wasn't sure. I just knew I was having fun. After our second Aperol Spritz, he asked if I wanted to grab a bite. I said yes. We ended up going to seven different venues that night. The date ended eight hours later with pizza and our first kiss.

After our first date, Paul deleted his dating apps. I stopped looking at mine but didn't delete them. I recall, after two weeks of dating, the thought came to mind that I should just check out who was messaging me on the apps. I thought about acting a bit aloof and mysterious toward Paul. But then I stopped myself. What was I thinking? Why would I punish this guy by hedging, by playing games, when he was showing up so beautifully? Both his words and actions were showing me that he was investing in building a relationship. I had to shake off the remnants of bad habits I still had kicking around, which were fear based, not love based.

I decided to continue listening to my heart, which was saying a loud YES.

At age thirty-seven, I met the man whom I would not only fall in love with but commit to standing in love with. The former is fleeting; the latter is a practice. The former you have no control over, but the latter you choose. Love is an action. It's something that is created with another person.

Looking back, I realize that each relationship, each rejection, each heartache, was a bridge. Sure, maybe I had to cross the same old bridge a few times over in order to finally learn the lesson. Eventually, I crossed enough bridges to get to where I am today—love as a state of being. This is love for myself that gives me the capacity to share love with another. Perhaps that's the greatest lesson of all: I was born with that love; it's always been inside me. No matter what plot twists I may experience, that love has been and always will be right here.

IT'S MONDAY MORNING AT RENEW, and we are about to have our last session together. The women are in high spirits, laughing and chatting before my session starts. We start off with a check-in and go around the circle with each person sharing one word to describe how she's feeling and a key takeaway she's learned.

"I'm feeling hopeful," Sheena says. "I came here thinking it was because of my ex, and now I'm like, 'Uh, what's his name?'" She chuckles. "I've realized that this is about me. It's about my patterns of codependence, and I'm going to take a break from dating and focus on investing in me."

"I feel grateful," says Jenny, tearing up. "The support of everyone here has been so incredible. I've got a lot of work to do. And I'm a bit anxious about going home and having to deal with it all. But I feel good that I have tools to help me."

"I'm feeling all sorts of things. Empowered, excited, scared," says Priya. "I want to let go of judgment and fear, which I think have been ruling my life. I think realizing I have an anxious attachment style and that's not my fault and that I can become more secure was big for me."

The women continue going around the circle sharing their experiences and key lessons learned over the weekend. There is a buzz in the air; they feel alive, bubbling with a positive force of energy. To witness the transformation of the women in just a few days is mind-blowing. It's this exact moment, when I see their smiling faces and eyes lit up, feeling empowered to make changes in their life, I am reminded that I'm exactly where I should be. This is what I was meant to do. As a last exercise, I take them outside, encouraging them to walk barefoot on the grass so they can feel grounded in nature. The sun is shining bright, and there's a cool breeze in the air.

Jon Hopkins's song "Immunity" is playing on repeat in the background. Other than the music, this is a silent exercise, and the most powerful. I set the guidelines for the exercise:

"We will each take a turn standing in the center and making eye contact with each person standing on the outside. Everyone on the outside of the circle, send supportive and loving energy to the person in the middle. See her in her fullest potential. See her for all the possibilities and dreams she has in store for her. When it's your turn to go in the middle, try not to rush and really soak it in. Put your hand to your heart if that helps you anchor the moment. Your only job is to receive the love."

Cindy is first to stand in the center. She's standing tall and smiling. You can feel the other women's supportive energy and how much they are rooting for her. When she makes her way through the circle to me, we lock eyes and I can feel her gratitude. She nods her head, acknowledging me. Her one look expresses a million words. I nod back and smile. I know she's got this.

One by one, the women take their turn. Some put their hand to their heart, anchoring the feeling of love. Not one is able to complete the circle without tears. But these are different tears. These are tears of feeling profoundly seen, supported, held, understood, acknowledged, and loved. I see each woman and recognize how beautiful, powerful, and strong she is. And then it's my turn. I step into the middle, and this time, it's my turn to practice receiving love. I make eye contact with Priya first. I can feel her gratitude. I can feel her love. I take a deep breath and soak it in. What an honor it is, to be a part of their journey and a character in their new story.

With tears still streaming down my face, nose running and all, I share my last thoughts.

"This is love. Romantic love is just one form of it. The love shared throughout this weekend, the compassion and empathy for one another, is love in action. You all feel it, you've all connected to it; it's inside you, it's in your cells. Hold on to this moment, and in the times when you need a reminder, tap back into this feeling of love. You are loved. You are love."

EXERCISE: Update Your Story

Chapter by chapter, this book has challenged some of your old perspectives and has taken you through different exercises in order to help you practice the skill of reframing. We started the book with an exercise where you took your ten-point story and refined it to five points, removing the interpretations, assumptions, and cognitive distortions in between.

We know how powerful our stories are in shaping our lives. My intention was for you to begin this book with one story and finish with another—a narrative that serves you now and in your future.

In this last exercise, review the five-point story you wrote from chapter one. This time, you get to add five points. You can choose to add lessons you've learned, perspective shifts, the meaning you've now derived from the breakup, and even possibilities for the future.

In this updated story you're not the victim of what happened. No, in this 2.0 version you are the heroine of an epic adventure. You loved and your heart got bruised, and that catapulted you on a journey to learn about yourself, heal old wounds, and shift limiting beliefs.

When you finish this new story, compare it to the original ten-point story you started with. What do you notice? What has changed?

This was never just about the ex. It was always about you.

THIS IS THE BEGINNING

Congratulations for making it to the end of this book and the beginning of your next life chapter. I know there were probably some passages that stirred up some uncomfortable emotions. It takes courage to look inside yourself, take accountability, and choose change.

You cannot change your destination in an instant, but you can choose to change your direction right now.

Without a doubt there will be ups and downs as you move forward. Becoming more aware and more conscious is not easy. But it's worth it. When your eyes open, you can't go back to the life before. Pain was your catalyst to seek change, and inspiration will be the fuel to maintain momentum.

Your life is one great choose-your-own-adventure story. You are the author.

All the heartaches, the hardships, the heroes, and the villains—they've all been critical to the plot. From the ones who let you down to the ones who touched your soul—that's character development.

Your scars add wisdom.

When things don't go as planned, when you feel lost in the ebbs, remember, it's just another plot twist. After all, you're still writing your story. Make it one worth telling.

Here's to your new beginning, renewed.

ACKNOWLEDGMENTS

First and foremost I want to thank my family. My sisters, Alice and Anita, who played school with me and taught me how to read and spell. Alice—your Save the Ocean cake and mango book initiatives really paid off. My mom, Mee Ping, who supported my Archie comic book obsession and let me pursue every extracurricular activity I wanted—thank you for your love and belief in me. My dad, Kay Mau, who supported my education and passed on his entrepreneurial savvy. My aunts Anna, Laura, Mirian, and Rosie, and my uncle Roberto, who treated me like I was one of their own and gave me a childhood of play and fun.

To my partner, Paul—words cannot describe the appreciation and love I have for you. Thank you for your support, for encouraging me, and for holding my hand during the hard times. Your love helps me stand even taller, and reach even further.

To my chosen family—you know who you are. Thank you being my greatest cheering squad.

A note of appreciation to Arash—thank you for being a part of this journey.

A huge thank you to Carrie Thornton. You were my compass while writing this book, and I am grateful for your vision, insight, and guidance in transforming this into a manuscript I'm proud of. Thank you to the team at HarperCollins for your enthusiastic professionalism in getting this book together—it takes a village and I'm fortunate you're in mine. Special thanks to Mandy Stadtmiller and Kimberly Miller for your support in editing.

Thank you to my agent, Meredith Miller, for championing my book; to Mary Pender for seeing the big "picture," and to the team at United Talent Agency. I'd like to acknowledge and thank Marc Gerald and Kim Koba, who first contacted me with the idea to turn my concept into a book.

Thank you to Neil Strauss—for your friendship, for encouraging me when I was self-conscious about my writing, and for inviting me to that dinner that changed the course of my career. Adam Robinson, thank you for your genius ideas and the inspiring chats. Matt Mullenweg, thank you for your loving support and for always cheering me on. To the Mupps—you've been a big part of my growth, and life is sweeter with you both and our adventures together.

Thank you to all the facilitators at Renew, who have poured their passion, heart, and soul into sharing their wisdom and being such an integral part of the healing journey for so many women. Shout-out to those who have been critical to Renew's growth: Kieran Swanson, Erika Laurion, Taryn Kristal, Jennifer Maloney, Patrycja Slawuta, Gina Marie, Maria Soledad, Alicia Marie, and Puneet Grewal. Special thanks to the teachers who shared their insight in shaping the curriculum and content of this book: Dr. Naomi Arbit, Dr. Erica Matluck, Dr. Elaina Zendegui, Trish Barillas, Nicole Boyar, Cynthia Dennis, Susan Spiegel Solovay, Lauren Harkness, Amy Jo Goddard, and Colette.

Thank you to the women who have participated in Renew for

trusting me with your hearts and for showing up so courageously. A special thank-you to the women who were interviewed for this book— your strength in transmuting your pain into strength and wisdom is inspiring, and your stories will no doubt help others in their healing journey.

NOTES

CHAPTER 1

1. Alice Boyes, "What Is Psychological Shock? And 5 Tips for Coping," *Psychology Today,* March 6, 2018, https://www.psychologytoday.com/intl/blog/in-practice/201803/what-is-psychological-shock-and-5-tips-coping.

2. Paul W. Eastwick et al., "Mispredicting Distress Following Romantic Breakup: Revealing the Time Course of the Affective Forecasting Error," *Journal of Experimental Social Psychology* 44, no. 3 (2008): 800-807, doi: 10.1016/j.jesp.2007.07.001.

3. Korin Miller, "OK, but Seriously, How Long Does It Take to Get Over a Breakup?," *Glamour,* May 28, 2019, https://www.glamour.com/story/how-long-should-it-take-to-get-over-my-ex.

4. Gary W. Lewandowski Jr. and Nicole M. Bizzoco, "Addition Through Subtraction: Growth Following the Dissolution of a Low Quality Relationship," *The Journal of Positive Psychology* 2, no. 1 (2007): 40–54, doi: 10.1080/17439760601069234.

5. Helen E. Fisher et al., "Reward, Addiction, and Emotion Regulation Systems Associated with Rejection in Love," *Journal of Neurophysiology* 104, no. 1 (July 2010): 51–60, doi: 10.1152 /jn.00784.2009.

6. Meghan Laslocky, "This Is Your Brain on Heartbreak," *Greater Good Magazine,* February 15, 2013, https://greatergood.berkeley .edu/article/item/this_is_your_brain_on_heartbreak.

7. Ibid.

8. Meghan Laslocky, *The Little Book of Heartbreak: Love Gone Wrong Through the Ages* (New York: Plume, 2013), 99.

9. "New Theory of Synapse Formation in the Brain," *ScienceDaily,* October 10, 2013, https://www.sciencedaily.com/releases/2013 /10/131010205325.htm.

10. Jill Bolte Taylor, *My Stroke of Insight* (London: Hachette, 2009), 153.

11. Amir Levine and Rachel S. F. Heller, *Attached: The New Science of Adult Attachment and How It Can Help You Find and Keep Love* (New York: TarcherPerigee, 2012), 166.

12. David R. Hamilton, "Does Your Brain Distinguish Real from Imaginary?," *David R. Hamilton* (blog), October 30, 2014, https:// drdavidhamilton.com/does-your-brain-distinguish-real-from -imaginary/.

13. "Cognitive Distortion," Wikipedia, https://en.wikipedia.org/wiki /Cognitive_distortion.

14. Ryan Martin, "What Is Overgeneralizing? How It's Defined and Why You Should Never Do It," *Psychology Today,* August 1, 2019, https://www.psychologytoday.com/us/blog/all-the-rage/201908 /what-is-overgeneralizing.

15. Ayelet Boussi, "Cognitive Strategies for Getting Through a Breakup," Cognitive Therapy for Women, January 3, 2019, http://www.ctwomen.org/blog/2019/1/3/cognitive-strategies-for-getting-through-a-breakup.

16. Collin M. Parkes, "Bereavement in Adult Life," *British Medical Journal* 316, no. 7134 (March 1998): 856–59.

17. "Understanding Anger," *Gooey Brains* (blog), http://gooeybrains.com/2016/08/02/understanding-anger/.

18. Sue Johnson and Kenneth Sanderfer, *Created for Connection: The "Hold Me Tight" Guide for Christian Couples* (Boston: Little, Brown, 2016), 54.

19. Lisa A. Phillips, "The Blistering Break-Up," *Psychology Today*, May 2015, https://www.psychologytoday.com/intl/articles/201505/the-blistering-break?collection=1076803.

20. Coco Ballantyne, "Can a Person Be Scared to Death?," *Scientific American*, January 30, 2009, http://www.scientificamerican.com/article/scared-to-death-heart-attack/.

21. David Puder, "Polyvagal Theory Simplified," *Psychiatry & Psychotherapy* (podcast), July 9, 2018, https://psychiatrypodcast.com/psychiatry-psychotherapy-podcast/polyvagal-theory-understanding-emotional-shutdown.

22. Jenn Tomomitsu, "How to Release Trauma: Shake Like a Gazelle," Medium, December 4, 2019, https://medium.com/@j.tomomitsu/shake-like-a-gazelle-how-to-release-trauma-abebf51eb747.

23. "Video: Breathing Exercises: 4-7-8 Breath," Weil, https://www.drweil.com/videos-features/videos/breathing-exercises-4-7-8-breath/.

24. Mark Hyman Rapaport, Pamela Schettler, and Catherine Bresee, "A Preliminary Study of the Effects of a Single Session of Swedish

Massage on Hypothalamic-Pituitary-Adrenal and Immune Function in Normal Individuals," *Journal of Alternative and Complementary Medicine* 16, no. 10 (October 2010): 1079–88, doi: 10.1089/acm.2009.0634.

25. Mary E. Larimer et al., "Relapse Prevention: An Overview of Marlatt's Cognitive-Behavioral Model," *Alcohol Research & Health* 23, no. 2 (1999): 151–60.

26. Shahram Heshmat, "Why Cravings Occur: Craving and Trigger Factors," *Psychology Today,* January 7, 2015, https://www .psychologytoday.com/us/blog/science-choice/201501/why -cravings-occur.

27. Robert J. Zatorre and Valorie N. Salimpoor, "Why Music Makes Our Brain Sing," *New York Times,* June 7, 2013, https://www.nytimes .com/2013/06/09/opinion/sunday/why-music-makes-our-brain -sing.html.

28. Linda Graham, *Bouncing Back: Rewiring Your Brain for Maximum Resilience and Well-Being* (Novato, CA: New World Library, 2013), 174.

29. Richard J. Davidson et al., "Alterations in Brain and Immune Function Produced by Mindfulness Meditation," *Psychosomatic Medicine* 65, no. 4 (July 2003): 564–70, doi: 10.1097/01.PSY .0000077505.67574.E3.

30. Sue McGreevey, "Eight Weeks to a Better Brain," *Harvard Gazette,* January 21, 2011, https://news.harvard.edu/gazette/story/2011/01 /eight-weeks-to-a-better-brain/.

31. "Just a Passing Cloud—A Meditation for Unpleasant Thoughts," William R. Marchand MD, August 28, 2015, https:// williamrmarchandmd.com/just-a-passing-cloud-a-meditation-on -anxiety-provoking-thoughts/.

32. Jonathan Haidt, *The Happiness Hypothesis: Finding Modern Truth in Ancient Wisdom* (New York: Basic Books, 2006), 85.

33. Ibid, 94.

34. Jane Weaver, "Puppy Love—It's Better Than You Think," NBC News, n.d., http://www.nbcnews.com/id/4625213/ns/health-pet _health/t/puppy-love----its-better-you-think/#.XsdxvGgzaUl.

35. Robert A. Emmons and Michael E. McCullough, "Counting Blessings Versus Burdens: An Experimental Investigation of Gratitude and Subjective Well-Being in Daily Life," *Journal of Personality and Social Psychology* 84, no. 2 (2003): 377–89, doi: 10.1037/0022-3514.84.2.377; Sonja Lyubomirsky, Kennon M. Sheldon, and David Schkade, "Pursuing Happiness: The Architecture of Sustainable Change," *Review of General Psychology* 9, no. 2 (2005): 111–31, doi: 10.1037/1089-2680.9.2.111.

36. Rodlescia S. Sneed and Sheldon Cohen, "A Prospective Study of Volunteerism and Hypertension Risk in Older Adults," *Psychology and Aging* 28, no. 2 (2013): 578–86, doi: 10.1037/a0032718.

37. "Study Describes Brain Changes During Learning," *ScienceDaily*, October 20, 2000, https://www.sciencedaily.com/releases/2000 /10/001020092659.htm.

38. Gary Marcus, "Happy New Year: Pick Up a New Skill," *New Yorker*, December 20, 2012, https://www.newyorker.com/news/news -desk/happy-new-year-pick-up-a-new-skill.

39. Marcel Schwantes, "Want to Increase Your Happiness This Year? Science Says 1 Rare Habit Truly Stands Out," Inc., January 9, 2018, https://www.inc.com/marcel-schwantes/want-to-be-much -happier-starting-tomorrow-practice-this-1-habit-rarely-found -at-work.html.

40. Ioanna Roumeliotis, "Shawn Achor's 6 Exercises for Happiness," CBC News, April 22, 2015, http://www.cbc.ca/news/health /shawn-achor-s-6-exercises-for-happiness-1.3040937.

CHAPTER 2

1. Bethany Saltman, "Can Attachment Theory Explain All Our Relationships?" The Cut, July 2016, https://www.thecut .com/2016/06/attachment-theory-motherhood-c-v-r.html.

2. Sue Johnson, *Love Sense: The Revolutionary New Science of Romantic Relationships* (New York: Little, Brown, 2013), 86.

3. Ibid., 88.

4. Joyce Catlett, "Avoidant Attachment: Understanding Insecure Avoidant Attachment," PsychAlive, https://www.psychalive.org /anxious-avoidant-attachment/.

5. Ibid.

6. Ibid.

7. Alexandra Katehakis, "Distorted Love: Adult Attachment Styles and Love Addiction," The Meadows, March 6, 2017, https://www .themeadows.com/blog/distorted-love-adult-attachment-styles -and-love-addiction/.

8. Darlene Lancer, "How to Change Your Attachment Style," PyschCentral, October 8, 2018, https://psychcentral.com/lib/how -to-change-your-attachment-style/.

9. Levine and Heller, *Attached*, 119.

10. Catlett, "Avoidant Attachment."

11. Ibid.

12. "The Roots of Love Addiction," Love Addiction Treatment, https://www.loveaddictiontreatment.com/the-roots-of-love-addiction/.

13. Ibid.

14. Catlett, "Anxious Attachment."

15. April D. Hussar, "Are You Attracted to Your 'Emotional Opposite'?," *Self*, April 3, 2012, https://www.self.com/story/are-you-attracted-to-your-emot.

16. Berit Brogaard, "Attachment Styles Can't Change, Can They?," *Psychology Today*, February 12, 2015, https://www.psychologytoday.com/blog/the-mysteries-love/201502/attachment-styles-cant-change-can-they.

17. Amy Banks, *Wired to Connect: The Surprising Link Between Brain Science and Strong, Healthy Relationships* (New York: Penguin, 2015), 157.

18. Ibid.

19. Pia Mellody, *Facing Love Addiction: Giving Yourself the Power to Change the Way You Love* (New York: HarperCollins, 1992), 92.

20. "Putting Feelings into Words Produces Therapeutic Effects in the Brain," *ScienceDaily*, June 22, 2007, https://www.sciencedaily.com/releases/2007/06/070622090727.htm.

21. Ornish Living, "The Science Behind Why Naming Our Feelings Makes Us Happier," *HuffPost*, May 15, 2015, http://www.huffingtonpost.com/ornish-living/the-science-behind-why-na_b_7174164.html.

22. Ken Page, "Recognizing Your Attractions of Deprivation," *Psychology Today*, April 3, 2011, https://www.psychologytoday.com/ie/blog/finding-love/201104/recognizing-your-attractions-deprivation?amp.

23. Banks, *Wired to Connect*, 97.

CHAPTER 3

1. Courtney E. Ackerman, "Learned Helplessness: Seligman's Theory of Depression (+ Cure)," Positive Psychology, May 12, 2020, https:// positivepsychology.com/learned-helplessness-seligman-theory -depression-cure/.

2. "The Elephant Syndrome: Learned Helplessness," Performance Management Counseling, January 7, 2014, https://pmcounseling .wordpress.com/2014/01/07/the-elephant-syndrome-learned -helplessness/.

3. Craig Gustafson, "Bruce Lipton, PhD: The Jump From Cell Culture to Consciousness," *Integrative Medicine: A Clinician's Journal* 16, no. 6 (2017): 44-50.

4. Sharon Muggivan, *It's Not About You. So Get Over It.* (Bloomington: Xlibris Corporation, 2011), 10.

5. Maxwell Maltz, *Psycho-Cybernetics: Updated and Expanded* (New York: TarcherPerigee, 2015), 4.

6. Maxwell Maltz, *Psycho-Cybernetics: A New Way to Get More Living out of Life* (Englewood Cliffs, NJ: Prentice-Hall, 1960), 2.

7. Joe Dispenza, *Becoming Supernatural: How Common People Are Doing the Uncommon* (Carlsbad, CA: Hay House, 2017), 171.

8. Sanaz Talaifar and William B. Swann Jr., "Self-Verification Theory," in *Encyclopedia of Personality and Individual Differences*, eds. Virgil Zeigler-Hill and Todd K. Shackelford (Cham, Switzerland: Springer, 2017), doi: 10.1007/978-3-319-28099-8.

9. Maltz, *Psycho-Cybernetics*, 37.

10. Dispenza, *Becoming Supernatural*, 37.

11. Maltz, *Psycho-Cybernetics*, 37.

12. "When You Stop Looking and Start Becoming," *Dr. Joe Dispenza's Blog*, https://drjoedispenza.net/blog/mastery-es/when-you-stop-looking-and-start-becoming/.

13. Graham, *Bouncing Back*, 94.

14. *The Market for Self-Improvement Products & Services*, Research and Markets, October 2019, https://www.researchandmarkets.com/reports/4847127/the-us-market-for-self-improvement-products-and?utm_code=fvt93q&utm_medium=BW.

15. Jon Kabat-Zinn, *Coming to Our Senses: Healing Ourselves and the World Through Mindfulness* (New York: Hyperion, 2005), 407.

16. Neil Strauss, "A Big Misconception About Happiness," *Neil Strauss* (blog), March 17, 2017, https://www.neilstrauss.com/advice/your-happiness/.

CHAPTER 4

1. John Montgomery, "The Shocking Truth," *Psychology Today*, July 15, 2014, https://www.psychologytoday.com/us/blog/the-embodied-mind/201407/the-shocking-truth.

2. Bessel van der Kolk, *The Body Keeps the Score: Brain, Mind, and Body in the Healing of Trauma* (New York: Penguin, 2014), 56.

3. Pia Mellody, *Facing Codependence: What It Is, Where It Comes from, How It Sabotages Our Lives* (New York: Harper & Row, 2003).

Nirmala Raniga, "Using Nonviolent Communication to Nurture Your Relationships," Chopra Center, February 5, 2014, https://chopra.com/articles/using-nonviolent-communication-nurture-your-relationships.

CHAPTER 5

1. Brené Brown, "Shame v. Guilt," *Brené Brown* (blog), January 14, 2013, https://brenebrown.com/blog/2013/01/14/shame-v-guilt/.

2. Rune Moelbak, "Shame: The Hidden Root of Most Psychological Problems," *Insight* (blog), August 30, 2015, http://www.bettertherapy.com/blog/shame/.

3. Holly VanScoy, "Shame: The Quintessential Emotion," PsychCentral, October 8, 2018, https://psychcentral.com/lib/shame-the-quintessential-emotion/.

4. Donald Nathanson, *Shame and Pride: Affect, Sex, and the Birth of the Self* (New York: W. W. Norton, 1994), 325.

5. Fred Wright, "Men, Shame, and Group Psychotherapy," *Group* 18, no. 4 (1994): 212–24, https://www.jstor.org/stable/41718776.

6. Robert Weiss, "Guilt = Good, Shame = Bad," *Psychology Today,* January 6, 2014, https://www.psychologytoday.com/us/blog/love-and-sex-in-the-digital-age/201401/guilt-good-shame-bad.

7. Tim Desmond, "Five Ways to Put Self-Compassion into Therapy," *Greater Good Magazine,* January 27, 2016, https://greatergood.berkeley.edu/article/item/five_ways_to_put_self_compassion_into_therapy.

8. "People with Self-Compassion Make Better Relationship Partners," UT News, October 8, 2012, https://news.utexas.edu/2012/10/08 /people-with-self-compassion-make-better-relationship-partners/.

9. Kristin Neff, "The Physiology of Self-Compassion," Self-Compassion, https://self-compassion.org/the-physiology-of-self -compassion/.

10. Jill Suttie, "Does Self-Compassion Make You Compassionate Toward Others?," Greater Good, June 1, 2018, https://greatergood .berkeley.edu/article/item/does_self_compassion_make_you _compassionate_toward_others.

11. Kristin Neff, "Tips for Practice," Self-Compassion, https://self -compassion.org/tips-for-practice/.

CHAPTER 6

1. "Romanticism," Wikipedia, https://en.wikipedia.org/wiki /Romanticism.

2. Alain de Botton, "How Romanticism Ruined Love," ABC Religion & Ethics, July 19, 2016, https://www.abc.net.au/religion/how -romanticism-ruined-love/10096750.

3. Emily Lenneville, "What Physiological Changes Can Explain the Honeymoon Phase of a Relationship?," Scientific American, September 1, 2013, https://www.scientificamerican.com/article /what-physiological-changes-can-explain-honeymoon-phase -relationship/.

4. "2/10: 'It's Destiny!' Most Americans Believe in Soul Mates," Marist Poll, February 10, 2011, http://maristpoll.marist.edu/210 -its-destiny-most-americans-believe-in-soul-mates/#sthash .BYki309S.rYzOYvz7.dpbs.

5. Raymond C. Knee et al., "Implicit Theories of Relationships: Moderators of the Link Between Conflict and Commitment," *Personality and Social Psychology Bulletin* 30, no. 5 (2004): 617–28, doi: 10.1177/0146167203262853.

6. Albert Wakin and Duyen B. Vo, "Love-Variant: The Wakin-Vo I.D.R. Model of Limerence," paper presented at the 2nd Global Conference: Challenging Intimate Boundaries, Freeland, UK, 2008.

7. Michael J. Rosenfeld and Reuben J. Thomas, "Searching for a Mate: The Rise of the Internet as a Social Intermediary," *American Sociological Review* 77, no. 4 (2012): 523–47, doi: 10.1177/0003122412448050.

8. David Sack, "Limerence and the Biochemical Roots of Love Addiction," *HuffPost,* June 6, 2012, https://www.huffpost.com /entry/limerence_b_1627089.

9. Alexandra Katehakis, "The Link Between Adult Attachment Styles and Sex and Love Addiction," *Psychology Today,* September 6, 2011, https://www.psychologytoday.com/us/blog/sex-lies -trauma/201109/the-link-between-adult-attachment-styles-and -sex-and-love-addiction.

10. Ibid.

11. "What Are the Most Common Indicators of Love Addiction," The Ranch, February 5, 2013, https://www.recoveryranch.com /articles/what-are-the-most-common-indicators-of-love -addiction/.

12. Rob Weiss, "The Neuroscience of Love and Love Addiction," Addiction.com, January 4, 2015, https://www.addiction.com/blogs /expert-blogs/neuroscience-love-love-addiction/.

13. "Love Addiction," Robert Weiss PhD, https://www
.robertweissmsw.com/about-sex-addiction/love-and-relationship
-addiction/.

14. Lindsay Mattison, "Researchers Say Craving for Ex Is Similar to an
Addict's Craving for Drugs," Lifehack, n.d., https://www.lifehack
.org/531836/researchers-say-craving-for-similar-addicts-craving
-for-drugs.

15. Emanuel Jauk et al., "How Alluring Are Dark Personalities? The
Dark Triad and Attractiveness in Speed Dating," *European Journal
of Personality* 30, no. 2 (2016): 125–38, doi: 10.1002/per.2040.

16. Drake Baer, "Narcissists Get More Dates," The Cut, June 23, 2016,
https://www.thecut.com/2016/06/narcissists-get-more-dates.html.

17. Megan Beauchamp, "What Is Gaslighting in Relationships? An
Expert Explains," MyDomaine, February 23, 2020, https://www
.mydomaine.com/gaslighting-in-relationships.

18. Helen E. Fisher, Arthur Aron, and Lucy L. Brown, "Romantic
Love: A Mammalian Brain System for Mate Choice," *Philosophical
Transactions of the Royal Society of London. Series B, Biological
Sciences* 361, no. 1476 (2006): 2173–86, doi: 10.1098
/rstb.2006.1938.

19. Alan Booth and James M. Dabbs Jr., "Testosterone and
Men's Marriages," *Social Forces* 72, no. 2 (1993): 463–77, doi:
10.2307/2579857.

20. Shelley D. Lane, *Interpersonal Communication: Competence and
Contexts,* 2nd ed. (New York: Routledge, 2010), 283.

21. Helen E. Fisher et al., "Defining the Brain Systems of Lust,
Romantic Attraction, and Attachment," *Archives of Sexual Behavior*
31, no. 5 (2002): 413–9, doi: 10.1023/A:1019888024255.

22. Helen E. Fisher, "Broken Hearts: The Nature and Risks of Romantic Rejection" in Ann C. Crouter and Alan Booth, eds., *Romance and Sex in Adolescence and Emerging Adulthood: Risks and Opportunities* (Mahwah, NJ: Lawrence Erlbaum Associates, 2006), 3–28.

23. Helen E. Fisher, "Lust, Attraction, and Attachment in Mammalian Reproduction," *Human Nature* 9, no. 1 (1998): 23–52, doi: 10.1007 /s12110-998-1010-5.

CHAPTER 7

1. "Familiarity Increases Liking," *ScienceDaily,* https://www .sciencedaily.com/terms/exposure_effect.htm.

CHAPTER 8

1. John Bradshaw, *Homecoming: Reclaiming and Championing Your Inner Child* (New York: Bantam, 1990), 18.

2. "*In a Different Voice,*" Wikipedia, https://en.wikipedia.org/wiki /In_a_Different_Voice.

3. Kerry Lusignan, "5 Things Men Can Do to Strengthen Their Relationship," The Gottman Institute, July 27, 2016, https://www .gottman.com/blog/five-things-men-can-do-to-strengthen-their -relationship/.

4. Nancy K. Dess, "Tend and Befriend," *Psychology Today,* September 1, 2000, https://www.psychologytoday.com/us/articles/200009 /tend-and-befriend.

CHAPTER 9

1. Andrew Trees, *Decoding Love: Why It Takes Twelve Frogs to Find a Prince, and Other Revelations from the Science of Attraction* (New York: Avery, 2009), 200.

2. Dess, "Tend and Befriend."

3. Elizabeth L. Paul and Kristen A. Hayes, "The Casualties of 'Casual' Sex: A Qualitative Exploration of the Phenomenology of College Students' Hookups," *Journal of Social and Personal Relationships* 19, no. 5 (2002): 639–61, doi: 10.1177/0265407502195006.

4. Fisher, "Lust, Attraction, and Attachment in Mammalian Reproduction," 23–52.

5. Jena Pincott, *Do Gentlemen Really Prefer Blondes? Bodies, Behavior, and Brains—The Science Behind Sex, Love, and Attraction* (New York: Bantam Dell, 2008), 167.

6. Ibid., 156.

7. Neil Strauss, *The Game: Penetrating the Secret Society of Pickup Artists* (New York: HarperCollins, 2005), 126.

8. David R. Hawkins, *Letting Go: The Pathway of Surrender* (New York: Hay House, 2012), 19.

CHAPTER 10

1. Christine Evangelou, *Stardust and Star Jumps: A Motivational Guide to Help You Reach Toward Your Dreams, Goals, and Life Purpose* (self-pub., Amazon Digital Services, 2016), Kindle.

ABOUT THE AUTHOR

Amy Chan is the founder of Renew Breakup Bootcamp, a company that takes a scientific and spiritual approach to healing the heart. She has been featured in the *New York Times, Fortune, Marie Claire, Glamour,* on CNN.com, and more. She has appeared on national television programs such as *Good Morning America, Nightline,* and *The Doctors.* She's the editor-in-chief of the online relationship magazine JustMyType.ca and has been a relationship columnist for over a decade. *Observer* calls her "a relationship expert whose work is like that of a scientific Carrie Bradshaw." Her work has been published in the *Huffington Post,* Medium, *Darling Magazine, 24 Hours,* and the *Vancouver Sun.*